VISUAL QUICKSTART GUIDE

DHTML

FOR THE WORLD WIDE WEB

Jason Cranford Teague

 Peachpit Press

Visual QuickStart Guide
DHTML for the World Wide Web
Jason Cranford Teague

Peachpit Press

1249 Eighth Street
Berkeley, CA 94710
(510) 524-2178
(510) 524-2294 (fax)

Find us on the World Wide Web at: http://www.peachpit.com

Peachpit Press is a division of Addison Wesley Longman

Copyright © 1998 by Jason Cranford Teague

Editor: Simon Hayes
Copy Editor: Carol Henry
Production Coordinators: Lisa Brazieal, Amy Changar
Compositor: Margaret Copeland—Terragraphics
Indexer: Ann Longknife of Creative Solutions

ISBN: 0-201-35341-5

0 9 8 7 6 5 4 3 2 1

Printed and bound in the United States of America

Special thanks to:

Tara my soul mate and best critic.

Simon, the best (and most patient Editor) in the business.

Carol for catching all of my mistakes.

Mom, Dad, and Nancy for making me who I am.

Pat and Red, my biggest fans.

Charles Dodgson (Lewis Carroll) for writing *Alice in Wonderland*

Matt Johnson, Douglas Adams, The Cure, New Model Army, The Cocteau Twins, The Cranes, The Smiths, Bauhaus, The Sisters of Mercy, Bad Religion, The Sex Pistols, This Mortal Coil, and Dead Can Dance whose noise helped keep me from going insane while writing this book.

TABLE OF CONTENTS

TABLE OF CONTENTS

INTRODUCTION

So you want to learn how to make your Web pages more exciting... more interesting... more dynamic—but you don't have all day. Creating Web pages used to be simple. You learned a few tags, created a few graphics, and presto: Web page. Now with streaming video, CGI, Shockwave, Flash, and Java, Web pages and their design may seem overwhelming to anyone not wanting to become a computer programmer.

Enter Dynamic HTML, a suite of technologies that give you—the Web designer—the ability to add pizzazz to your Web pages as quickly and easily as HTML does. With Dynamic HTML you don't have to rely on plug-ins that the visitor might not have, or complicated programming languages (except maybe a little JavaScript). For the most part, Dynamic HTML is created the same way as HTML and requires no special software to produce.

Who is this book for?

If the title of this book caught your eye, you're probably already well acquainted with the ins and outs of the Internet's most popular off shoot, the World Wide Web—or perhaps just a severely confused arachnophile. In order to understand this book, you will need to be familiar with the HyperText Mark-up Language. You don't have to be an expert, but you should at least know the difference between a <P> tag and a <BR> tag. In addition, several of the chapters call for more than a passing knowledge of JavaScript.

That said, the more knowledge about HTML and JavaScript you can bring to this book, the more you will be able to get out of it.

What is Dynamic HTML?

I'll let you in on a little secret: There really isn't *a* DHTML. At least, not in the way that there is *an* HTML or *a* JavaScript. HTML and JavaScript are specific, easily identified technologies for the Web. Dynamic HTML, on the other hand, is a marketing term coined by both Netscape and Microsoft to describe a series of technologies introduced in the 4.0 versions of their Web browsers, to enhance the "dynamic" capabilities of those browsers.

So the real question is, what makes a Web page dynamic? There is, of course, substantial debate on this topic, but we can agree on a few things.

1. Dynamic documents allow the designer to control how the HTML displays the Web pages' content.

2. Dynamic documents react and change with the actions of the visitor (the person using the Web site).

3. Dynamic documents can exactly position any element in the window, and change that position after the document has loaded.

4. Dynamic documents can hide and show content as needed.

What is an element?

In HTML, an element is any object on the screen that can be independently controlled using JavaScript. If you have done any work at all with Web coding, then you have used HTML elements. These elements comprise any content on the screen that is surrounded by HTML tags and then identified either by a name, ID, or array position.

The flavors of DHTML

Unfortunately, Netscape and Microsoft have differing ideas about exactly what technologies should be used to make HTML more dynamic. Fortunately for us, the specifications of these two companies do overlap, as shown in **Figure I.1.** And this area of overlap is what this book is primarily about. Why? Because the World Wide Web was founded on a very simple premise: the display of Web documents should be indifferent to the software being used.

Evolution and progress mean newer browsers have had to add technologies not supported by legacy (older) browsers. Still, there is an important tenet supporting the idea of being able to use the Web regardless of whose binary code you happen to be running. Cross-browser capability is what the Web is all about, and for good reason.

Cross-Browser DHTML

The following technologies will run pretty much identically, regardless of the DHTML browser being used. (Exceptions are noted throughout this book.)

1. **Cascading Style Sheets (CSS), Level 1**

   CSS allows you to define how HTML tags should display their content.

2. **Cascading Style Sheets-Positioning (CSS-P)**

   With CSS-P you can exactly position HTML elements anywhere in the window, as well as control the visibility of those elements.

3. **JavaScript 1.2**

   JavaScript allows you to create simple code to control the behavior of Web page elements.

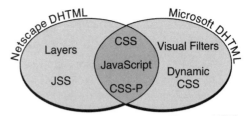

Figure I.1 Where the two versions of Dynamic HTML intersect is cross-browser DHTML. It is this area that will be most useful to us and to which most of the book is dedicated.

What DHTML *should* be

Although there is no official or even standard definition of Dynamic HTML, a few things are undeniably part of the DHTML mission:

1. DHTML should make use of HTML tags and scripting languages, without requiring the use of plug-ins or any software other than the browser.

2. Like HTML, DHTML should work (or at least have the potential to work) with all browsers and on all platforms.

3. DHTML should enhance the interactivity and visual appeal of the Web page.

Netscape-Specific DHTML

Netscape has brought several new technologies to the table hoping to create more dynamic Web pages. Unfortunately, these technologies will never become standards because CSS does most of the same things and is endorsed by the W3C.

1. **JavaScript Style Sheets**

   Like CSS, JSS allows you to define how HTML tags display their content; but JSS uses a JavaScript syntax.

2. **Layers**

   Like CSS-P, layers allow you to control the position of elements on the screen and their visibility.

Microsoft-Specific DHTML

Much of the Microsoft-specific DHTML is based on proprietary Microsoft software, such as ActiveX technology. Since ActiveX is owned by Microsoft, it is unlikely that it will ever be a cross-browser technology.

1. **Visual Filters**

   Visual filters let you perform visual effects on graphics and text in your document. If you have ever worked with Photoshop filters, you'll understand the similar ways of visual filters.

2. **Dynamic CSS**

   With Internet Explorer you can not only change the positions of elements on the screen, you can change their visual appearance as well.

The DHTML browsers

The only browsers considered DHTML capable are Netscape Navigator 4.x and Internet Explorer 4.x—the so-called 4.0 browsers. We can also safely assume that any of the browsers coming after these will be DHTML capable, as well. Parts I and II of this book address these fourth-generation browsers. Chapters 12 and 13 apply to Navigator 4, and Chapters 14 and 15 apply to Internet Explorer 4. In addition, although Internet Explorer 3 is not a DHTML browser, it can use CSS Level 1 but not CSS-Positioning. Thus Part I of the book is also applicable to IE 3.

Legacy browsers

A large percentage of browsers still used today will not run DHTML code. This means your Web pages will have to work both with and without DHTML, if you do not want to turn off a significant portion of your potential audience. It's a good idea to always test your Web pages in as many different Web browsers as possible, before going live on the Web.

The flavors of DHTML

CSS and DHTML

By the beginning of the next millennium, a scant two years away, the Web will probably bear no more resemblance to its current incarnation than a telephone does to an aldus lamp. The technologies used to create Web pages will continue to evolve, especially in the visual range.

One thing Web design has always lacked however, especially for anyone used to the controls available in desktop layout programs such as PageMaker and Quark, is exact control over the position and appearance of the HTML elements on the screen.

Cascading Style Sheets,—the key component of cross-browser DHTML technology and a central topic of this book—allow for just such control over our Web pages. Although the concept of control may not seem as jazzy and dynamic as the ability to make graphics move around on the page, CSS has the potential to do for Web layout what word processors did for print publication. In addition, the dynamic capabilities of cross browser DHTML are all predicated on the use of Cascading Style Sheet-Positioning.

The future of CSS

The CSS version on which this book is based is CSS Level 1. The next version, CSS Level 2, was released March 24, 1998. So why don't we use CSS2 in this volume? Because CSS2 has yet to be implemented in any of the browsers available as I write this book.

Don't worry, though—learning CSS2 after using CSS1 shouldn't be difficult. For the most part, CSS2 simply refines and improves the capabilities of its predecessor, without significantly changing the syntax.

JavaScript and DHTML

JavaScript has been around for a while now and is widely accepted as the standard means of adding functionality to Web pages. If you are unfamiliar with JavaScript, I recommend *The Visual Quickstart Guide to JavaScript, 2nd Edition* by Tom Negrino and Dori Smith (Peachpit Press, 1998), not just because it happens to be a part of this series but because it helped me with many questions that came up as I wrote this book.

JavaScript is, as its name says, a scripting language that allows you to script (give instructions to) your Web page about how to behave when certain things happen on the screen. DHTML relies on the capabilities of JavaScript in order to move elements on the screen, cause elements to appear and disappear, and change their appearance.

JavaScript and DHTML

Tools you need to create DHTML

The great thing about Dynamic HTML is that, like HTML, you don't need any special or expensive software in order to create it. All DHTML code is just text and can be edited using a program such as Simple Text (Mac OS) or WordPad (Windows OS). You do need to have one of the 4.0 browsers, however, in order to run most DHTML code. (see the earlier sidebar, "The DHTML browsers").

There are a couple of programs, in addition, that will make life with DHTML much easier by automating many of the tedious and repetitious tasks associated with Web design.

Figure I.2 Macromedia's Dreamweaver

Macromedia's Dreamweaver

www.macromedia.com

This powerful program (see **Figure I.2**) provides menus for creating CSS without having to dirty your fingers with the actual code. Despite its excellent WYSIWYG editor, Dreamweaver does not include a very robust HTML code editor, it's basically no more sophisticated than Note Pad or SimpleText. However, Dreamweaver can automatically launch your code into the HTML editor of your choice.

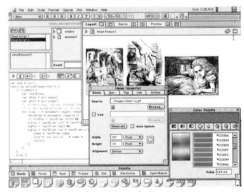

Figure I.3 CyberStudio from GoLive

GoLive's CyberStudio

www.golive.com

Despite the fact that this program is only available on the Macintosh platform, CyberStudio is my program of choice for Web development (see **Figure I.3**). This feature-rich program helps you edit your Web page in a variety of ways, including WYSIWYG as well as HTML code, and a special JavaScript editor. In addition, the 3.0 version CyberStudio includes extensive CSS and DHTML abilities, making life that much easier.

The code used in this book

For clarity and precision in this book, I have used several layout techniques to help you see the difference between the text of the book and the code.

Code will look like this:

```
<STYLE>

    P { font-size: 12pt; }

</STYLE>
```

The HTML code is always in uppercase, while all CSS and JavaScript code is in lowercase. In addition, quotes in the code will always appear as straight quotes (" or ') not curly quotes (" " or '). There is a good reason for this, since curly quotes, also called smart quotes, will cause the code to fail.

Important lines of code that we are discussing on a certain page will be emphasized by appearing in red.

When you type in a line of code, the computer can run the line as long as needed, but in this book we have to break lines of code to make them fit. When that happens, I use this gray arrow (→) to indicate that the line of code is continued from above, like this:

```
.title { font: bold 28pt/26pt times, serif;
→color: #FFF; background-color: #000;
→background-image: url(bg_title.gif); }
```

Save your fingers

I hope you'll be using a lot of the code from this book in your Web pages, but watch out—retyping information can lead to errors. Some books include a fancy-shmancy CD-ROM containing all the code from the book, and you can pull it off that disk. But guess who pays for that CD? You do. And they aren't cheap.

But if you bought this book you already have

access to the largest resource of knowledge
ever to exist: the Web. And that's exactly
where you can find the code from this book:

www.webbedenvironments.com/dhtml/index.html

This is my support site for the *Visual Quickstart
Guide to DHTML*. You can download the code
and any important updates and corrections.
In addition, the site includes other articles I
have written about the Web.

Also be sure to visit Peachpit Press' support site
for the book: www.peachpit.com/vqs/DHTML.

If you do type in the examples from the
book, you might find that some do not work
without the support files I used to create
them. No worries—at the support site you
will find the various examples, which you
can either view live or download for use on
your own computer.

You have DHTML questions? I have DHTML
answers. You can contact me at:

vqs-dhtml@webbedenvironments.com

Table 1.1

Relative Length Values			
NAME	TYPE OF UNIT	WHAT IT IS	EXAMPLE
em	EM dash	Width of the letter M for that font	3em
ex	x-height	Height of the lowercase x of that font	5ex
px	Pixel	Based on the monitor's resolution	125px

Table 1.2

Absolute Length Values			
NAME	TYPE OF UNIT	WHAT IT IS	EXAMPLE
pt	Point	Generally used to describe font size. 1pt = 1/72 of an inch.	12pt
pc	Picas	Generally used to describe font size. 1pc = 12pt.	3pc
mm	Millimeters		25mm
cm	Centimeters		5.1cm
in	Inches	1 inch = 2.54cm	2.25in

Values and units in this book

A CSS property always has an associated value, which determines how it will behave. These values will come in various forms, depending on the need of the property. Some values are straightforward—a number is a number—but others will have special units associated with them.

Length values

Length values come in two varieties:

* Relative lengths (see **Table I.1**), which will vary depending on the computer being used

* Absolute values (see **Table I.2**), which will remain constant regardless of the particular hardware and software.

I generally recommend using point sizes to describe font sizes, and pixels to describe other length values. These units are pretty much the standards being used today.

Color values

There are a variety of ways to describe color on the screen (see **Table I.3**), but most of these descriptions are just different ways of telling the computer how much red, green, and blue is in that particular color.

Percentages

Many of the properties in this book can have a percentage as their value. The behavior of this percentage value will depend on the particular property being used.

URLs

A Uniform Resource Locator (URL) is the unique address of something on the Web. This "resource" could be an HTML document, a graphic, a CSS file, a JavaScript file, a sound or video file, a CGI script, or a variety of other file types. URLs can be either **local,** which simply describes the location of the resource relative to the current document; or **global,** which describes the absolute location of the resource on the Web and begins with http://.

✔ Tip

- Certain colors will always display properly on any monitor. These are called the **browser-safe colors.** You'll find them fairly easy to remember because their values stay consistent. For hex, you can use any combination of 00, 33, 66, 99, CC, or FF. For numeric values, use 0, 51, 102, 153, 204, or 255. For percentages, use 0, 19, 38, 61, 81, or 100.

Table 1.3

Color Values

NAME	WHAT IT IS	EXAMPLE
#RRGGBB	Red, Green, and Blue hexcode value of a color (00-99,AA-FF)	#CC33FF or #C3F
rgb (#R,#G,#B)	Red, Green, and Blue numeric values of a color (0-255)	rgb(204,51,255)
rgb(R%,G%,B%)	Red, Green, and Blue percentage values of a color (0%-100%)	rgb(81%,18%,100%)
name	The name of the color	Purple

CSS Basics

Figure 1.1 The World Wide Web Consortium:
http://www.w3.org

It's no big secret: HTML is not a designer's dream come true. Then again, HTML was never intended to deliver high-concept graphic content and multimedia. In fact, it was never really intended to be anything more than just a glorified universal word-processing language delivered over the Internet—and a pretty limited one at that.

Over time new tags and technologies have been added to the Web which allow finer control over the appearance of Web documents—things such as tables, frames, justification controls, and JavaScript. Still there are a lot of layout effects that Web designers have to hack together using slow loading graphics rather than fast loading code. Not a very elegant system.

So when Web developers started clamoring for the World Wide Web consortium (**Figure 1.1**) to add greater control over Web page design, Cascading Style Sheets were introduced to fill the void left by straight HTML.

In this chapter you will learn how Cascading Style Sheets work and the principles involved in creating them. Then, in subsequent chapters, you will learn how to use all of the individual properties.

What is a style?

Most Word processors today include a way to make changes to text not just on a word-by-word basis, but throughout an entire document—using *styles*.

Styles work by collecting all of the different properties—bold, italic, font size, etc.—that you want to apply to similar types of text—titles, headers, captions, etc.—and giving these groups of properties a common name. Say you want all of the section titles in your document to be 14pt, Times, and italic. You would assign all of those properties to a style called Section Title.

With that style established, whenever you type in a section title all you have to do is set the style for the title to be of type Section Title, and all of the style's properties are applied to the text in one fell swoop (see **Figure 1.2**). No fuss, no mess. And, even better, if you decide later that you really wanted all of those titles to be 18pt instead of 14pt, you just change the definition of Section Title, and it will change the appearance of all text marked with that style throughout the document.

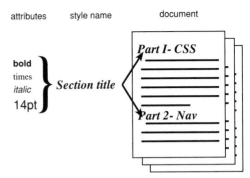

Figure 1.2 Styles being applied to a word processing document.

bold
times
italic
14pt
} **<P>...</P>**

Figure 1.3 Attributes can be assigned to HTML tags.

What are Cascading Style Sheets?

Cascading Style Sheets (CSS) bring the same "one-stop shopping" convenience for setting styles that is available on most word processors to the Web. You can set a Cascading Style Sheet in one central location to affect the appearance of HTML tags on a single Web page, or across an entire Web site.

Although the CSS methodology works with HTML, it is not HTML. Rather, CSS is a completely separate code that is used to enhance the abilities of HTML by allowing you to redefine the way preexisting HTML tags work (see **Figure 1.3**).

For example, the paragraph tag container, <P>...</P>, basically does one thing: It puts a space between two paragraphs. Using CSS, we can change the nature of the paragraph tag, so that it also sets all of the text contained within it to 12pt size, uses the Times font, indents the first line of the paragraph five spaces, and any variety of other effects.

Although Cascading Style Sheets have been around for a while, you may just now be discovering them. Microsoft has at least partially supported them since Internet Explorer 3.0, but it was not until the 4.0 browsers were released (Internet Explorer 4.0 and Netscape Navigator 4.0) that CSS became a going concern.

✔ Tips

- Cascading Style Sheets are not the only type of style sheet available for the Web; for instance, there are also JavaScript Style Sheets. However, CSS is the most commonly used style sheet and has been endorsed by the World Wide Web Consortium.

HTML 4.0

The latest version of the Hypertext Markup Language, HTML 4.0, was released in December 1997 by the World Wide Web Consortium. HTML 4.0 includes the style sheet methodology, which was previously maintained as a separate standard, as part of the HTML specification. This does not mean that CSS is HTML; it simply means that HTML is now reliant on the capabilities of CSS.

Understanding CSS rules

The best thing about Cascading Style Sheets is that they are amazingly simple to set up. No plug-ins, no fancy software—just *rules*.

A CSS rule defines what the HTML should look like and how it should behave in the browser window.

Rules can be set up to tell a specific HTML tag how to display its content (see page 21). Or you can create generic rules which can then be applied to tags at your discretion (see pages 22 and 24).

The parts of a rule:

All rules, regardless of where they are located, have the following three parts (see **Table 1.a**):

1. **Selectors** are the alpha/numeric characters that identify this rule. The selector can be an HTML tag selector, a class selector, or an ID selector.

2. **Properties** are what is being defined. There are several dozen different properties, each one responsible for an aspect of the page content's behavior and appearance.

3. **Values** are assigned to a property to define its "nature." A value can be a keyword such as "yes" or "no," or a number or a percentage. The type of value used will depend solely on the property it is being assigned to. The property and value together are known as the *definition*.

✔ Tip

- Although Navigator 4.x and Internet Explorers 3.x and 4.x all support CSS, none of these browsers supports all of the CSS capabilities. When using CSS, always check Appendix A to see if a particular property is supported by a browser.

Where to put CSS rules

Rules can be set up in three different places (see **Table 1.b**):

- In an HTML tag within the body of your document. This is called **inline.**

- In the head of a document. This is called **embedded**.

- In an external document that is then linked or imported into your HTML document(s). This is called **external**.

The position of a rule in relationship to the document will determine the scope of the rule's effect on the document or even on the whole Web site.

Table 1.a

Required Contents of Style Rules

PART	WHAT IT IS	EXAMPLES	FOR MORE INFORMATION
Selector	Letters and/or numbers that identify the rule.	H1, coolThing, layer1	Understanding selectors-Page XXX
Property	Name given to a particular style.	font-size	The definition: properties and values-Page XXX
Value	Value assigned to the property.	12pt, black, 115%	Units and abbreviations in this book-Page XXX

Table 1.b

A CSS Rule Can Be Included in any of Three Different Places

LOCATION	HOW INCLUDED	WHAT IT AFFECTS	FOR MORE INFORMATION
Inline	As part of an HTML tag.	That tag in that instance.	Adding CSS to individual HTML tags-Page XXX
In the head	As part of a style definition in the head of the document.	All instances of that tag in that document.	Adding rules to an HTML document-Page XXX
In an external file	As part of a style definition in a text file.	Can be imported or linked to any HTML document affecting the tags in that HTML document.	Setting up an external CSS file-Page XXX

Understanding CSS rules

Understanding selectors

In CSS rules, the selectors are the "gateways" between definitions and the HTML tags to which the rules will be applied.

Selectors come in three basic forms:

1. **HTML selectors** are the text portion of an HTML tag. For example, H3 is the selector for the <H3> tag. HTML selectors are used to define the behavior of that specific HTML tag (see **Creating a CSS rule with an HTML selector**, page 21).

2. **Class selectors** set up a class with whatever name you want. A class is a "free agent" selector that can be applied to any HTML tag at your discretion. Since it can be applied to multiple HTML tags, a class selector is the most versatile type of selector (see **Defining a class selector**, page 22).

3. **ID selectors** work a lot like class selectors, in that they can be applied to any HTML tag. ID selectors, however, are usually applied only once on the page to a particular HTML tag (see **Defining an ID selector**, page 24).

✔ Tips

- Don't confuse the selector of an HTML tag with its attributes. For example, in the following tag, IMG is the selector and SRC is an attribute.

    <IMG SRC="picture.gif">

- The <BR>, <FRAMESET>, and <FRAME> tags cannot be used as selectors.

- Although the paragraph <P> tag is often used without its closing </P> tag, to be defined using CSS the closing tag must be included.

Tags or selectors: What's the big difference?

An HTML selector is the text part of an HTML tag, the part that tells the browser what type of tag it is. So when you define an HTML selector using CSS, you are in fact *redefining* the HTML tag. Although the two ideas, tag and selector, seem identical, they aren't: If you used the full HTML tag—brackets and all—in a CSS rule, the tag would not work. So it's important to keep these two ideas separate.

Understanding selectors

Table 1.3

Selectors for Block-Level Tags

SELECTOR	HTML USE	SELECTOR	HTML USE
BLOCKQUOTE	Quote style	H1-7	Header levels 1-7
CENTER	Center text	LI	List item
DD	Definition	OL	Ordered list
	description	P	Paragraph
DFN	Defined term	TABLE	Table
DIR	Directory list	TR	Table row
DIV	Logical division	TD	Table data
DL	Definition list	TH	Table head
DT	Definition term	UL	Unordered list

Table 1.4

Selectors for Inline Tags

SELECTOR	HTML USE	SELECTOR	HTML USE
A	Anchored link	STRIKE	Strikethrough
B	Boldface	SPAN	Localized style-
BIG	Bigger text		formatting
CITE	Short citation	STRONG	Strong emphasis
CODE	Code font	SUB	Subscript
EM	Emphasis	SUP	Superscript
FONT	Font appearance	TT	Typewriter
I	Italic	U	Underline text
PRE	Preformatted text		

Table 1.5

Selectors for Replaced Tags

SELECTOR	HTML USE	SELECTOR	HTML USE
IMG	Image embed	SELECT	Select input area
INPUT	Input object	TEXTAREA	Text input area
OBJECT	Object embedding		

Kinds of tags

Not all CSS definitions can be applied to all HTML selectors. It depends on which HTML tag is associated with the selector. Besides the BODY tag, there are three basic types of HTML tags:

Types of HTML tags:

1. **Block Level** places a line break before and after the element.

2. **Inline** tags have no line breaks associated with the element.

3. **Replaced** tags have set or calculated dimensions (width and height).

The HTML selectors associated with these types of tags are shown in **Tables 1.3** through **1.5**.

The type of tag to which you apply the definition will determine what CSS properties can be applied to the tags. For the most part, this will be pretty obvious. For example, you wouldn't expect the text-indent property, which indents the first line of a paragraph, to apply to an inline tag such as bold. When you do need some help in this area, though, **Appendix A** tells you which properties can be used with a particular kind of HTML tag.

The definition: properties and values

After the selector, the rest of a CSS rule consists of the properties and their values which together we will refer to as a definition. **Table 1.6** lists the general property categories and where you can go to find the specific properties. **Figure 1.4** illustrates the general syntax of a definition.

✔ Tip

- Although you do not have to include a semicolon with the last definition in a list, experience shows that adding this semicolon can prevent heartache later. If you decide to add something to the definition and forget to put in the required semicolon before the addition, you may cause that rule to fail completely. Not just that one definition, but all of the definitions in the rule will fail to be used (see **Troubleshooting CSS**, page 38).

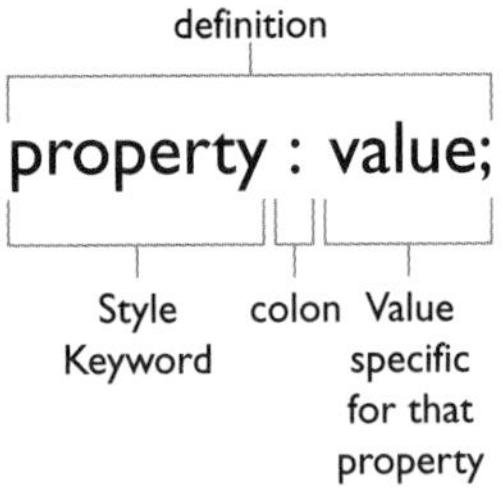

Figure 1.4 General syntax for a CSS property definition.

Table 1.6

CSS Properties		
PROPERTY	**WHAT YOU CONTROL**	**FOR MORE INFORMATION**
Fonts	Letter form, size, boldface, italic	Chapter 2
Text	Kerning leading, alignment, case	Chapter 3
Lists	Bullets, indentation	Chapter 4
Colors	Borders, text, bullets, rules, backgrounds	Chapter 5
Backgrounds	Behind the page or behind a single element on the page	Chapter 5
Margins	Margins, padding, borders, width, height	Chapter 6
Positioning	Exact placement on the screen	Chapter 7

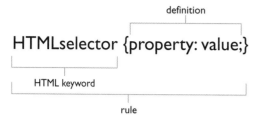

definition

HTMLselector {property: value;}

HTML keyword

rule

Figure 1.5 General syntax for CSS rules with an HTML selector.

Code 1.1 The bold tag gets a new look.

```
B
  {
    font: bold 16pt times,serif;
    text-decoration: underline;
  }
```

Figure 1.6 Now bold **really** stands out.

Creating a CSS rule with an HTML selector

Most HTML tags already have built-in properties. Take the bold tag, for example; its built-in property makes text bold.

By adding new definitions to the bold tag's selector, B, we can make the <B>...</B> pair have any effect we want. **Figure 1.5** shows the general syntax for a complete CSS rule using an HTML selector; while **Code 1.1** shows one possible way to redefine the bold tag and **Figure 1.6** shows what the redefined bold tag looks like in a browser.

To define an HTML selector:

1. B {

Start with the HTML selector whose properties you want to define, and then add a { bracket to open your definition list, as shown in **Code 1.1**.

2. font: bold 16pt times,serif;
text-decoration: underline;

Type in your property definition(s); (see **The definition: properties and values** page 20). You can add as many definitions as you want, but the properties have to work with the HTML tag in question. For instance, text indent won't work with bold.

3. }

Close your definition list with a } bracket. Forget this and it will ruin your day!

✔ Tips

■ Once you redefine an HTML selector this way, all of its tags throughout the entire document will be affected automatically.

■ The syntax is slightly different for redefining an individual HTML tag within a document.

21

Defining a class selector

Using a class selector gives you the ability to set up an independent style that can then be applied to any HTML tag.

Unlike an HTML selector, which works automatically, definitions given to a class will only work if the class is indicated in an actual HTML tag. **Figure 1.7** shows the general syntax for a CSS class rule.

To define a class selector:

1. .huge {

Type a period and a class name; then open your definition with a { bracket. The class name can be anything you choose as long as it is letters and numbers. In **Code 1.2** we will create the class called "huge."

Huge is an **independent class**, so it can be used with any HTML tag you want—with one stipulation: The properties set for the class must work with the type of tag you use it in.

2. font-size: 42pt

Type your definition for this class. Here we have decided to change the font-size property to 42 point.

3. ;}

Type a semicolon and a } bracket to close your rule.

dot   CSS definition

.classname {property: value;}

the name of your class selector

Figure 1.7 General syntax for an independent class.

Code 1.2 Using Classes. The first class, extra, is associated with the bold tag and is thus a dependent class. The second class, huge, is independent and can therefore be used with any tag.

```
B.extra {font-style: italic; font-size: 18pt;}
.huge {font-size: 42pt;}
```

Code 1.3 The classes must be included with an HTML tag before they work, and extra *must* be used with the bold tag.

```
<HTML>
  <BODY BGCOLOR="#FFFFFF">
    Look, this is <B>really</B>,
    <B class="extra">really</B>,
    <BIG class="huge">really</BIG> important.
  </BODY>
</HTML>
```

Figure 1.8 General syntax for an HTML selector with a class.

Figure 1.9 The extra and huge classes as they will appear in a browser.

To use your class in an HTML tag:

A class will not work until it is specified within an HTML tag within a document, like this:

1. `<BIG CLASS="huge">...</BIG>`

Now we will use the huge class to make big really *big*. We can use huge with any tag, though, as shown in **Code 1.3**. The results of all of this is shown in **Figure 1.9**.

✔ Tip

■ You can mix a class with ID and inline rules (see **Adding CSS to individual HTML tags**, page 27) within an HTML tag.

Dependent classes

A class can also be directly associated with an HTML selector, in which case it is a *dependent class*. That means the class selector can only be used with that particular HTML tag. **Figure 1.8** shows the basic syntax for a dependent class.

It's unlikely you would want to have a class associated with an HTML selector, unless you needed to use the same name for a class but define it differently for various HTML tags—for instance, P.cool as opposed to H1.cool.

Defining a class selector

Defining an ID selector

Like the independent class selector, the ID selector can be used to create unique styles that are independent of any particular HTML selector. Thus they can be assigned to any applicable HTML tag, as shown in **Figure 1.10**

To define an ID selector:

1. #area1 { position: relative; margin-left: 9em;
→color: red;}

ID rules always start with a number sign and then a name for your ID selector. The name can be a word, or any set of letters or numbers you choose; take a look at **Code 1.4.** You can use an ID with any type of property, but ID selectors are best used with the positioning properties to define a particular element in the screen.

To use your ID in an HTML tag:

An ID will not work until it is specified with an HTML tag within a document.

1. <SPAN ID="area1" >...</SPAN>

Add the ID attribute to an HTML tag, as shown in **Code 1.5.** The value for the ID attribute will be the name of the ID selector you created, as explained just above. Notice, though, that the number sign is not included. **Figure 1.11** shows the results of this code.

✔ Tips

- The difference between IDs and classes will become apparent after you've learned more about using CSS positioning, and after you've used IDs to create CSS elements. IDs are used to give each element on the screen a unique name and identity. This is why an ID is typically used only once, for one element in a document.

number sign   CSS definition

#IDname {property: value;}

name for your ID selector

Figure 1.10 General syntax for ID selectors.

Code 1.4 This sets up a an ID selector called area1, which will give associated text a left margin of 9 em units.

```
#area1 { position: relative; margin-left: 9em;
→color: red;}
```

Code 1.5 The ID selector is assigned using the span tag.

```
<HTML>
  <BODY BGCOLOR="#FFFFFF">
    <P>'Well!' thought Alice to herself...<P>
    <SPAN ID="area1">Down, down, down... </SPAN>
    <P>Let me see...</P>
  </BODY>
</HTML>
```

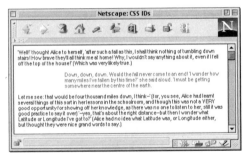

Figure 1.11 The paragraph has been moved over 9 em units.

Code 1.6 All the header tags are given the same set of definitions; in addition, the <H1> tag is set to be larger than the rest.

```
                        code
<HTML>
  <HEAD>
    <STYLE TYPE="text/css">
      H1, H2, H3 ,H4, H5, H6 {
font: bold 18pt/20pt helvetica,sans-serif;
}
      H1 {font-size:26pt;}
    </STYLE>
  </HEAD>
  <BODY BGCOLOR="#FFFFFF">
    <H1>Header Level 1</H1>
    <H2>Header Level 2</H2>
    <H3>Header Level 3</H3>
    <H4>Header Level 4</H4>
    <H5>Header Level 5</H5>
    <H6>Header Level 6</H6>
  </BODY>
</HTML>
```

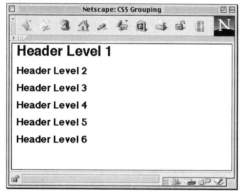

Figure 1.12 All the header tags display identically, except for <H1>.

Giving several HTML selectors the same definition

If you have two or more HTML selectors that you want to have the same definitions, just put the selectors in a list separated by commas (see **Figure 1.12**). You can define qualities in the list, and then add additional rules for each HTML selector individually if you like.

To group definitions together:

1. H1, H2, H3, H4, H5, H6 { font: bold
   →18pt/20pt helvetica,sans-serif;}

   Type in the list of HTML selectors separated by commas as shown in **Code 1.6**. These tags will all get the same definition.

2. H1 {font-size:26pt;}

   If you want to, you can then add or change definitions for each selector separately.

✔ Tips

■ Grouping selectors together like this can save a lot of time and repetition. But be careful—by changing the value of any of the properties, you change that value for every tag in the list.

■ You can also have class selectors (dependent or independent) and/or ID selectors in the list, in addition to the HTML selectors.

Putting selectors into context

When a tag is surrounded by another tag, one inside another, we call the tags *nested*. In a nested set, the outer tag is called the parent and the inner tag the child. We can use CSS to create a rule for a tag if it is the child of another particular tag or tags. For example, if you want all boldface type to appear on a pink background within <P> tag, but on a red background when it is in a <BLOCKQUOTE>, you would need to set up a definition based on the tag's *context*.

To set up a contextual selector

1. P B { background: pink;}

Type in the HTML selector of the parent tag and then a space, as demonstrated in **Code 1.7**. You can type in as many HTML selectors as you want for as many different parents as the nested tag will have, but the last selector in the list is the one that is defined as the nested tag.

2. <P>... <B>...</B></P>

Now if, and only if, the bold tag occurs within a paragraph (**Code 1.8**) will the pink background appear. You can see how it looks in **Figure 1.13**.

✔ Tip

- Like grouped selectors, contextual selectors can include class selectors (dependent or independent) and/or ID selectors in the list, as well as HTML selectors.

Code 1.7 Setting the contextual selectors in a file called titles.css

```
P B { background: pink;}
```

Code 1.8 Here, the bold tag is within a paragraph, which fulfills the context.

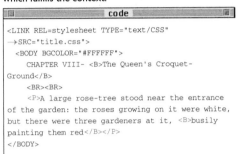

```
<LINK REL=stylesheet TYPE="text/CSS"
→SRC="title.css">
  <BODY BGCOLOR="#FFFFFF">
    CHAPTER VIII- <B>The Queen's Croquet-
Ground</B>
    <BR><BR>
    <P>A large rose-tree stood near the entrance
of the garden: the roses growing on it were white,
but there were three gardeners at it, <B>busily
painting them red</B></P>
</BODY>
```

Figure 1.13 Bold is pink in the paragraph, but not pink outside of a paragraph.

Code 1.9 The <P> tag is set to be double-spaced, but this gets overridden in the second <P> tag in the code.

```
code
<HTML>
  <HEAD>
    <STYLE TYPE="text/css">
        P {font-size: 10pt; line-height: 18pt;}
    </STYLE>
  </HEAD>
  <BODY BGCOLOR="#FFFFFF">
<P>the Queen was in a furious passion, and went
stamping about, and shouting 'Off with his head!'
or 'Off with her head!' about once in a minute.</P>
<P STYLE="line-height: 12pt; margin-left: 30px;"
align="right">'They're dreadfully fond of
beheading people here; the great wonder is, that
there's any one left alive!'</P>
<P>She was looking about for some way of escape,
and wondering whether she could get away without
being seen, when she noticed a curious appearance
in the air.</P>
  </BODY>
</HTML>
```

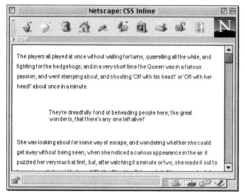

Figure 1.14 When **Code 1.9** is loaded into a browser, it looks something like this.

Adding CSS to individual HTML tags

CSS means never having to set the appearance for each and every tag individually. But what if you *want* to set a tag individually? No problem. Using CSS in a single tag will only affect that tag in that one particular case. This comes in handy when you want to override any definitions set in the head of the document.

To set the properties of a particular HTML tag:

1. <P STYLE="

   Include the style attribute in the HTML tag of your choice, which can be any HTML tag that CSS can define. In **Code 1.9** we're using the paragraph tag.

2. font-size: 10pt; line-height: 18pt;"

   Type in your property definition(s) and make sure to close the definition list with a quote mark.

3. </P>

   Close the tag pair with the corresponding end tag, if necessary. **Figure 1.14** shows what this will look like in a browser.

✔ Tips

- Although we do not gain the benefit of the universal style changes, using CSS in individual HTML tags is nevertheless very useful when you want to override universally defined styles. (See **Determining the cascade order** at the end of this chapter.).

- You can also define the <BODY> tag as described in this section. But be careful— this can lead to more problems than it's worth (see the sidebar, **Dealing with ubiquitous properties** on page 34).

Adding CSS to an HTML document

The main use for CSS is to define style rules for an entire document. To do this, we include our style rules in the head of the document nested within a *style container*.

To set the style for tags in an HTML document:

1. `<STYLE TYPE="text/css">`

   This text opens a CSS style container within the head of your HTML document.

2. `P {font: normal 12pt/16pt times,serif;}`

   `P HR {color: red;}`

   `.coolText {color: lime;}`

   Type in your CSS rule(s), which can be any of the following rule types:

   - An HTML *selector*
   - A *class selector*
   - An *ID selector*
   - A *group of selectors*
   - A *group of contextual selectors*
   - An *imported CSS file*

3. `</STYLE>`

   Close the style definition by typing one end tag.

✔ Tips

- You don't have to include `TYPE="text/css"`, because the browser should be able to determine the type. This TYPE statement is recommended, however, to allow browsers that do not support a particular type of style sheet to avoid the code. It also clarifies to other humans the type being used.

- You can employ the HTML comment tags to hide CSS from non-CSS browsers (see the sidebar, **Hiding CSS from non-CSS browsers**).

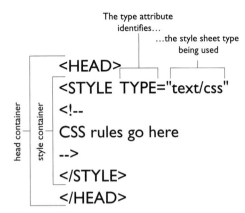

The type attribute identifies...

...the style sheet type being used

```
<HEAD>
<STYLE TYPE="text/css"
<!--
CSS rules go here
-->
</STYLE>
</HEAD>
```

head container

style container

Figure 1.15 The parts of a style section

Hiding CSS from non-CSS browsers

You can never know who will be looking at your Web page and what type of browser they'll be using. In order to prevent Cascading Style Sheets from messing up the display of your document in non-CSS browsers, you can use the HTML comment tags to "hide" the CSS code from older browsers. This is only necessary if the style sheet is defined within the `<HEAD>` of your document (see **Figure 1.15**).

Mixing and matching files

To get the exact layout you need, you can mix and match CSS files from a variety of sources into a single document. For instance, you might color code the sections of your site. You can have one master CSS file that controls the general appearance for the entire site, and then each section can have its own CSS file to set that section's color.

✔ Tips

■ Although the external CSS filename can be anything you want it to be, it's a good idea to use a name that will remind you of what these styles are for. For instance, navigation.css is probably a more helpful name than ss1.css.

■ You do not have to use the ".css" extension with CSS files. We could have just called this file "filename" and it would have worked just as well. However, adding the extension can prevent confusion.

■ A CSS file should not contain any HTML tags or other content, with the exception of comments and imported styles (see **Importing external CSS files**, page 31).

Setting up an external CSS file

A major benefit of CSS is that you can create a style sheet for use not just with a single HTML document, but throughout an entire site. This external style sheet can be applied to a hundred different HTML documents— without having to retype the information.

Establishing an external CSS file is a two-step process. First, set up the rules in a text file; and then link or import this file into an HTML document

To set up an external CSS file:

1. Create a new file, using a word processor or other software that allows you to save as a text file. NotePad or SimpleText will do.

2. H1, H2 {font: bold 18pt/18pt helvetica,sans-
   ⟶serif;}

   H1 {color: blue;}

   #layer1 {position: relative;}

   Type in your CSS rule(s) based on the following rule types:

   • An HTML *selector*
   • A *class selector*
   • An *ID selector*
   • A *group of selectors*
   • A group of *contextual selectors*
   • An *imported CSS file*

3. Save this document as filename.css, where filename is whatever you wish to call this file, and .css is an extension to identify the file type.

4. As shown on the next few pages, to use this external CSS file to affect the tags in an HTML document, you either need to link the document to the CSS file or import the CSS file.

Linking to external CSS files

External style sheet files can be used with any HTML file, through the <LINK> tag. Linking a CSS file affects the document just as if the styles had been typed directly into the head of the document. **Figure 1.16** shows the general syntax for linking style sheets.

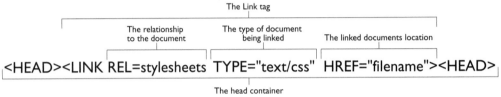

Figure 1.16 A linked style sheet.

Linking an external CSS file to an HTML document

1. <LINK

Within the head of your HTML document, open your link tag and then type a space.

2. REL=stylesheets

Tell the browser that this will be a link to a style sheet. (*Note:* No quotes are needed.)

3. TYPE="text/css"

Define the type of style sheet being imported.

4. HREF="filename"

Specify the location, either global or local, of the CSS file to be used, where filename is the full path and name (including extension) of your CSS document .

5. >

Close the LINK tag with a chevron.

6. <LINK REL=stylesheets TYPE="text/css"
→HREF="filename2">

Repeat steps 1–7 to add as many style sheets links as you want.

✔ Tip

■ Linked style sheets in Navigator 4.0 often disappear if the document has to be reloaded from the computer's cache. This is mostly an annoyance, but it may confuse visitors. There is no fix for this problem.

Tells the document
to import . . .

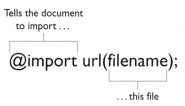

@import url(filename);

. . . this file

Figure 1.17 The *@import* statement general syntax.

Importing external CSS files

Another way to bring external style sheets into a document is the @import statement. Although this method is not yet fully supported in Netscape 4, it can be used to put external CSS files into an HTML document file as well as into other external CSS files for Internet Explorer. **Figure 1.17** shows the general syntax for the import statement.

To import a CSS document into an HTML document:

1. Create an external CSS file (see **Setting up an external CSS file**).

2. <STYLE TYPE="text/css">

Within the head of your HTML document, open a style container.

3. @import url(filename);

Import the CSS file. The **filename** is the URL of the CSS document to be used. The URL can be global, in which case it would start with http://; or it could be local, pointing to a file on the same computer.

4. @import url(filename2);

Repeat step 3 for as many external CSS documents as you want to link.

5. EM {font: italic bold 18pt/18pt;}

You can also include additional CSS rules here, if needed. (see **Adding CSS to an HTML document** on page 28).

6. </STYLE>

Close the style definition with a style end tag.

✔ Tip

■ Since the @import statement is currently only supported by Internet Explorer 4.x, using it is somewhat impractical unless you know that everyone looking at your Web page is using IE.

To import one CSS document into another CSS document:

1. Within the external CSS document, type @import url(filename); The filename is the location, either global or local, of the CSS document to be used. This file will now be used if the document containing it is either linked to or imported into an HTML document.

2. Repeat step 1 for as many CSS documents as you wish to import.

Adding comments to CSS

Like any other part of an HTML document, style sheets can have comments. A comment will not have any effect on the code; the purpose of comments is to make notes in your code or give guidance to anyone looking at your code. Comments can be included in the head of an HTML document or in an external CSS file as shown in **Code 1.10**.

Including multilined comments within a style sheet:

1. /*

To open a comment area within a style sheet, type a slash and an asterisk.

2. tag= HTML tags
required= required attributes
optional= optional attributes

Type in your comments. You can use any letters or numbers, symbols, and even line breaks (i.e. Return or Enter keypresses).

3. */

Close your comment by typing an asterisk and a slash.

✔ Tips

- You cannot have comments within other comments.

- The double slashes of a single-line comment often stand out better when you're skimming through a document, making them easier to find.

Code 1.10 CSS with comments

```
// Sets the general appearance of code tags
CODE
        {
        color: #FF6600;
        font-family: monaco,courier,monospace;
        font-size: 10pt;
        line-height: 12pt;
        margin-left: 2em;
        }
/* While this sets the appearance of special cases
for code
        tag= HTML tags
        required= required attributes
        optional= optional attributes */
CODE.tag { color: #CC6666;}
CODE.required { color: #66CC66;}
CODE.optional { color: #6666CC;}
```

Including single-line comments within a style sheet:

If your comment is only one line, you can use a slightly different format:

1. //

Start a comment line by typing two slashes.

2. blah blah blah...

Type in your comments. In this format, you can use any letters or numbers, and symbols; however, you cannot include any line breaks.

Code 1.11 An independent class selector and ID selector are created and then applied in the HTML to a <SPAN> and <DIV> tag.

```
code
<HTML>
  <HEAD>
    <STYLE TYPE="text/css">
        .paragraph {font: 10pt/18pt helvetica,
→sans-serif; width: 150px;}
        .emphasis {font: bold 14pt/18pt times,
→serif; background color:aliceblue;}
    </STYLE>
  </HEAD>
  <BODY BGCOLOR="#FFFFFF">
  <DIV CLASS="paragraph">By the time she had caught
the <SPAN CLASS="emphasis">flamingo</SPAN> and
brought it back, the fight was over, and both the
<SPAN CLASS="emphasis">hedgehogs</SPAN> were out
of sight: 'but it doesn't matter much,' thought
Alice, 'as all the arches are gone from this side
of the ground.' So she tucked it away under her
arm, that it might not escape again, and went back
for a little more conversation with her
friend.</DIV>
  </BODY>
</HTML>
```

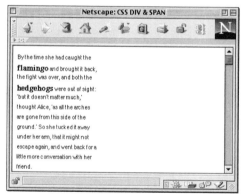

Figure 1.18 The results of the **Code 1.11** in a browser.

Making your own tags with <DIV> and <SPAN>

You learned in this chapter how to change the styles of existing HTML tags in **Adding CSS rulers to individual tags**. But the majority of HTML tags contain some predefined properties that you either have to accept or redefine.

What if you want to start from scratch? Although you can't create your own HTML tags, per se, you can use either the <SPAN> or <DIV> tags, along with classes and IDs, to get pretty close. **Code 1.11** shows how this works.

Using the <DIV> tag

Since the <DIV> tag's only inherent property is that it has a break above it and below it, it's useful for creating a paragraph style tag without having to upset the <P> tag.

Using the <SPAN> tag

The <SPAN> tag, on the other hand, has no inherited properties; it serves as a blank slate for the purposes of creating our own style. <SPAN> is perfect for creating your own inline elements, and for creating positionable layers using ID selectors (which we will discuss in **Chapter 7**).

✔ Tip

■ Both <DIV> and <SPAN> can be defined just like any other HTML selector (page 21). Doing this, however, would limit both tags to only one set of properties. Instead, we can use a class or ID selector with either tag to load in just those properties needed for a particular element in our Web page.

Making your own tags with <DIV> and <SPAN>

Inheriting properties from parents

No, this is not the Visual Quickstart Guide to real estate. HTML tags will generally get the styles of any tags they are nested within (i.e their parent). This is called *inheritance* of styles. For example, a color set for the BODY selector will be used as the color for all tags in the body.

In some cases, a property will not be inherited by its nested tags—for example, obvious properties such as margins, width, and borders. You will probably have no trouble figuring out which properties are inherited and which are not. You wouldn't expect every nested element to have the same amount of padding as its parent, for instance. If you have any doubts, though, check out **Appendix A**. Here you'll find a list of all the properties, as well as whether they are inherited or not.

Code 1.12 Setting the body tag as shown in this code sets attributes throughout the document.

```
<HTML>
  <HEAD>
    <STYLE TYPE="text/css">
      BODY {font: 16pt/20pt times,serif; color:
→red; background-color: white;}
    </STYLE>
  </HEAD>
  <BODY>
    <P>The Queen had only one way of settling all
difficulties, great
    or small. 'Off with his head!' she said,
without even looking round.</P>
    <P><FORM ACTION="head.html" METHOD="get">
    <SELECT NAME="SelectName" SIZE="4" MULTIPLE>
      <OPTION VALUE="one">First Head
      <OPTION VALUE="two">Second Head
      <OPTION VALUE="three">Third Head
    </SELECT> </P>
    <P> <BR>
    <INPUT TYPE="RESET" VALUE="Leave head On.">
<INPUT TYPE="SUBMIT" VALUE="OFF WITHHEAD!">
</P></FORM>
  </BODY>
</HTML>
```

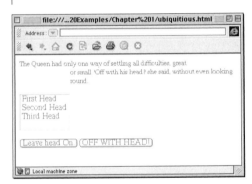

Figure 1.19 The results of setting attributes throughout the document as done in Code 1.12.

Dealing with ubiquitous properties

Be careful when defining the body tag.

BODY {font: 16pt/20pt times,serif; color: red;
→background color: white;}

With this one simple line, you have control over the appearance of everything on the screen.

The problem with this example is that in Internet Explorer the font property will apply to *all* fonts on the screen—including teletype, preformatted text, and the headings. The color property applies to just the text color, but the color of everything on the screen—including tables, and horizontal rules **(Figure 1.19)**.

So consider very carefully what you define for the <BODY> tag.

Code 1.13 Overturning our inherited properties.

```
code

<HTML>
  <HEAD>
    <STYLE>
      B, I { font-weight: normal;}
      P { font-weight: bold;}
    </STYLE>
  </HEAD>
  <BODY BGCOLOR="#FFFFFF">
    <P>Alice was not a bit hurt, and she jumped up
on to her feet in a moment: she looked up, but it
was all dark overhead; before her was another long
passage, and the White Rabbit was still in sight,
hurrying down it.<I> There was not a moment to be
lost: away went Alice like the wind, and was just
in time to hear it say, as it turned a corner, 'Oh
my ears and whiskers, how late it's
getting!'</I></P>
    <B>She was close behind it when she turned the
corner, but the Rabbit was no longer to be seen:
she found herself in a long, low hall, which was
lit up by a row of lamps hanging from the roof.</B>
  </BODY>
</HTML>
```

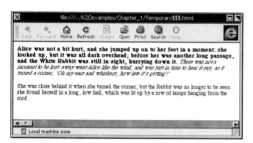

Figure 1.20 The results of **Code 1.13** displayed in Internet Explorer

Managing preexisting or inherited property values

By redefining a selector, you do not cause it to lose any of its inherent attributes. A tag redefined using CSS will keep its already specified properties. All of those properties will display, unless the specific preexisting properties that make up its appearance are changed.

For instance, with CSS you could make the <B> tag a larger font size and italic, like so:

B {font-size: larger; font-style: italic;}

But even though it is not specified in the CSS definition, this text would still be bold. You could, however, set the <B> tag not to be bold by changing the font-weight property, like so:

B {font-weight: normal;}

thus overriding the <B> tag's natural state (see **Code 1.13**).

Properties that are inherited from a parent tag (see **Inheriting properties from parents**, previous) can likewise be overturned simply by explicitly resetting the property in question in the nested tag's definition list, either in the head style list or directly in a particular tag.

Figure 1.20 shows how this all works. Both italic and bold have been set to font-weight normal, and paragraphs will display in bold. When italic is used in the paragraph, it will not be bold.

✔ Tip

■ Navigator is a bit uncooperative when it comes to getting rid of preexisting values. You can adjust them, but you can't override them completely. For instance, even if we set the bold tag's font-weight to normal, it would still appear bold in Navigator.

Determining the cascade order

Within a single Web page, you may have style sheets linked, imported, embedded, or even inlined.

If that's not enough, some browsers plan to eventually allow visitors to have their own style sheets, which they can use to override yours. Of course, it's guaranteed that style sheets from two or more of these sources being used simultaneously will conflict. Who comes out on top? Why do you think they call them *Cascading* Style Sheets?

Determining the cascade order

The following rules determine the cascade order when style sheets conflict.

1. **The existence of the !important attribute**

    !important will give the associated property top billing when being displayed. If both the page author and the visitor have included !important in their definitions, the author's definition wins out. (See the sidebar). Therefore, be cautious when using !important because you might override special colors or font sizes needed by a visitor who is visually challenged.

2. **The source of the rules**

    An author's style sheets will override a visitor's style sheets unless the visitor's uses the !important value.

3. **Specificity**

    The more specific a rule is, the higher its cascade priority. So, the more HTML, class, and ID selectors a particular rule has, the more important it is. In determining this priority, ID selectors count as 100, classes count as 10, and HTML selectors are only worth 1. With this formula, the selectors OL OL OL.cool would be

Using !important

The !important value can be added to a definition in order to give it the maximum weight when determining the cascade order. Insert it into your definition like so:

selector {property: value !important;}

Any property receiving a definition like this will always be used.

weighted at 13 (1+1+1+10=13), while P would only be 1. This priority setting may seem a bit silly, but it allows context-sensitive and ID rules to carry more weight and thus ensures that they will be used.

4. **Last one in the pool wins**

If all else fails, CSS gives priority to the last rule listed, in order. This is especially useful if you include a definition in line to override style settings listed in the head.

Troubleshooting CSS

All too often, you will carefully set up your style sheet rules, go to your browser, and see… nothing. There are plenty of simple things that can prevent your style sheet rules from working properly, so don't panic.

Check the following:

1. Are the properties you are using available for your platform and browser? Many properties will be unsupported on Internet Explorer and/or Netscape Navigator, depending on the operating system being used. Check **Appendix A** to see if the property works with the intended browser and OS.

2. Are there any typos in your selector? If you forget the opening period or number sign (#) for classes and IDs, they won't work.

3. Are there any typos in the properties? Typos in one property can cause the entire rule to fail.

4. Are the values that you are using permitted for that property? Using improper values may cause a definition to fail or behave unpredictably.

5. Are you missing any semicolons? A missing semicolon at the end of a definition will cause the entire rule to fail.

6. Did you open *and* close the definition list with curly brackets? If not, there is no telling what will happen.

7. Did you remember to close all of your multiline comment tags? If not, the entire CSS is treated as a comment.

8. Are the HTML tags themselves set correctly in the document? Remember, you have to use an end **</P>** in order for the paragraph tag to work properly with CSS.

Code 1.14 Can you spot the first 7 mistakes in this code?

```
/* This will never work!
P
  {
  font: normal 10pt18pt helvetica, sans-serif;
  color: #CCCCCC
  marginleft: 3em;
  word-spacing: 2px;
  text-indent: yes;


hyperText
  {
  background-color: fred;
  background-image: url(../images/bg.gif);
  }
```

9. If your rules are in the head, did you use the style tag correctly? Typos in the style tag mean that none of the definitions get used.

10. If you are linking or importing style sheets, are you retrieving the correct file? Check the exact path for the file.

11. Do you have multiple, perhaps conflicting rules for the same tag? Check your cascading order.

If all else fails, try these ideas:

1. Delete the rule and retype it. Sometimes when you can't see what's wrong, retyping it from scratch may fix it.

2. Test the same code on an alternate browser and/or OS. It's possible that a property is buggy and doesn't work correctly on your browser. It's even possible that that browser will not allow that property to work with that tag for some reason.

3. Give up and walk away from the project. Just joking, though you might want to think about taking a 15 minute break before looking at the problem again.

4. If nothing else works, try a different solution to the design problem.

Troubleshooting CSS

CSS FONTS

Typography is one of our most important tools for presenting nice, clean-looking documents. (For that matter, type is our best tool for presenting chaotic, grungy-looking documents.) The fonts you use go a long way toward getting your message across in just the way you want — whether that message is classical or grunge or anything in between. Boldfacing, italic, and other typographic effects help designers guide a visitor's eye around the page.

Cascading style sheets give you the ability to control the appearance of fonts, also known as the *letterforms*, in your Web pages. But with CSS you can set more than just the font family, boldface and italic attributes, and the seven type sizes available through HTML. CSS allows you to go a step farther and set generic font families, various levels of boldness, different types of italic, and any font size desired using the standard point notation used in the print world.

Setting the font

The font you use to display your text can make a powerful difference in how the reader perceives your message. Some fonts are easier to read on the screen, while others look better when printed. The font element allows you to determine the visual effect of your message by choosing the font for displaying your text. **Figure 2.1** shows some of the more commonly used fonts.

To define the font in a rule:

1. H3 {

Begin your rule by typing a selector to define. In **Code 2.1** we are using H3.

2. font-family:

Type in the property name and a colon.

3. times

Type the name of the font you want to use.

4. , "new york", palatino

If you want to, you can type in a list of fonts separated by commas.

5. , serif

After the last comma, type the name of the generic font family for the particular style of font you are using. These generic families are listed in **Table 2.2**. Although including this value is optional, it's a good idea to do it.

6. ;}

Don't forget to close your rule with a semicolon. You can then add any other definitions to the rule, as needed, and a } bracket to close.

Times   Helvetica

Arial   `Courier`

Figure 2.1 Some common fonts.

Code 2.1 You can specify as many fonts as you like in your definition. In this example, Level 3 headers will appear in Times or another serif font. Paragraphs will be in Helvetica, Arial, or another sans-serif font.

```
code
<HTML>
  <HEAD>
  <STYLE TYPE="text/css">
    H3 {font-family: times, "new york", palatino,
→serif;}
    P {font-family: helvetica, arial, sans-serif}
  </STYLE>
  </HEAD>
  <BODY BGCOLOR="#FFFFFF">
    <H3>CHAPTER I<BR>
    Down the Rabbit-Hole</H3>
    <P>Alice was beginning to get ...</P>
  </BODY>
</HTML>
```

Setting the font

Table 2.2

Generic Font Values	
VALUE	EXAMPLES
serif	Times, New York, Garamond
sans-serif	Arial, Helvetica, Geneva
cursive	Zapf-Chancery, Ribbon
fantasy	Decorative fonts, such as Western
monospace	Courier or Monaco

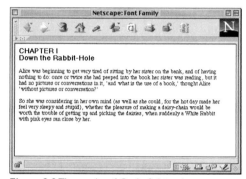

Figure 2.2 The results of **Code 2.1** in a browser.

✔ Tips

- When you provide a list of fonts, the browser will try to use the first font listed. If that one isn't available to the browser, it will work through the list until it encounters a font that is installed on the visitor's computer. If there are no matches, the browser will display the text in the user's default font. The advantage to specifying a generic font is that the browser will try to display the text in the same style of font, even if none of the specific ones you list are available.

- Fonts that contain a space in their names must be enclosed in quotation marks. Example: "New York"

- Most computers have the following fonts built in : Times, Arial or Helvetica, and Courier.

- Both Internet Explorer 4.0 and Navigator 4.0 allow you to download a particular font to the visitor's computer, and then specify the font using the family-name property. However, the principal browsers accomplish the font downloading differently.

Setting the font

Setting the font size

HTML gives you seven different font sizes, but these are all relative to a default size set by the visitor. With CSS you can specify the size of the text on the screen using several different notations or methods, including the traditional point-size notation, percentage, absolute size, or even a size relative to the surrounding text. **Figure 2.3** shows text in different sizes.

To define the font size in a rule:

1. BODY {

Open your rule by typing the selector for which you want to define a font size. Remember to open the definition with a { bracket. In **Code 2.2** we are defining the appearance of the body tag.

2. font-size:

Type the font size property and a colon.

3. 12pt

Type a value for the font size, which could be any of these options:

- A length unit, usually the font size in points.

- An "absolute expression" that describes the font size. The expressions are: xx-small, x-small, small, medium, large, x-large, xx-large.

- smaller or larger, to describe the font size in relation to its parent element (see **Inheriting properties from parents**, page 34).

- A percentage, representing how much larger the text is in proportion to the size of its parent element; for example, 75%.

4. ;}

Close the rule by typing a semicolon. (You can then add any other definitions to this rule as needed, and then a } bracket to close.)

6pt 12pt 24pt 48pt

Figure 2.3 A few different point sizes.

Code 2.2 In this example, all text within the <BODY> tag will be rendered at 12pt size — except for Level 3 headers, in which text will be "larger" than 12pt.

```
<HTML>
  <HEAD>
    <STYLE TYPE="text/css">
      BODY {font-size: 12pt;}
      H3 {font-size: larger;}
    </STYLE>
  </HEAD>
  <BODY BGCOLOR="#FFFFFF">
    <H3>CHAPTER II<BR>The Pool of Tears</H3>
    <P>'Curiouser and curiouser!' cried Alice (she
was so much surprised, that for the moment she
quite forgot how to speak good English); 'now I'm
opening out like the largest telescope that ever
was! Good-bye, feet!' (for when she looked down at
her feet, they seemed to be almost out of sight,
they were getting so far off).</P>
  </BODY>
</HTML>
```

Setting the font size

Figure 2.4 The results of **Code 2.2** in a browser.

✔ Tips

- Although the maximum size font you can use will be dependent on the visitors' computer, try to stay under 500pt size to be safe.

- Don't limit yourself to the small letters available with HTML. With CSS you can create dramatic effects for titles using large letters that will download as quickly as any other text.

Setting the font size

Making text italic

Two kinds of styled text —italic and oblique—are often confused. An *italic font* refers to a special version of a particular font, redesigned with more pronounced serifs and usually a slight slant to the right. *Oblique text* is simply a font that is slanted to the right by the computer. With the font-style element you can define a font as either italic, oblique, or normal. When a font is set to italic and does not have an explicit italic version, the font will default to oblique. **Figure 2.5** shows italic and oblique ext.

To set font-style in an HTML tag:

1. <P STYLE="

Begin your rule by typing the selector to which you want font-styles to apply. In this case, we will be setting up a style rule within an individual HTML tag (see **Code 2.3**).

2. font-style:

Type the font-style property name and a colon.

3. italic

Type the value for the font-style. Your options are:

- italic, which will display the type in an italic version of the font.
- oblique, which will slant the text to the right.
- normal, which will override any other styles set.

4. ;">

Finish the rule by typing a semicolon, a quote mark, and close the HTML tag with a chevron.

normal   *italic   oblique*

Figure 2.5 Italic or oblique?

Code 2.3 The paragraph tag has been set up to display the text in italic. In addition, a class called "speech" is provided; when invoked, the class will neutralize the italic font-style.

```
code
<HTML>
  <HEAD>
    <STYLE TYPE="text/css">
      .speech {font-style: normal;}
    </STYLE>
  </HEAD>
  <BODY BGCOLOR="#FFFFFF">
    <P STYLE="font-style: italic;">
    <SPAN CLASS="speech">'I wish I hadn't cried so
much!'</SPAN>
    said Alice, as she swam about, trying to find
her way out.
    <SPAN CLASS="speech">'I shall be punished for
it now, I suppose, by being drowned in my own
tears! That will be a queer thing, to be sure!
However, everything is queer to-day.'</SPAN>
    </P>
  </BODY>
</HTML>
```

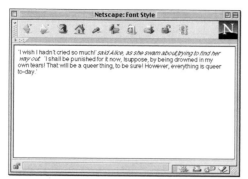

'I wish I hadn't cried so much!' *said Alice, as she swam about,trying to find her way out.* 'I shall be punished for it now, I suppose, by being drowned in my own tears! That will be a queer thing, to be sure! However, everything is queer to-day.'

Figure 2.6 The results of **Code 2.3** in a browser.

✔ Tips

■ The oblique font style does not work with Navigator. Use italic instead.

■ Many Web designers underline words to draw visual attention to them. I recommend using italic or oblique text, instead.Underlining will often cause the page to look cluttered; more importantly, underlined text might be confused with hypertext links!

■ Italicized text generally fits into a more compact space than does non-italic (called "roman" in traditional typesetting terms), and so could be used to save screen space. But be careful — at very small point sizes, italic can be more difficult to read on the screen.

Making text italic

Bold, bolder, boldest

In straight HTML, text is either bold or not. With CSS there are several more options which allow you to set different levels of boldness for text. Many fonts have various *weights* associated with them; these weights have the effect of making the text look more or less bold. CSS can take advantage of this. **Figure 2.7** shows what bold text looks like.

To define bold text in a CSS rule:

1. P B {

Begin your rule by typing the selector to which you want to apply font-styles. In all rules, the selector can be an HTML selector, or a class or ID selector (see **Code 2.4**). Here we will define the font-weight for the bold tag when it is nested in a paragraph tag.

2. font-weight:

Type the font-weight property name and a colon.

3. bold

Type the value for the font-weight property, using one of these options:

- bold, which sets the font to be bold-faced.
- bolder or lighter. which will set the font's weight to be bolder or lighter relative to its parent element's weight.
- A value from 100 to 900, in increments of 100. This will increase the weight based on alternative versions of the font as available.
- normal, which will override other weight specifications.

4. ; }

As always, close your definition by typing a semicolon and a } bracket.

bold   normal

Figure 2.7 Bolder or lighter

Code 2.4 The first rule in this example of two rules sets text in bold tags that are nested within paragraph tags to appear bolder, and the second sets text in bold tags on their own to appear like normal text.

```
<HTML>
  <HEAD>
    <STYLE TYPE="text/css">
      P B {font-weight:bold;}
      B {font-weight: normal;}
    </STYLE>
  </HEAD>
  <BODY BGCOLOR="#FFFFFF">
    <P>It was all very well to say <B>'Drink
me,'</B> but the wise little Alice was not going to
do that in a hurry. 'No, I'll look first,' she
said, 'and see whether it's marked <B>"poison"</B>
or not'.</P>
    <B>'What a curious feeling!' said Alice; 'I
must be shutting up like a telescope.'</B>
  </BODY>
</HTML>
```

Font-weight numbers

Most fonts will not have nine different weights. So if you specify a font-weight value that is not available, another weight will be used based on the following system:

400 and **500** may be used interchangeably.

100–300 will use the next lighter weight, if available, or the next darker otherwise

600–900 will use the next darker weight, if available, or the next lighter otherwise

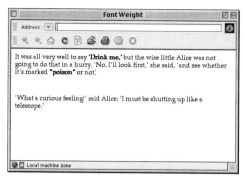

Figure 2.8 The results of **Code 2.4** in a browser.

✔ Tip

- Use font-weight to add emphasis to text, but use it sparingly. If everything is bold, then nothing stands out.

Bold, bolder, boldest

Creating minicaps

Minicaps are very useful for emphasizing titles. With minicaps, lowercase letters are converted to uppercase, but in a slightly smaller size than the regular uppercase letters. **Figure 2.9** shows titles using minicaps.

To make a rule for minicaps:

1. P.curioser {

Type a selector to begin your rule. If you use a class selector, as we do in **Code 2.5**, the class name can be any word you choose. Remember, though, that you can only use this class with the paragraph tag.

2.   font-variant:

Type the font-variant property name and a colon.

3.   small-caps

Type the value of the font-variant property, using one of these options:

- small-caps, which will set lowercase letters as smaller version of true uppercase letters.

- normal, which will override other font-variant values that might be inherited.

4. ; }

Don't forget: Always close your definition by typing a semicolon and a } bracket.

✔ Tips

■ At this writing, the font-variant property is supported only in Internet Explorer 4.0 — and the only change to your text will be conversion to regular uppercase (not true minicap).

■ Why use minicaps if they don't show up in any browsers? Future browsers will be able to display this property and it will not interfere with current browsers.

Normal   MINICAPS

Figure 2.9 Minicaps

Code 2.5 Using a dependent class, we set the P tag to display minicaps.

```
<HTML>
  <HEAD>
    <TITLE>Font Variant</TITLE>
    <STYLE TYPE="text/css">
      P.curiouser {font-variant: small-caps;}
    </STYLE>
  </HEAD>
  <BODY BGCOLOR="#FFFFFF">
    <P CLASS="curiouser">'What a curious feeling!'
said Alice; 'I must be shutting up like a
telescope.'</P>
    <P>And so it was indeed: she was now only ten
inches high, and her face brightened up at the
thought that she was now the right size for going
through the little door into that lovely garden.
First, however, she waited for a few minutes to see
if she was going to shrink any further: she felt a
little nervous about this; 'for it might end, you
know,' said Alice to herself, 'in my going out
altogether, like a candle. I wonder what I should
be like then?' And she tried to fancy what the
flame of a candle is like after the candle is blown
out, for she could not remember ever having seen
such a thing.</P>
  </BODY>
</HTML>
```

■ Other font-variants, such as condensed, expanded, and other customizable variations, are planned for inclusion in future CSS specifications. Stay tuned.

Code 2.6 This example sets Level 3 headers to be italic, bold, 14pt size, in minicaps, and in a sans-serif font.

```
                        code
<HTML>
   <HEAD>
      <STYLE TYPE="text/css">
        H3 {font: italic small-caps bold 14pt
  →helvetica,arial,sans-serif;}
      </STYLE>
   </HEAD>
   <BODY BGCOLOR="#FFFFFF">
      <H3>CHAPTER II<BR>
      The Pool of Tears</H3>
      <P>'Curiouser and curiouser!' cried Alice (she
was so much surprised, that for the moment she
quite forgot how to speak good English); 'now I'm
opening out like the largest telescope that ever
was! Good-bye, feet!'...</P>
   </BODY>
</HTML>
```

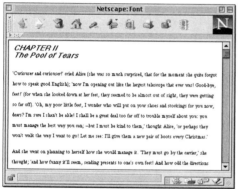

Figure 2.10 The results of **Code 2.6** in a browser.

✔ Tips

- You don't have to specify all of the values for this property to work. Since all of the values are of different types, the browser will know which are which. Instead, just leave the value out completely.

- Line-height is not a font attribute per se. Nevertheless, it can be included in this definition because font size and line height are typographically interdependent.

Setting multiple font values

Although it is possible to set different font elements independently, it is often useful — not to mention more concise — to put all font elements into a single definition. To do this we use the font property.

To define several font attributes simultaneously in a rule:

1. H3 {

   Type a selector for the rule. Don't forget to open your definition by typing a { bracket. In **Code 2.6** we will be defining the appearance of level 3 headers.

2. font:

   Type the property name and a colon.

3. italic

   Type a **font-style** value and a space.

4. small-caps

   Type a **font-variant** value and a space.

5. bold

   Type a **font-weight** value and a space.

6. 14pt

   Type a **font-size** value.

7. /36pt

   Type a forward slash, a **line-height** value, and a space (see **Adjusting the leading** on page 36).

8. helvetica, arial, sans-serif

   Type a **font-family** value.

9. ;}

   Finish your rule by typing a semicolon, add any other definitions that you want for this rule, and finally a } bracket to close it.

CSS TEXT CONTROL

A lot of designers coming to the Web started out designing for print. Although the days of wet ink and image trapping may be far behind us, wouldn't it be nice to have that same precise control over the text in a web page that you had with printed paper?

Although HTML gives you limited control over layout, with tags such as **<CENTER>** and **<P>**, with CSS you have more opportunities to manage the arrangement of text: You can set line spacing within a paragraph, indention, various alignments, spacing between letters, and much more.

Adjusting the kerning (letter spacing)

Adjusting the kerning (letter spacing)

Kerning refers to the amount of space between letters in a word. More space between letters will often improve the readability of the text. On the other hand, too much space can make reading more difficult because individual words appear less distinct on the page.

To define kerning:

1. .stretch {

Type a selector and open your definition with a { bracket. Here we are using a class selector.

2. letter-spacing:

Type the letter-spacing property and a colon.

3. 2em

Type a value for the letter-spacing property, using either:

- A length value, such as 2em, which sets the absolute space between letters.

- normal, which overrides inherited spacing attributes.

4. ; }

Close your rule with a semicolon, and then add a closing } bracket.

✔ Tips

- Currently, letter spacing is only available on Internet Explorer 4.0 for Windows 95.

- A positive value for letter spacing adds additional space to the default amount; and a negative value closes up the space. A value of 0 does not add or subtract space but prevents justification of the text.

Code 3.1 The stretch class puts an additional two em spaces between each letter.

```
<HTML>
  <HEAD>
    <STYLE TYPE="text/css">
    .stretch {letter-spacing: 2em; font-
→weight:bold;}
    </STYLE>
  </HEAD>
  <BODY BGCOLOR="#FFFFFF">
  <P>An enormous puppy was looking down at her with
large round eyes, and feebly <SPAN
CLASS="stretch">stretching</SPAN> out one paw,
trying to touch her. 'Poor little thing!'...</P>
  </BODY>
</HTML>
```

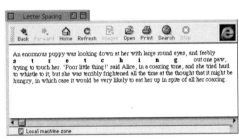

Figure 3.1 This text does what it says.

Adjusting word spacing

Just like letter spacing, adjusting word spacing can both help and hinder. Adding a little spacing between words on the screen can help make your text easier to read, but too much space interrupts the path of the reader's eye across the screen and therefore interferes with reading.

Currently, word spacing is not supported in either Internet Explorer or Navigator, so it's not really that useful. Stay tuned.

To define word spacing:

1. P {

Begin your rule by typing the selector you will use.

2.   word-spacing:

Type the property name and a colon.

3.   5px

Set the value for word spacing, using either:

- A length value representing the amount of space between words; for example, 5px.
- normal, which overrides inherited values.

4. ; }

Finish off your definition with a semi-colon, and end it with a closing } bracket.

✔ Tip

- A positive value for word spacing adds additional space to the default, and a negative value closes up the space. A value of 0 neither adds nor subtracts space but prevents justification.

Adjusting leading (line height)

Anybody who has ever typed a term paper knows that it usually has to be double-spaced. This is done to make reading easier and to allow space for comments to be written on the page. In addition, adding space between lines can be used for dramatic effect, by creating areas of negative space between the text. The line-height property adds space between the *baselines* (the bottoms of most letters) of lines of text.

To define leading in a rule:

1. BODY {

Type the selector for which you want to define line height, and open your definition with a { bracket.

2.   line-height:

Type the property name and a colon.

3.   1.5

Type the value for the line height, using one of these options:

- A number to be multiplied by the font size to get the spacing value; for instance, 2 for double-spacing.

- A length unit; for instance; 24pt. The space for each line of text is set to this size regardless of the designated font size. (So if the font size is set to 12pt and the line height is set to 24pt, the text will be double-spaced.)

- A percentage, which sets the line height proportional to the font size.

- normal, which overrides inherited spacing values.

4. ; }

Don't forget to close your rule with a semicolon, and a } bracket.

Code 3.2 In this example, all text within the body of the document will get line-spacing of one-and-a-half lines (one-and-one-half times that of single-line spacing)—except for blockquotes within paragraphs, which will be single-spaced.

```
                        code
<HTML>
  <HEAD>
    <STYLE TYPE="text/css">
      BODY {line-height: 1.5;}
      P BLOCKQUOTE {line-height: 100%;}
    </STYLE>
  </HEAD>
  <BODY BGCOLOR="#FFFFFF">
    <P>Alice took up the fan ...<P>
    <BLOCKQUOTE>'Dear, dear! How queer everything
is to-day!...'</BLOCKQUOTE>
    <P>And she began thinking...<P>
  </BODY>
</HTML>
```

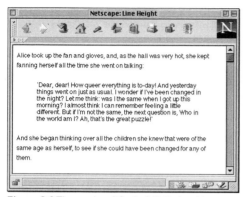

Figure 3.2 The results of **Code 3.2** displayed in a browser.

✔ Tips

- Adding space between lines of text is encouraged in order to enhance legibility —especially in large amounts of text. Generally, a line height of 1.5 to 2 times the font size is appropriate for most text.

- To double-space text, set the line-height value as either 2 or 200%. Likewise, 3 or 300% will result in triple-spaced text.

- Line height can also be defined in the font property (see **Setting multiple font values** on page 51).

Justifying the text (left, right, and center)

Traditionally, text is either aligned at its left margin or fully justified (often called "newspaper style," where text is aligned at both left and right margins). In addition, for added emphasis or special effect, text can be centered in the screen or even right-justified. The text-align property gives you control over the text's alignment and justification.

To define text alignment:

1. BODY {

Type the selector and a { bracket. Here we will be aligning all text in the body of our document.

2. text-align:

Type the property name and a colon.

3. right

Set one of the following alignment styles:

- left to align the text on the left margin.
- right to align the text on the right margin.
- center to center the text within its area.
- justify to align the text on both the left and right sides.

4. ; }

Type a semicolon, then other definitions as needed, and then a closing } bracket to end the rule.

✔ Tip

- Fully justifying text may get some strange results, because spaces between words must be added in order to make each line the same length. In addition, there is considerable debate as to whether full justification actually helps or hinders readability.

Code 3.3 This example sets all text in the body to be right-aligned, unless it is given the class "quote" that sets it to be left-aligned.

```
<HTML>
  <HEAD>
    <STYLE TYPE="text/css">
      BODY {text-align: right;}
      .quote {text-align: left;}
    </STYLE>
  </HEAD>
  <BODY BGCOLOR="#FFFFFF">
    <P>As she said this ...</P>
    <P CLASS="quote">'How can I have done
that?'</P>
    <P>she thought. </P>
    <P CLASS="quote">'I must be growing small
again.' </P>
    <P>She got up and went ...</P>
  </BODY>
</HTML>
```

Figure 3.3 Text within the <BODY> tag is aligned on the right side unless it has the class **quote**, in which case it is left-aligned.

Code 3.4 Superscripting the speed of light.

```
                    code
<HTML>
  <HEAD>
    <STYLE TYPE="text/css">
      H2 {font-size: 75pt;}
      H2.superscript {vertical-align: super;
→ font-size: 35pt;}
    </STYLE>
  </HEAD>
  <BODY BGCOLOR="#FFFFFF">
    <H2>e=mC
    <SPAN CLASS="superscript">2</SPAN></H2>
  </BODY>
</HTML>
```

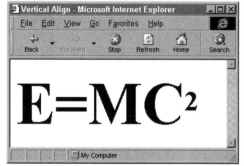

Figure 3.4 e equals m C squared.

Table 3.1

Setting Element's Position Relative to Parent Element	
TYPE THIS	TO GET THE ELEMENT TO ALIGN LIKE THIS
top	Top to highest element in line
middle	Middle to middle of parent
bottom	Bottom to lowest element in line
text-top	Top to top of parent element's text
text-bottom	Bottom to bottom of parent element's text

Aligning text vertically

With the vertical-align property you can specify the position of inline elements relative to the rest of the text, either above or below. This means that vertical-align can only be used with inline element selectors—these are tags without a break before or after them, such as the anchor tag <A>, image tag <IMG>, bold <B>, and italic <I> tags.

Currently, vertical-align is not supported in Navigator; nor is it supported in Internet Explorer except in version 4.0, which recognizes only the sub and super values.

To define vertical alignment:

1. H2 {

Type a selector to begin your rule.

2. vertical-align:

Type the property name and a colon.

3. super

Type a value for the vertical alignment of the text. Choose one of these options:

- baseline, which places the text on the baseline (its natural state).

- sub, which subscripts the text below the baseline.

- super, which superscripts the text above the baseline.

- A relative value from **Table 3.1** which sets the element's alignment relative to its parent's alignment. For example, to have the top of your text aligned with the top of the parent element's text, type text-top.

- A percentage value, which raises or lowers the element's baseline proportional to the parent element's font size. For example, type 25%.

4. ; }

Type a semicolon, other definitions, and then the } bracket to close your rule.

59

Indenting paragraphs

At last the Web can do paragraph indents! Indenting the first word of a paragraph several spaces (traditionally five) is the time-honored method of introducing a new paragraph. On the Web, however, indented paragraphs haven't worked because most browsers compress multiple spaces into a single space. Instead, paragraphs have been separated by an extra line-break.

Now, with the text-indent property you can specify extra spaces at the beginning of the first line of text in a paragraph.

To define text indentation in a rule:

1. P {

Start your rule with the selector of your choice. Here we are going to indent all paragraphs on the page.

2.   text-indent:

Type the property name and a colon.

3.   2em

Type a value for the indention, using either of these options:

- A length value, for example 2em. This amount will create a nice, clear indent.

- A percentage value, which indents the text proportional to the paragraphs width. For example, type 10%.

4. ; margin:0; }

Close this rule by typing a semicolon, (then any other definitions for this selector), and then the closing } bracket. I set the margin to 0 in order to override the P tags natural tendency to add space between paragraphs.

Code 3.5 All paragraphs in this passage will be indented two em spaces, a "respectable" indention.

```
<HTML>
  <HEAD>
    <STYLE TYPE="text/css">
       P {text-indent: 2em; margin:0;}
    </STYLE>
  </HEAD>
  <BODY BGCOLOR="#FFFFFF">
    <P>'Ugh!' said the Lory, with a shiver.</P>
    <P>'I beg your pardon!...'</P>
    <P>'Not I!' said the Lory hastily.</P>
    <P>'I thought you did,' said the Mouse...</P>
    <P>'Found what?' said the Duck.</P>
    <P>'Found it,' the Mouse replied rather
crossly...</P>
    <P>'I know what &quot;it&quot; ...</P>
  </BODY>
</HTML>
```

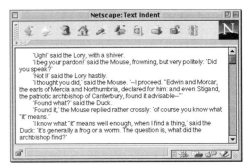

Figure 3.5 Real Indented paragraphs; no need for the extra line breaks.

Code 3.6 The class **name**, if invoked, will force words to be displayed in initial caps.

```
                        code
<HTML>
  <HEAD>
    <STYLE TYPE="text/css">
      .name {text-transform: capitalize;}
    </STYLE>
  </HEAD>
  <BODY BGCOLOR="#FFFFFF">
    <P CLASS="name">george jetson</P>
    <P CLASS="name">fred flintstone</P>
    <P CLASS="name">ralph cramden</P>
    <P CLASS="name">gomez adams</P>
    <P CLASS="name">diana prince</P>
    <P CLASS="name">robert dobbs</P>
    <P CLASS="name">homer simpson</P>
  </BODY>
</HTML>
```

Figure 3.6 The list of names is correctly capitalized.

Controlling text case

Often when you're dealing with dynamically generated output, you can never be sure if the text will be produced in uppercase, lowercase, or a mixture. With the **text-transformation** property, you can control the ultimate case of the text no matter what it is to begin with.

To define the text case:

1. .name {

Start off by typing in a selector. Since we can't be sure which tags will need to have the letter case controlled, let's set this up as an independent class.

2. text-transform:

Type the property name and a colon.

3. capitalize

Type one of the following values for how you want the text treated:

- **capitalize** sets the first letter of each word in uppercase.

- **uppercase** forces all letters to be uppercase.

- **lowercase** forces all letters to be lowercase.

- **none** overrides inherited text case values and leaves the text as is.

4. ; }

Close with the obligatory semicolon, and } bracket.

✔ Tips

- If you want specific text to be in uppercase, you should type it in as uppercase, so that older browsers won't get left out.

- The **text-transform** property is probably best reserved for formatting text that is being created dynamically. For instance, if the names in a database are all uppercase, you can use **text-transform** to make them more legible when displayed.

Controlling text case

Decorating the text

Text decoration allows you to adorn the text with one of four different looks. Used to add emphasis, these decorations will attract the reader's eye to important areas or passages in your Web page.

To decorate a selector's text:

1. EM {

Begin by choosing the selector whose text you want to embellish.

2. text-decoration:

Type the property name and a colon.

3. underline

Type a value for the decoration style; choose one of the following:

- underline places a line beneath the text.
- overline places a line above the text.
- line-through places a line through the middle of the text.
- blink causes the text to blink on and off.
- Typing none as the value will override decorations set elsewhere.

4. overline underline blink

If you want to, and as long as the first value is not none, you can have multiple text decorations by adding additional values in a list separated by spaces.

5. ; }

Close this definition with a semicolon, type any other rules you want, and then close the rule with a bracket.

Code 3.7 In this example we set the emphasis tag to be underlined unless it is included within a paragraph, in which case it gets the line through the middle.

```
<HTML>
  <HEAD>
    <STYLE TYPE="text/css">
      EM {text-decoration: underline;}
      P EM {text-decoration: line-through;}
    </STYLE>
  </HEAD>
  <BODY BGCOLOR="#FFFFFF">
    <EM>CHAPTER IV<BR>
    The Rabbit Sends in a Little Bill</EM>
    <P>It was the White Rabbit, trotting slowly
back again, and looking anxiously about as it
went, as if it had lost something; and she heard it
muttering to itself <EM>'The Duchess! The Duchess!
Oh my dear paws! Oh my fur and whiskers! She'll get
me executed, as sure as ferrets are ferrets! Where
can I have dropped them, I wonder?'</EM> Alice
guessed in a moment that it was looking for the fan
and the pair of white kid gloves...</P>
  </BODY>
</HTML>
```

Decorating the text

Figure 3.7 The title is underlined, but the emphasized text in the paragraph is crossed out. Notice that the text is oblique, despite the fact that we didn't explicitly give this instruction. This is because Navigator naturally sets the <EM> tag as oblique, despite any added properties. If needed, we could override this by setting **font-style: normal;** (see page 46).

✔ Tips

■ The blink value is not supported in Internet Explorer.

■ The overline value is not supported in Navigator.

■ Many visitors don't like blinking text, especially on Web pages where they spend a lot of time. Use this decoration sparingly.

■ Setting text-decoration: none; will not override link underlines if they're set in the visitor's browser. Sorry.

Decorating the text

Controlling white spaces

As mentioned in the section on indents, browsers in the past have collapsed multiple spaces into a single space unless the <PRE> tag was used. CSS lets you allow or disallow the collapsing of spaces, as well as designate whether text can break at a space (similar to the <NOBR> HTML tag).

To define white space for a selector:

1. P {

Set up your selector.

2. white-space:

Type the property name and a colon.

3. pre

Type one of the following values to designate how you want spaces in text to be handled:

- pre preserves multiple spaces.
- nowrap prevents line wrapping without a break tag.
- normal allows the browser to determine how spaces are treated. This usually forces multiple spaces to collapse into a single space.

4. ; }

Finish off your definition.

✔ Tips

- Internet Explorer does not support the white-space property.

- Navigator does not support the nowrap option for white-space.

- The text content of any tag that receives the nowrap value will run horizontally as far as it needs, regardless of the window's width. The user may be forced to scroll horizontally to read all of the text, which is usually frowned upon.

Code 3.8 Paragraphs will preserve the spacing as indicated within the HTML, but if given the class **.collapse**, multiple spaces become one.

```
<HTML>
  <HEAD>
    <STYLE TYPE="text/css">
      P {white-space: pre;}
      .collapse {white-space: normal;}
    </STYLE>
  </HEAD>
  <BODY BGCOLOR="#FFFFFF">
    <P>A L      I C E        ' S        R I G H
    T F OO T, E S       Q . </P>
    <P CLASS="collapse">H      E     A  R T H R
U    G      ,</P>
    <P>(WITH ALICE'S LOVE).              <IMG
SRC="../images/alice08a.gif" WIDTH="200"
HEIGHT="131"></P>
  </BODY>
```

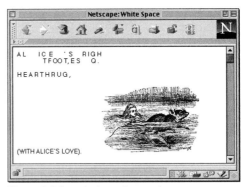

Figure 3.8 Even the image is spaced over.

USING THE LIST STYLE PROPERTIES

One useful feature of HTML is its ability to set up lists that will automatically number or bullet themselves. You set up the list and the browser takes care of the rest. When you add additional items to the list, the layout adjusts automatically when it's rendered in the window. However, the choices available are fairly limited with HTML.

CSS gives you a lot more choices, providing control over the type of marker used to denote your list items, which can be a bullet or an alphanumeric character. You can also create your own bullets and make lists with "hanging" indents.

The bad news is that many of these features are not supported in either Navigator or Internet Explorer. In addition, for the features that Navigator does support it does not allow you to use just any HTML tag, but will only allow you to redefine the LI tag. Hopefully that will change in the near future.

Setting the bullet style

The list-style property gives you control over the type of bullet to be used for list items—not just circles, discs, and squares, but letters and numerals and dots. (Oh my!)

To define the bullet style:

1. LI.grocery {

Type in the selector you are defining. For this example we'll set up a dependent class called grocery that is associated with the list tag. It's important to remember that in Navigator we can only change the list tag with these properties.

2.   list-style-type:

Type in the list-style-type property and a colon.

3.   disc

Type in one of the marker style names listed in **Table 4.1**.

Or type none if you want no marker at all to appear.

4. ;}

Close the definition.

✔ Tips

■ Currently, list-style-type can only be used with list tags <LI>. This is at odds with the official CSS specs, which state that *any* HTML tag can be used to make a list as long as it includes the definition display: list-item; in the same rule. Hopefully this conflict will be cleared up in future versions of DHTML browsers.

■ It's a good idea always to include the list-style-type property, because image loading may be turned off by the user, or a bullet image may not load for some reason, or the list-style-image property may be set to none.

Code 4.1 Two classes are created to help with the shopping list. The grocery class uses discs as its bullet, and computer uses squares.

```
<HTML>
  <HEAD>
    <STYLE TYPE="text/css">
      LI.grocery {list-style-type: disc;}
      LI.computer {list-style-type: square;}
    </STYLE>
  </HEAD>
  <BODY BGCOLOR="#FFFFFF">
    <H3>Shopping list</H3>
    <UL>
    <LI CLASS="grocery">Butter
    <LI CLASS="grocery">Milk
    <LI CLASS="grocery">Cereal
    <LI CLASS="computer">5GB Hard drive
    <LI CLASS="grocery">Orange juice
    <LI CLASS="grocery">Cat food
    <LI CLASS="computer">40MB RAM
    <LI CLASS="grocery">Soup
    </UL>
  </BODY>
</HTML>
```

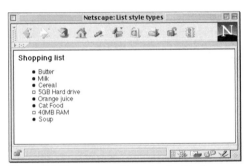

Figure 4.1 The computer items stand out in the shopping list because they use a unique bullet.

Table 4.1

Selectors for Block-Level Tags	
NAME	**APPEARANCE** (VARIES DEPENDING ON SYSTEM)
disc	●
circle	○
square	■
decimal	.
upper-roman	I
lower-roman	i
upper-alpha	A
lower-alpha	a

Code 4.2 Here, lists are set to display with a hanging indent unless given the class inside, which will cause the text to run flush with the bullet.

```
                    code
<HTML>
  <HEAD>
    <STYLE TYPE="text/css">
      LI {list-style-position: outside;
→width="200px";}
        .inside {list-style-position: inside;}
    </STYLE>
  </HEAD>
  <BODY BGCOLOR="#FFFFFF">
    <UL>
      <LI>'A knot!' said Alice...
      <LI CLASS="inside">'I shall do nothing...
      <LI>'I didn't mean it!' ...
      <LI>The Mouse only growled in reply.
    </UL>
  </BODY>
</HTML>
```

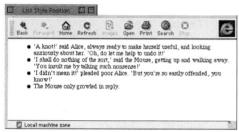

Figure 4.2 The results of **Code 4.2** in a browser.

Creating a hanging indent

Often the text of an item in a bulleted list is longer than one line. Using the list-style-position property, you can specify the position of wrapping text in relation to the bullet. Wrapped text that will be indented to start underneath the first letter of the first line of text is called a *hanging indent*.

To define the line position for wrapped text in a list item:

1. .inside {

Set up your selector. For this example, we'll create an independent class called "inside" which, when used with a list tag, will make the listed text fall flush with the bullet.

2. line-style-position:

Type in the list-style-position property and a colon.

3. inside

Type one of the following keywords to determine how you want the text indented:

- inside sets subsequent lines of wrapped text aligned with the bullet.

- outside sets subsequent lines of wrapped text aligned with the first letter in the first line of the text.

4. ;}

Close the definition with a semicolon and a } bracket.

✔ Tips

- Navigator does support the list-style-position property.

- Generally, bulleted lists that have a hanging indent (outside position) stand out much better than those without a hanging indent (inside position).

Creating a hanging indent

Creating your own bullets

You're not limited to the preset bullet styles built into the browser (see page 66). You can also use your own graphics as bullets, in GIF, JPEG, and PNG (for supporting browsers only) formats. You will first need to create the graphic in a program such as Adobe PhotoShop.

To define your own graphic bullet:

1. LI

   Start your definition with a list selector.

2. list-style-image:

   Type in the line style image property name.

3. url(../images/bullet1.gif)

   To include your own bullet, you have to tell the browser where your bullet graphic is located. This location is either the complete Web address or the local filename of the image. In this example, ../images/ →bullet1.gif is a local address that goes up one directory level and then into a directory called images, and uses a graphic called bullet1.gif.

4. Or type none, which instructs the browser to override any inherited bullet images.

5. ;}

   Close the definition with a semicolon. Then type in any other definitions for this rule and close it with a } bracket.

✔ Tips

- Navigator does not support the list-style-image property.

- Graphical bullets are a great way to enhance the appearance of your page while minimizing download time.

Code 4.3 These list items will have an image in front of them rather than a standard bullet.

```
<HTML>
  <HEAD>
    <STYLE TYPE="text/css">
      LI {
  list-style-image : url(../images/bullet1.gif);
}
    </STYLE>
  </HEAD>
  <BODY BGCOLOR="#FFFFFF">
    <P>Things to do</P>
    <UL>
      <LI>write book
      <LI>make examples
      <LI>edit book
      <LI>take holiday in bahamas
      <LI>drink pina colladas
    </UL>
  </BODY>
</HTML>
```

Figure 4.3 The various parts of the list are indicated by a graphical arrow.

Creating your own bullets

Code 4.4 Here, all of the *list-style* properties are set at once.

```
                        code
<HTML>
  <HEAD>
  <STYLE TYPE="text/css">
    LI {
  list-style: circle  outside url(bullet1.gif);
}
  </STYLE>
  </HEAD>
  <BODY BGCOLOR="#FFFFFF">
    <H3>Places to go</H3>
      <LI>London
      <LI>Paris
      <LI>Tokyo
      <LI>New York
      <LI>Slippery Creek
  </BODY>
</HTML>
```

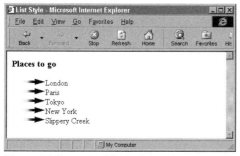

Figure 4.4 *The results of* **Code 4.4** *in a browser.*

Setting multiple values for the list-style property

You can set all of the attributes for a list in one line of code by using the list-style property. This property allows you access to the list-style-type, list-style-position, and line-style-image properties.

To define multiple list-style attributes for a selector simultaneously:

1. LI {

Set up the list item selector to be redefined.

2. list-style:

Type in the list-style property.

3. circle

Type a list-style-type value and a space.

4. outside

Type a list-style-position value and a space.

5. url(bullet2.gif)

Next, type a list-style-image value.

6. ;}

Close the definition with a semicolon, then type in any other definitions for this rule, and close it with a } bracket.

✔ Tips

■ Navigator does not recognize list-style-position or list-style-image values. Bummer.

■ Since each of the multiple values above is of a different type, not all values must be present for this definition to work. Values omitted will be set to the default.

■ If the visitor has turned off graphics in the browser, or if a graphical bullet does not load for some reason, the browser will use what you have set for list-style-type instead.

USING THE COLOR AND BACKGROUND PROPERTIES

HTML has allowed us to set background colors and graphics almost since its beginnings. However, this was limited only to the background of the entire Web page. You could play around with the background colors of table cells, but this was still very confining.

CSS gives designers the ability to define the background color and graphic for any element on the page, giving you much greater versatility when it comes to designing your Web pages. In fact, this may be the most significant advancement that CSS offers.

Setting colors

By using the color property you can set the color appearance for an element. Text, borders, and even horizontal rules within that tag will be the color you set.

To define the color:

1. .fj43 {

Begin your rule by typing a selector to define, in **Code 5.1** we are using an independent class selector which can be used to apply our definitions to any HTML tag.

2. color:

Type the name of the color property and a colon.

3. red

Next type in a value for the color you wish this element to appear in.

4. ;}

Do not forget to close your definition with a semi-colon. You can then add any other definitions to this rule that you want and a } bracket to close it.

✔ Tips

■ Setting all parts of a tag to a single color might lead to problems where selectors which control elements you don't want to be that color are set anyway, so consider what selectors you set this property for carefully (see **Inheriting properties from parents**, page 34).

■ A tag's border color is also set by the color property, but can be overwritten by the border-color property (see **Setting the border's color**, page 96).

Code 5.1 An ID selector called fj43 is set to the color red.

```
<HTML>
  <HEAD>
     <TITLE>Color</TITLE>
     <STYLE TYPE="text/css">
        .fj43 {color: red;}
     </STYLE>
  </HEAD>
  <BODY BGCOLOR="#FFFFFF">
     <H3 CLASS="fj43">CHAPTER V<BR>
     Advice from a Caterpillar</H3>
     <P>The Caterpillar and Alice ...<P>
  </BODY>
</HTML>
```

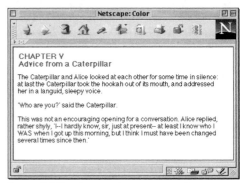

CHAPTER V
Advice from a Caterpillar

The Caterpillar and Alice looked at each other for some time in silence: at last the Caterpillar took the hookah out of its mouth, and addressed her in a languid, sleepy voice.

'Who are you?' said the Caterpillar.

This was not an encouraging opening for a conversation. Alice replied, rather shyly, 'I--I hardly know, sir, just at present-- at least I know who I WAS when I got up this morning, but I think I must have been changed several times since then.'

Figure 5.1 The chapter title appears in red.

Code 5.2 Four different elements are given their own unique background colors.

```
                      code
<HTML>
  <HEAD>
    <STYLE TYPE="text/css">
      BODY {background-color: #FF6666;}
      H4 {background-color: #FF9999;}
      P {background-color: #FFCCCC;}
      B {background-color: #FFFFFF;}
    </STYLE>
  </HEAD>
  <BODY>
    <H4>CHAPTER VI<BR>
    Pig and Pepper</H4>
    <P>For a minute or two she stood looking at
the house, and wondering what to do next, when
suddenly a footman in livery came running out of
the wood- (she considered him to be a footman
because he was in livery: otherwise, judging by
his face only, <B>she would have called him a
fish</B>)—and rapped loudly at the door with his
knuckles...</P>
  </BODY>
</HTML>
```

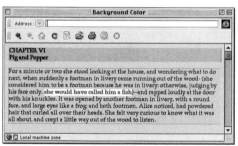

Figure 5.2 The results of **Code 5.2** in a browser.

Setting background colors

The ability to set the background color for an HTML page has been around almost since the first web browsers. However, with CSS you can define not only the background color for the entire page, but behind individual elements as well.

To define the background color for a selector:

1. BODY {

   Start your rule with the selector you want to define.

2. background-color:

   Start your definition by typing in the property and a colon.

3. #FF6666

   Type in a value for the color you want the background to be.

4. Or you could type transparent which tells the browser to use the default color set by the browser.

5. ;}

   Always close your definitions with a semi-colon. You can then add any other definitions to this rule that you want and a } bracket to close the rule.

✔ Tips

- Background color is not fully supported in Internet Explorer 3.0 for Windows. However, background color can be set in the background property (see **Setting multiple background values** on page 81) which does work in Internet Explorer.

- Although background colors are not inherited, since the default state for an elements background is transparent, its parent elements background-color will show through.

Setting a background image

With CSS you can define not only the background image for the entire page, but the image behind individual elements as well. So, you might set the background image for the entire page, and then have a different background image behind a title or text input field.

To define a background image:

1. #para1 {

Set up the selector you want to define. Here we will set a background image for and ID selector.

2. background-image:

Type in the name for background image property and a colon.

3. url(../images/background_rough.gif)

Let the browser know where the file you want to use as the background is, either a complete web address or local filename. In this case ../images/background_brick.gif which instructs the browser to go up a directory level to look in a directory called images for the file background_brick.gif. Close the url specification by typing).

4. Or type none which instructs the browser not to use a background image.

5. ; padding: 10px; font: bold 12pt/14pt hel →vetica,sans-serif; color: black;}

Close your definition with a semi-colon. You can then add any other definitions to this rule that you want and a } bracket to close the rule.

Code 5.3 The <BODY> tag is set to have one background image, while paragraphs will have a different image behind them.

```
                        code
<HTML>
  <HEAD>
    <STYLE TYPE="text/css">
      #para1 {background-image:
→url(../images/background_rough.gif); padding:
→10px; font: bold 12pt/14pt helvetica,sans-
→serif; color: black;}
        BODY {background-image:
→url(../images/background_brick.gif);}

    </STYLE>
  </HEAD>
  <BODY>
    <P ID="para1">Very soon the Rabbit noticed
Alice...<P>
  </BODY>
</HTML>
```

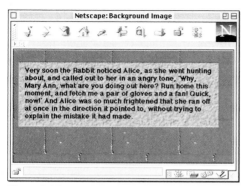

Figure 5.3 The Web page has a brick pattern in it, but behind the paragraphs is a rough grainy texture.

✔ Tips

- Like background-color, background-image is not fully supported in Internet Explorer 3.0 for Windows. However, background color can be set in the background property which does work in Internet Explorer.

- The ability to place graphics behind any element on the screen is a very powerful tool for designers, and frees them from the constraints of always having to create new graphics whenever text changes (see **Creating headlines with graphic backgrounds**, page 126).

- Since the default state for an elements background is none, the parent elements background image (or color) will show through unless background color or background image is set.

Setting a background image

Setting a background image's repetition

Sometimes a repeating background can be really annoying. It may repeat where it's not wanted or you may only want it to tile in one direction. CSS gives you supreme control over how background graphics appear using the background-repeat property.

To control background repeating:

1. BODY {

   Type in the selector you are going to set the background for. Here we will be setting the background for the entire document through the body tag.

2. background-image: url(../images/
   →background_rough.gif); background-color:
   →#CC6666;

   In order to set a background image's repetition, you have to set a background image. It also helps to set the background color which will show up anywhere that the background image does not repeat.

3. background-repeat:

   Start your definition by typing in the background repeat property.

4. no-repeat

   Next, type in a keyword that tells the browser how you want the repetition of the background treated:

   - repeat instructs the browser to repeat the graphic throughout the background of the element.

   - repeat-x instructs the browser to repeat the background graphic only horizontally. In other words, the graphic will repeat in one straight horizontal line along the top of the element.

Code 5.4 The <BODY> tag is given a background, but it will only appear once in the top left corner of the window...

```
                          code
<HTML>
  <HEAD>
    <STYLE TYPE="text/css">
      BODY {background-color: #CC6666;
→background-image:url(../images/background
→_rough.gif); background-repeat: no-repeat;}
      H2 {width: 120px; margin: -5px; font-size:
→18pt; line-height: 28pt;}
    </STYLE>
  </HEAD>
  <BODY LINK="#000066">
    <H2 STYLE="margin-bottom: 30px;">CHAPTER
IX<BR>
    The Mock Turtle's Story</H2>
    <P>'You can't think how glad I am to see you
again, you dear old thing!'</P>
  </BODY>
</HTML>
```

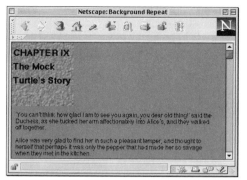

Figure 5.4 ...which provides a nice backdrop for the page title.

- repeat-y instructs the browser to repeat the background graphic only vertically. In other words, the graphic will repeat in one straight vertical line along the left side of the element.

- no-repeat in which case the background graphic will not tile, but only appear once.

5. ;}

Close your definition with a semi-colon and a } bracket.

✔ Tips

- Any background space that does not have a background graphic will be filled with the background color (see **Setting the background colors**, page 73).

- You can use the repeat-y value to create side bars (see **Creating a side bar**, page 127).

- You can use the repeat-x property to put a different background behind the top of your document (see **Creating a title bar**, page 130).

Setting a background image's repetition

Positioning a background on the screen

A background graphic can be given an initial position. This positioning can be applied to block-level elements or any element for which the exact size is known (such as img, input, textarea, select, and object), and offsets the background from the top left corner of that element by however much you want.

To define the position of a background graphic:

1. .body {

   Set up the selector you want to use. In **Code 5.5a** we're setting up an independent class that can be used to put a "watermark" background graphic behind an HTML tag on the screen.

2. background-color: #CC6666;

   background-image: url(../images/back
   →ground_rough.gif);

   To position a background graphic, you have to have define where the background graphic is. It also helps to give a background color which will appear anywhere the graphic does not.

3. background-position:

   Start your definition by typing in the letter spacing property and a colon.

4. 75px 75px

   You can define the position of a background numerically or by percentages:

   Type in **two length values** separated by a space. The first number tells the browser the distance from the left of the edge, while the second value specifies the position from the top.

Code 5.5a *The rule for the class watermark is set up in an external file called alice.css that gets used in...*

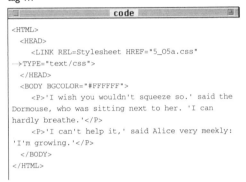

```
.body
 {
 background-color: #CC6666;
 background-image:
 url(../images/background_rough.gif);
 background-position: 75px 75px;
 }
```

Code 5.5b ...this document through the <LINK> tag ...

```
<HTML>
 <HEAD>
  <LINK REL=Stylesheet HREF="5_05a.css"
→TYPE="text/css">
 </HEAD>
 <BODY BGCOLOR="#FFFFFF">
  <P>'I wish you wouldn't squeeze so.' said the
Dormouse, who was sitting next to her. 'I can
hardly breathe.'</P>
  <P>'I can't help it,' said Alice very meekly:
'I'm growing.'</P>
 </BODY>
</HTML>
```

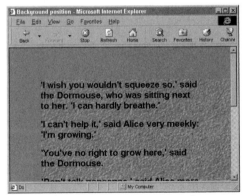

Figure 5.5 ...for display on the screen in a browser window. The offset creates a nice space at the top and left of the screen.

Or type **two percentage values** separated by a space, for example 25% 35%. The first percentage indicates the horizontal position proportional to the elements size, while the second value indicates the vertical position proportional to the elements size.

5. ;}

Close your definition with a semi-colon. You can then add any other definitions to this rule that you want and a } bracket to close the rule.

✔ Tips

■ Background positioning currently only works in Internet Explorer 4.0.

■ You can mix percentage and length values in the same definition, but you cannot mix length or percentages with plain English keywords.

Positioning in plain English

background-position: center top;

You can also define the position using keywords to position the graphic relative to the size of the window:

1. Type in a horizontal position keyword: left, center, right.

2. Next type a space and then type in a vertical position keyword: top, center, bottom.

Fixing backgrounds on the screen

Sometimes you want the background to just stand still and the rest of the content to travel over the top of it. In other words, you want it to be fixed in relation to the other elements on the screen. To do this use the background-attachment property. The drawback is that this property does not work yet with Navigator.

To define the background graphics attachment for a selector:

1. BODY{

Set up the selector you want to use. In **Code 5.6** we're setting whether the background will repeat or not in the document.

2. background-image: url(../images/
→background_rough.gif);

To position a background graphic, you have to have define where the background graphic is. It also helps to give a background color which will appear anywhere that the graphic does not.

3. background-attachment:

Start your definition by typing in the background-attachment property and a colon.

4. fixed

Now type in a keyword instructing the browser how to treat the background when scrolling:

- fixed which instructs the browser to not scroll the background content with the rest of the elements.

- or scroll which will instruct the background graphic to scroll with the element.

5. ;}

Close your definition.

Code 5.6 The background is attached and then fixed in place.

```
<HTML>
  <HEAD>
    <TITLE>Background Attachment</TITLE>
    <STYLE TYPE="text/css">
      background-image:
      url(../images/background_rough.gif);
      background-repeat: repeat-x;
      background-attachment: fixed;
    </STYLE>
  </HEAD>
  <BODY BGCOLOR="#FFFFFF">
    <P>The Fish-Footman began by producing from
under his arm a great letter, nearly as large as
himself, and this he handed over to the other,
saying, in a solemn tone, 'For the Duchess. An
invitation from the Queen to play croquet.' The
Frog-Footman repeated, in the same solemn tone,
only changing the order of the words a little,
'From the Queen. An invitation for the Duchess to
play croquet.'</P>
    <P>Then they both bowed low, and their curls
got entangled together.</P>
    <P>Alice laughed so much at this, that she had
to run back into the wood for fear of their hearing
her; and when she next peeped out the Fish-Footman
was gone, and the other was sitting on the ground
near the door, staring stupidly up into the
sky.</P>
  </BODY>
</HTML>
```

Code 5.7 All of the background properties for the <BODY> tag are set in one line.

```
                    code
<HTML>
  <HEAD>
    <STYLE TYPE="text/css">
      BODY {background: pink
→url(../images/background_brick2.gif) repeat-y
→fixed right top;}
      P {margin-left: 125px; font: 12pt/18pt
helvetica,sans-serif;}
        H2 {width: 100px; color:white;}
    </STYLE>
  </HEAD>
  <BODY BGCOLOR="#FFFFFF">
    <H2>CHAPTER XII<BR>
    Alice's Evidence
    </H2>
    <P>'Here!' cried Alice...P>
  </BODY>
</HTML>
```

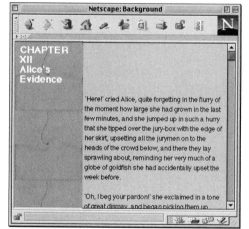

Figure 5.6 The results of **Code 5.7** displayed in a browser.

Setting multiple background values

Sometimes it's useful to set all of the background values in a single line. Sometimes it's even necessary because some browsers don't recognize all of the background properties, but will understand this one. Background can be applied to any selector and is not inherited.

To define multiple background values:

1. BODY {

   Set up the selector you want to work with. In **Code 5.7**, we're dealing with the body tag.

2. background:

   Start your definition by typing in the letter spacing property and a colon.

3. pink

   Type a **background-color value** and a space.

4. url(../images/background_brick2.gif)

   Type a **background-image value** and a space.

5. repeat-y

   Type a **background-repeat value** and a space.

6. fixed

   Type a **background-attachment value** and a space.

7. right top

   Next type a **background-position value**.

8. ;}

   Close your definition.

CSS MARGINS
AND BORDERS

In the physical world, atoms are the building blocks for all larger objects. Every different type of atom—element—has its own unique properties, but when bonded with other atoms they create larger structures with properties different from the parts.

Likewise, HTML tags are the building blocks of your Web page. Each tag has its own unique abilities, and can be combined together to create a whole Web page that is greater than the parts.

Whether the tag is by itself or nested deep within other tags, each one can be treated as a discrete "element" on the screen and controlled using CSS.

We use the concept of *the box* as a metaphor to understand and describe the various things that you can do to an HTML element in a window. This box has several properties—including margins, borders, padding, width, and height—which can be influenced by CSS.

Understanding the element's box

The term *element* is used to refer to the various parts of an HTML document that are set off by HTML container tags. For example:

<P>My Word!</P>

is an HTML element.

In addition, replaced tags such as the image tag create elements on the screen by placing on object onto the screen (see **Kinds of tags** in Chapter 1, page 19).

Let's take a closer look at what makes up an element's box.

Parts of the Box

All elements have four sides: top, bottom, left, and right (**Figure 6.1**). These four sides make up the element's box, to which CSS properties can be applied. Each side of the box has a

- margin: the space between the outermost edge of the element and other elements.
- border: the rule (line) that surrounds the element; this is often invisible.
- padding: the space between the border and the content of the element.

Element boxes also have a width and height. The width is the distance from the outer edge of the left border to the outer edge of the right border. The height is the distance from the top of the top border to the bottom of the bottom border. If you leave width and height undefined, these distances will be determined by the browser. (See **Setting the width and height of an element** on page 101.)

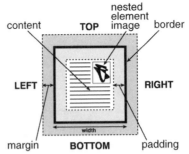

Figure 6.1 Understanding the box. An element block has a margin, a border, and padding, on four sides around its central content. The element's width and height can be defined by the author or can be left to the browser's discretion.

Tags or containers?

You'll see the term *HTML tag* used a lot, not only in this book but all over the Web. A *tag* is a marker used by HTML (for instance, the <BLOCKQUOTE> tag) that tells the browser to do something. Very often a tag also has an associated closing tag that is designated with a / character (for instance, </BLOCKQUOTE> is the closing blockquote tag). The closing tag shows the browser when to stop doing something. These two tags collectively are known as a *container*. But more often than not, the entire container will be referred to with the term *tag*.

```
<P>To be or not to be <I>that<I> is
the question.</P>
```

Figure 6.2 Parents and children. In this code, <P>...</P> is the parent element to <I>...</I>. Thus <I>...</I> is <P>...</P>'s child.

The Content

At the center of the box is the *content*. All the other CSS properties (**font, text, color, background** and **lists**) apply to this area. (*Note:* Background properties also apply to the padded area of an element's box.) The content includes all text, lists, forms, images, and embedded objects that are included between the opening and closing container tags.

Nested Elements

When one tag is enclosed by another tag, this is referred to as a *nested* element as shown in **Figure 6.2.** The children of an element are those elements nested within it. An element's parent is the element that it is nested within. A single element may have many parents if it is nested within an element that is in turn nested within other elements.

✔ Tips

■ Any inline element that is given a box property will appear as a block-level element (that is, it will get a line break before and after it).

■ CSS properties will generally apply themselves to all nested tags within a particular tag (see **Inheriting properties from parents** in Chapter 1, page 34).

Setting element margins

The margin property allows you to set the space between that element and others in the window by specifying one to four values that correspond to either all four sides together, the top/bottom and left/right sides as pairs, or all four sides independently. **Figure 6.3** shows margins in action used to provide negative space around the text on the left and right sides.

To define the margins:

1. BODY {

   Type your selector. In **Code 6.1** (shown on the next page) we are setting a margin for everything on the page by using the body tag's selector.

2.   margin:

   Start your definition by typing in the margin property and a colon.

3.   5em

   Now type in a value for the margin, which can be any of the following:

   • A length value.

   • A percentage, which creates a margin proportional to the parent element's width.

   • The value auto, which returns control of the margins to the browser's discretion.

4. ;}

   Close this definition with a semicolon. If you want, you can then add other definitions for this rule, or close the rule with a } bracket. **Figure 6.3** shows what this margin will look like.

Code 6.1 The body of the page gets a 5em margin, so that all text on the page stays that distance from the edge of the page. The only exception is the level 5 header, which receives a -5em margin, effectively negating the body margin for that tag.

```
                        code
<HTML>
 <HEAD>
 <STYLE TYPE="text/css">
    BODY {margin: 5em;}
    H5 {margin: -5em;}
 </STYLE>
 </HEAD>
 <BODY BGCOLOR="#FFFFFF">
    <H5>CHAPTER VII<BR>
    A Mad Tea-Party</h5>
    <P>There was a table set ...</P>
 </BODY>
</HTML>
```

Many values at once

If you want to set several margins, you can enter up to four different values separated by spaces. For example:

5em auto 5em 25%

1. One value sets the margin for all four sides.

2. Two values set the top/bottom margins and left/right margins.

3. Three values set the top margin, the left and right margins (the same), and the bottom margin.

4. Four values set each individual margin: top, right, bottom, and left.

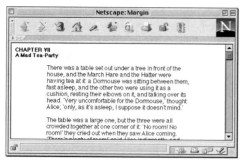

Figure 6.3 Although the text in paragraphs is 5em from the edge of the screen on the left and right, the header is over to the left where it would normally be.

✔ Tips

- Be careful when setting negative margins around a hypertext link. If one element has margins that cause it to cover the link, the link will not work as expected.

- Navigator only permits negative values for the top and bottom margins.

- When setting proportional margins, be aware that you might get very different results depending on the size of the user's window. What looks good at a resolution of 640x480 might be a mess at larger screen sizes.

Setting negative margins

H5 {margin: -5em;}

Although you can use negative margins to create interesting effects for overlapping pieces of text, this method is often frowned upon because the various browsers will present different results. Overlapping text is better achieved using CSS positioning (see Chapter 7, **CSS Positioning**).

Setting element margins

Setting individual margins

You can set just one side of the box's margin without having to worry about the other three margins. This is especially useful when used with an inline style for overriding margins set elsewhere. In **Figure 6.4,** several different margins have been set for the different sides of the elements.

To define an individual margin:

1. **.left {**

   Set up the selector you want to use to control your document. In **Code 6.2** we are setting up a class called left that can then be applied to whatever HTML tag we want.

2. margin-

   Start your definition by typing in the **margin** property and a hyphen.

3. left

   Select the side of the element box for which you want to set the margin. Type its name, either **top**, **bottom**, **left**, or **right**, and then type a colon.

4. 5em

   Now type a value for that side's margin, which can be any of the following:

   • A length value.

   • A percentage, which creates a margin proportional to the parent element's width.

   • **auto**, which returns control of the margins to the browser's discretion.

5. **;}**

   Close this definition with a semicolon. You can then add more definitions that you need for this rule and close the rule with a } bracket.

Code 6.2 The body has a margin setting of 2em, but then four classes are established—left, right, top, bottom—that will adjust the margin on those sides.

```
code
<HTML>
  <HEAD>
  <STYLE TYPE="text/css">
    BODY {margin: 2em;}
    .left {margin-left: 5em;}
    .right {margin-left: 4em;}
    .top {margin-top: -1em;}
    .bottom {margin-bottom: -1em;}
  </STYLE>
  </HEAD>
  <BODY BGCOLOR="#FFFFFF">
    <P>Alice looked all round the table, but there
was nothing on it but tea. 'I don't see any wine,'
she remarked.</P>
    <P CLASS="left">'There isn't any,' said the
March Hare.</P>
    <P CLASS="bottom">'Then it wasn't very civil
of you to offer it,' said Alice angrily.</P>
    <P CLASS="right">'It wasn't very civil of you
to sit down without being invited, 'said the March
Hare.</P>
    <P CLASS="top">'I didn't know it was your
table,' said Alice; 'it's laid for a great many
more than three.'</P>
  </BODY>
</HTML>
```

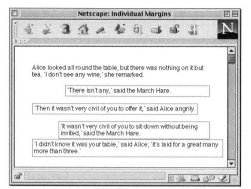

Figure 6.4 The first paragraph is positioned normally within the body since it has no class associated with it, but the next four paragraphs move to different positions depending on each one's associated class. Note: The elements' borders have been turned on so that you can better see how the margins interact.

✔ Tips

- The auto value doesn't work for margin-right and margin-left on Internet Explorer or Navigator.

- Use these side-by-side margin properties to override the ubiquitous margins set using the margin property (see the earlier section on **Setting element margins** on page 86).

Setting padding around an element

At first sight, padding seems to have an effect identical to margins: It adds space around the element's content. The difference is that padding sets the space between the border of the element and its content, rather than between the element and the others on the screen. Take a look at **Figure 6.5** to see an example of padding to separate the content from the border.

To define padding:

1. P {

Type in the selector for which you want to set up a CSS rule. In **Code 6.3** we are using the paragraph tag's selector.

2. padding:

Start your definition by typing in the padding property and a colon.

3. 10px

Next, type a value for the element's padding, which can be either of the following:

- A length value.
- A percentage, which creates padding proportional to the parent element's width.

4. ;}

Close this definition by typing a semi-colon, any additional definitions, and a } bracket.

Code 6.3 This code instructs P elements to have a 10-pixel top padding, a 5-pixel right padding, a 35% bottom padding, and a 40-pixel left padding.

```
code
<HTML>
  <HEAD>
  <STYLE TYPE="text/css">
    P {padding: 10px 5px 35% 40px;}
  </STYLE>
  </HEAD>
  <BODY BGCOLOR="#FFFFFF">
    <P>First it marked out a race-course, in a
sort of circle, ('the exact shape doesn't matter,'
it said,) and then all the party were placed along
the course, here and there...</P>
  </BODY>
</HTML>
```

Multiple values

padding: 10px 5px 35% 40px;

You can place up to four values within the padding property, separated by spaces:

1. One value sets the padding for all four margins.

2. Two values set the padding for the top/bottom and left/right pairs.

3. Three values set the top padding, the padding for the left and right sides (the same), and the bottom padding.

4. Four values set padding for each side individually: top, right, bottom, and left.

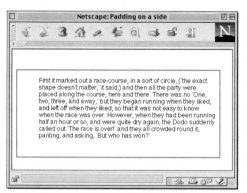

First it marked out a race-course, in a sort of circle, ('the exact shape doesn't matter,' it said,) and then all the party were placed along the course, here and there. There was no 'One, two, three, and away,' but they began running when they liked, and left off when they liked, so that it was not easy to know when the race was over. However, when they had been running half an hour or so, and were quite dry again, the Dodo suddenly called out 'The race is over!' and they all crowded round it, panting, and asking, 'But who has won?'

Figure 6.5 The results of **Code 6.3** in a browser. The border has been included so that you can see how the padding works.

✔ Tip

■ Padding and margins are easily confused, often because their results look the same if border is not visible. Remember: Margins separate one element from other elements, but padding is the space between the border and the content of the element.

Setting padding around an element

Setting padding on a side

You can set the padding on each side of the box individually if you like, which is useful for overriding values set by the padding property. **Figure 6.6**, shows the content hoping around in relation to the border depending on how the padding is set.

To define padding for one side of the box:

1. <P STYLE="

Type the selector for which you want to set a rule. In **Code 6.4**, we've set up our rule to affect the appearance of a single HTML tag, the paragraph tag. By doing this we can override padding set in the head of the document.

2. padding-

Type the padding property and a hyphen.

3. left:

Select the side of the element for which you're setting the padding. Type its name —top, bottom, left, or right—and then type a colon.

4. 0px

Type a value for the padding. You can choose one of the following::

- A length value.

- A percentage, which adds padding proportional to the parent element's width

- The value auto, which returns control of that side's padding to the browser's discretion.

5. ;">

Close this definition with a semicolon, add any more definitions you want to use with this HTML tag, and then close the rule with a quote mark and a closing chevron. **Figure 6.6** shows what this will look like in a browser window.

Code 6.4 Paragraphs will get a padding of 20 pixels all the way around. In the HTML, however, we override this margin in each of the <P> tags.

```
code
<HTML>
  <HEAD>
  <STYLE TYPE="text/css">
    P {padding: 20px;}
  </STYLE>
  </HEAD>
  <BODY BGCOLOR="#FFFFFF">
    <P STYLE="padding-left: 0px;">A large rose-
tree stood near the entrance of the garden: the
roses...</P>
    <P STYLE="padding-top: 0px;">Alice thought
this a very curious thing, and she went nearer
to...</P>
    <P STYLE="padding-right: 0px;">'I couldn't
help it,' said Five, in a sulky tone;</P>
    <P STYLE="padding-bottom: 0px;">On which Seven
looked up and said, 'That's right, Five!'</P>
  </BODY>
</HTML>
```

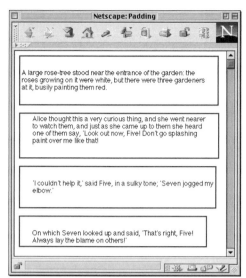

Figure 6.6 The results of **Code 6.4** in a browser.
Note: The element's borders have been turned on so that you can better see the effects of padding.

✔ Tips

- You can use these properties to override the padding property set using the padding property for a single side (see **Setting padding around an element** on page 90).

- Negative values are not allowed with padding.

Setting padding on a side

Setting the border width

The border width is a set of up to four values that will define the thickness of the rules (i.e. lines) that surround an element's content. If you do not set the border style or color, it will appear as a solid black line. **Figure 6.7** shows some examples of the border width where different sides have different widths.

To define the border width of an element:

1. P {

Type the selector and opening bracket.

2. border-width:

Type the border-width property and a colon.

3. 5px

Next, type one of the following values for the border width:

- A length value.
- A relative-size keyword; use either thin, medium, or thick.

4. ;}

Don't forget to close your definition with a semicolon and a } bracket.

✔ Tip

- The border-width property is not supported in Internet Explorer. Use the border property instead.

Code 6.5 *This code sets the border widths for the element to 5 pixels top, 10 pixels right, 20 pixels bottom, 40 pixels left.*

```
<HTML>
  <HEAD>
  <STYLE TYPE="text/css">
    P {border-width: 5px 10px 20px 40px;}
  </STYLE>
  </HEAD>
  <BODY BGCOLOR="#FFFFFF">
    <P>It was the White Rabbit, trotting slowly
back again,...</P>
  </BODY>
</HTML>
```

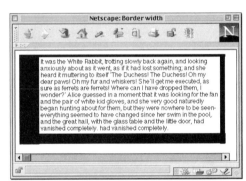

Figure 6.7 The results of **Code 6.5** in a browser window. Notice that the border automatically defaults to solid in Navigator even though a style was not set in the code. In Internet Explorer the border style has to be defined or else the border remains invisible.

Setting multiple values

border-width: 5px thick 20px 40px;

You can set one to four values:

1. One value sets the border width for all four sides.

2. Two values sets the border width for the top/bottom and left/right.

3. Three values sets the top border width, the border width for the left and right sides (the same), and the bottom border width.

4. Four values sets the border width for each side individually: top, right, bottom, and left.

Setting the border width

Code 6.6 This code is saved as an external CSS file called border_patrol.css.

```
                          code

    P {border: 5mm groove red;}
    .left {border-left-width: .5in;}
    .right {border-right-width: .5in;}
    .top {border-top-width: .5in;}
    .bottom {border-bottom-width: .5in;}
```

Code 6.7 Code 6.7 is then linked to this document,

```
                          code

<HTML>
  <HEAD>
  <LINK REL=stylesheet HREF="6_06.css">
  </HEAD>
  <BODY BGCOLOR="#FFFFFF">
     <P CLASS="left">'Now tell me, Pat, what's that
in the window?'</P>
     <P CLASS="right">'Sure, it's an arm, yer
honour!' (He pronounced it 'arrum.')</P>
     <P CLASS="top">'An arm, you goose! Who ever
saw one that size? </P>
     <P CLASS="bottom">'Sure, it does, yer honour:
but it's an arm for all that.'</P>
  </BODY>
</HTML>
```

Figure 6.8 The code produces this result in a browser. The general border size is 5 millimeters, but the class's left, top, bottom, and right can be used to override this on each side.

Setting the border width on a side

You can set each side's border width on an individual basis if you desire, which is useful for overriding width values set by the border-width property. In **Figure 6.8**, each element has its border widths set by the border property and then one of its sides set separately.

To define an individual side's border width:

1. .left {

Type a selector for this rule. For **Code 6.6** we will set up an independent class, which we can then use to control the margin of any HTML tag. (**Code 6.7**)

2. border-

Start your definition by typing in the border property and a hyphen.

3. left

Type the name of the side of the element whose border width you're setting: top, bottom, left, or right.

4. -width:

Let the browser know that you are setting the width, by typing a hyphen and then width.

5. .5in

Next, type a value for the border width:
- A length value.
- Or a relative size of thin, medium, or thick.

6. ;}

Lest we forget, close your definition with a semicolon and a } bracket.

✔ Tip

■ These border-width properties are not supported in Internet Explorer. Use the border property instead.

Setting the border color

Like most elements on a Web page, you can specify the color of an element's border. If left unspecified, this color will default to the user-defined color property. **Figure 6.9** shows a multicolored border. (OK, not really. But it would if we could print more than two colors).

To define the border color for a selector:

1. IMG {

Set up a selector for this rule. In **Code 6.8** we have entered the image tag's selector.

2. border-color:

Start your definition by typing in the border-color property and a colon.

3. red

Type a **color value,** which is the color you want the border to be. This can be the name of the color, a hex color value, or an RGB value.

4. ; border: 20px inset;}

Type in a closing semicolon for this definition. Then, for your border color to show up, you should include a border size definition.

Code 6.8 This code sets an image's top border red, the right border green, the bottom blue, and the left purple.

```
code
<HTML>
  <HEAD>
    <TITLE>Border Color</TITLE>
    <STYLE TYPE="text/css">
      IMG {border-color: red green blue purple;
→border: 20px inset;}
    </STYLE>
  </HEAD>
  <BODY BGCOLOR="#FFFFFF">
    <IMG SRC="../images/alice32a.gif" WIDTH="139"
HEIGHT="200">
  </BODY>
</HTML>
```

Multi-colored borders

border-color: red green blue purple;

You can type up to 4 values separated by spaces. This works just as it does for setting other element properties:

1. One value sets the border color for all four sides.

2. Two values set the border color for the top/bottom and left/right pairs.

3. Three values set the top border color, the border color for the left and right sides (the same), and the bottom border color.

4. Four values set the border color for each side individually: top, right, bottom, and left.

Figure 6.9 It's hard to see in a two-color book, but trust me—this border is a beautiful and vibrant multicolored extravaganza.

✔ Tips

- This property does not work in Netscape Navigator 4.

- Navigator does not allow border-color to be set on a per-side basis. Navigator will use the first value in the value list to set the color on all four sides.

Decorating the border

Not only can you set the border's color, but you can also choose from a small range of patterns for decorating your border. In **Figure 6.10** the border has been set to inset to make it appear to recess into the screen.

Navigator Note: The border-style property must be specified in order for the border to show up on the screen in Netscape browsers.

To set the border style for a selector:

1. P {

   Type the selector for which you're setting up this rule. In **Code 6.9** we'll be using the paragraph tag.

2.   border-style:

   Type the border-style property and a colon.

3.   inset

   Type the name of the style you want to assign to your border. (See **Table 6.2** for a complete list of available styles.)

   Or you can type none; which will prevent the border from appearing altogether.

4. Just like many other definitions in this chapter, you can define up to 4 border-style values separated by spaces.

5. ; border-width:5px;}

   Type a semicolon and then type in a border-width definition. Close it with a } bracket. Of course, you can also include other definitions before closing if you wish.

✔ Tips

- Dotted and dashed styles for borders are not supported in Navigator or Internet Explorer.

- Navigator does not allow decoration to be set on a per-side basis. The first value in the list will be used on all four sides.

Code 6.9 These paragraphs will have a border around them.

```
<HTML>
  <HEAD>
  <STYLE TYPE="text/css">
    P {border-style: inset; border-width:10px;}
  </STYLE>
  </HEAD>
  <BODY BGCOLOR="#FFFFFF">
    <IMG SRC="../images/alice06a.gif" WIDTH="163"
HEIGHT="200" ALIGN="left">
    <P>Alice remained looking...P>
  </BODY>
</HTML>
```

Figure 6.10 The results of **Code 6.9** in a browser. The border appears to be embossed into the screen.

Table 6.2

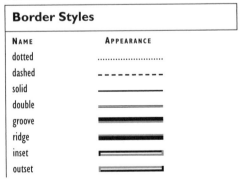

Border Styles	
NAME	**APPEARANCE**
dotted	....
dashed	- - - - - - - - -
solid	————————
double	═══════════
groove	▬▬▬▬▬▬▬▬
ridge	▬▬▬▬▬▬▬▬
inset	▭▬▬▬▬▬▬
outset	▬▬▬▬▬▭

Code 6.10 Both the <IMG> and <P> tags will get the same border.

```
                    code
<HTML>
  <HEAD>
    <TITLE>Border</TITLE>
    <STYLE TYPE="text/css">
      IMG, P {border: 20px double #990000;}
    </STYLE>
  </HEAD>
  <BODY BGCOLOR="#FFFFFF">
    <IMG WIDTH="151" HEIGHT="200"
SRC="../images/alice15a.gif">
      <P>This time Alice waited patiently until it
chose to speak again. In a minute or two the
Caterpillar took the hookah out of its mouth and
yawned once or twice, and shook itself.</P>
  </BODY>
</HTML>
```

Figure 6.11 The results of **Code 6.10** in a browser window. The border frames both the image and the text.

Setting multiple border values

To set any of the border attributes for all four sides of the box simultaneously, CSS provides the border property. Border can be used to set width, style, and/or color. As you can see in **Figure 6.11,** setting the border property in **Code 6.10** has dramatic effects on the look of the page.

To set multiple border attributes:

1. IMG, P {

   Type the selector(s) for which you want to create a rule. In **Code 6.10** we are defining both the image and paragraph tags at the same time.

2.   border:

   Type in the border property and a colon.

3.   20px

   Type a **border-width value** and a space.

4.   double

   Type a **border-style value** and a space.

5.   #990000

   Type a **border-color value** and a semi-colon.

6. ;}

   Close the definition with a semicolon, then any additional definitions for this rule, and then the } bracket. **Figure 6.11** shows you what this should look like in the browser.

✔ Tip

- Most browsers that do not support other border properties will usually support this one.

Setting multiple border values on a side

Each border side can also have all of its values set independently. **Figure 6.12** shows one possible way of doing this by setting a common border style all the way around and then augmenting an individual side.

To define multiple border attributes on a side for a selector:

1. .left {

Type the selector for which you're setting up this rule. In **Code 6.11** we are creating a rule for the independent selector called left.

2. border-

Start your definition by typing in the border property and a hyphen.

3. left:

Type the name of the side whose attributes you're specifying—top, bottom, left, or right—and then a colon.

4. 5px

Type a **border-width value** and a space.

5. double

Type a **border-style value** and a space.

6. red

Type a **border-color value**.

7. ;}

Close the definition with a semicolon, type in any additional definitions for this rule, and then close the rule with a } bracket.

✔ Tip

■ Navigator does not support this property. Instead, you'll need to control individual sides by accessing each side's specific properties one at a time.

Code 6.11 Each side can have its border attributes set independently.

```
<HTML>
  <HEAD>
  <STYLE TYPE="text/css">
    .left {border-left: 5px double red;}
    .right {border-right: 10px ridge red;}
    .top {border-top: 20px inset red;}
    .bottom {border-bottom: 40px outset red;}
    P {border: 5px groove black;}
  </STYLE>
  </HEAD>
  <BODY BGCOLOR="#FFFFFF">
    <P CLASS="left">'Now tell me, Pat, what's that
in the window?'</P>
    <P CLASS="right">'Sure, it's an arm, yer
honour!' (He pronounced it 'arrum.')</P>
    <P CLASS="top">'An arm, you goose! Who ever
saw one that size? Why, it fills the whole
window!'</P>
    <P CLASS="bottom">'Sure, it does, yer honour:
but it's an arm for all that.'</P>
  </BODY>
</HTML>
```

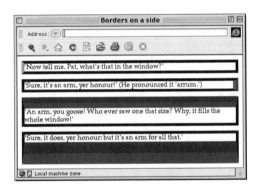

Figure 6.12 The results of **Code 6.11** in Internet Explorer. Each element has had a different border set individually.

Code 6.12 TEXTAREA is set to a 300-pixel width and 200-pixel height.

```
code

<HTML>
  <HEAD><TITLE>Width & Height</TITLE>
  <STYLE TYPE="text/css">
    TEXTAREA {width: 300px; height: 200px;}
  </STYLE>
  </HEAD>
  <BODY BGCOLOR="#FFFFFF">

  <FORM ACTION="geher.html" METHOD="get">
  <TEXTAREA >Alice remained looking...<TEXTAREA>
  </FORM>
  </BODY>
</HTML>
```

Setting the width and height of an element

The width and height of block-level and replaced elements can be specified using the width and height properties. Usually, the width and height are determined automatically by the browser, but you can override both the width and height properties, as shown in **Figure 6.13**.

To define the width and height:

1. TEXTAREA {

Type the selector for which you want to create a rule. In **Code 6.12** we are defining the dimensions of a form's text-entry field.

2. width:

Type in the width property and a colon.

3. 300px;

Type a value for the elements width, which can be any of the following:

- A length value.
- A percentage, which sets the width proportional to the parent element's width.
- auto, which uses the width calculated by the browser for the element. The width is usually going to be the maximum distance that the element can stretch to the right before hitting the edge of the window or the edge of a parent element.

4. height:

Type in the height property and a colon.

5. 200px

Type a value for the height of the element; for example, **200px** is a length of 200 pixels.

Or type **auto**, which uses a calculated height determined by the browser. The height will be however much space the element needs to display all of the content.

6. ;}

Close the definition with a semicolon, and any additional definitions for this rule. Close the rule by typing a } bracket.

✔ Tips

- You can resize an image (GIF or JPEG) using the width and height properties, and thus overriding the width and height set in the image tag. Doing this will more than likely create a severely distorted image. But that can also be a pretty neat effect.

- Use width and height to keep form fields and buttons a consistent size.

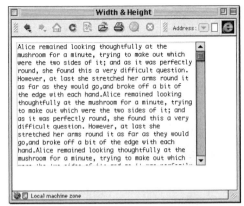

Figure 6.13 Text areas will always be 300x200 pixels.

Code 6.13 Any paragraph given the TNT class will float to the right.

```
HTML>
   <HEAD>
      <STYLE TYPE="text/css">
         P.tnt {float: right; font-weight: bold;
→width:275px; padding:1em;}
      </STYLE>
   </HEAD>
   <BODY BGCOLOR="#FFFFFF">
      <P CLASS="tnt">
      <IMG SRC="../images/alice37a.gif" WIDTH="100"
HEIGHT="136" ALIGN="right">One of the jurors
...</P>
      <P>The King and Queen of Hearts ...</P>
   </BODY>
</HTML>
```

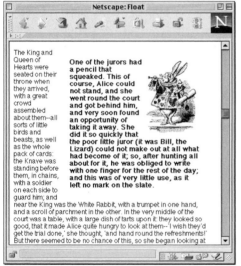

Figure 6.14 One element flows around the next.

Wrapping text around text (aka "floating")

Early on in the development of HTML, when the ability to have text flow around a graphic was added, designers everywhere were delighted. CSS takes this technique one step forward by letting you not only flow text around graphics, but also flow text around text and text around tables. This is accomplished by using the **float** property. **Figure 6.14** shows an example of text floating inside text.

To define the floating position of a selector:

1. P.tnt {

   Type your selector. In **Code 6.13** we have created a dependent class that can be used with the paragraph tag.

2. float:

   Start your definition by typing in the **float** property and a colon.

3. right

   Next, type a keyword to tell the browser which side of the screen the element should float to. Choose:

   - right to align this element to the right, causing other elements to wrap on the left.
   - left to align this element to the left, causing other elements to wrap on the right.
   - none, which defaults back to the parent element's alignment.

4. ; font-weight: bold; width:275px;
   →padding:1em;}

   Close the definition with a semicolon, and type in any additional definitions for this rule. In this example, for instance, we added properties to make our floating text larger and bolder. Finally, close the rule with a } bracket.

Preventing floating text

Sometimes you may find it necessary to override the float property. Similar to the clear attribute of the HTML break tag, the clear property allows you to specify whether you want to *deny* floating text to the left, right, or both sides of the element. In **Figure 6.15**, you can see how the second paragraph wraps around the first but the third appears beneath it.

To stop text floating:

1. .nextpart {

Type the selector for which you want to turn wrapping off. In **Code 6.14** we have set up an independent class that we can use with any HTML tag.

2. clear:

Type in the clear width property and a colon to start your definition.

3.   left

Choose the side or sides where you want to prevent floating. Type in left, right, or both, and then a semicolon.

Or you can type none, which overrides other clear properties.

4. ;}

Close the definition with a semicolon, and then close the rule with a bracket.

5. <P CLASS="next part">...</P>

Now whenever you use this class with an HTML tag, it will not wrap around other tags regardless of how their float property is set.

✔ Tips

■ Internet Explorer does not support the both option.

■ Use the clear command to force an element to appear below an element that would normally have been wrapped.

Code 6.14 Putting the clear property into a paragraph prevents it from wrapping around other elements.

```
<HTML>
  <HEAD>
    <TITLE>Clear</TITLE>
    <STYLE TYPE="text/css">
      .leftcol {float: left; font-size: 8pt;
  font-weight: bold; width:275px; padding:1em;}
      .nextpart {clear: left;}
    </STYLE>
  </HEAD>
  <BODY BGCOLOR="#FFFFFF">
    <P CLASS="left vol">
<IMG SRC="../images/alice22a.gif" WIDTH="100"
HEIGHT="147" ALIGN="left">&quot;You can really
have no notion how delightful it will be when they
take us up and throw us, with the lobsters, out to
sea!&quot;...</P>
    <P>&quot;What matters it how far we go?&quot;
his scaly friend replied. &quot;There is another
shore, you know, upon the other side...</P>
    <P CLASS="nextpart">Will you, won't you, will
you, won't you, will you join the dance? Will you,
won't you, will you, won't you, won't you join the
dance?&quot;'</P>
  </BODY>
</HTML>
```

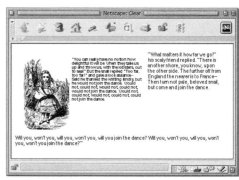

Figure 6.15 The last paragraph drops below the wrapped text.

Code 6.15 The display property is used along with the list properties to create CSS lists...In theory. MSIE does not support this property and Navigator does not require it for lists.

```
code
<HTML>
  <HEAD>
  <STYLE TYPE="text/css">
    .list {display: list-item;}
  </STYLE>
  </HEAD>
  <BODY BGCOLOR="#FFFFFF">
    <P>First came </P>
    <P CLASS="list">ten soldiers carrying clubs;
these were all shaped like the three gardeners,
oblong and flat, with their hands and feet at the
corners.</P>
    <P CLASS="list">next the ten courtiers; these
were ornamented all over with diamonds, and walked
two and two, as the soldiers did. </P>
    <P CLASS="list">After these came the royal
children; there were ten of them, and the little
dears came jumping merrily along hand in hand, in
couples: they were all ornamented with hearts. </P>
    <P CLASS="list">Next came the guests, mostly
Kings and Queens, and among them Alice recognised
the White Rabbit: it was talking in a hurried
nervous manner, smiling at everything that was
said, and went by without noticing her. </P>
    <P CLASS="list">Then followed the Knave of
Hearts, carrying the King's crown on a crimson
velvet cushion; and, </P>
    <P CLASS="list">last of all this grand
procession, came THE KING AND QUEEN OF HEARTS.</P>
  </BODY>
</HTML>
```

Telling the element how to display (or not)

The display property can be used to define whether an element includes line breaks above and below, is included inline with other elements, is treated as part of a list, or is displayed at all. For this example we have shown how display works if used to define a list. **Figure 6.16** shows how elements will be shifted to the right when set as list items.

To set the display mode for a selector:

1. .list {

Type in the name of the selector for which you want to use this rule. In **Code 6.15** we are setting up an independent class which can then be used to indent a list.

2. display:

Start your definition by typing in the display property and a colon.

3. list-item

Type a keyword that defines how this element will display. Choose one of these:

- list-item will place a list-item marker on the first line of text, as well as place a break above and below. This allows it to be used as part of a list.
- block will place a line break above and below the element.
- inline will cause the element to include no breaks.
- none will cause this element not to display at all in CSS browsers.

4. ;}

Close the definition with a semicolon, any additional definitions for this rule, and then the closing } bracket.

✔ Tips

■ Any elements given the value none will simply be ignored by a CSS browser. Be careful when using none, however. Although it is not an inherited attribute, none will turn off display of the element as well as any children elements within it.

■ Only Navigator 4.0 supports the none option.

■ The display property should not be confused with visibility (see page 150). The visibility property gives you control, through JavaScript, of whether an element appears on the screen or not.

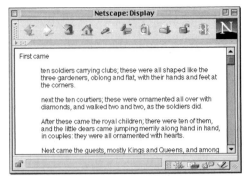

Figure 6.16 In Navigator the list gets indented even if it does not place bullet in front of each list element.

Telling the element how to display (or not)

CSS POSITIONING

A lot of people complain that the Web is too slow—the joke is that WWW stands for "The World Wide Wait." Part of the problem is that in order to construct an attractive web page, designers often use graphics simply to create text that will show up where the designer wants it.

Another design issue that affects the efficiency of page display is the use of tables to create columns, or to assemble graphics jigsaw fashion. Tables take a fair amount of calculation time to set up on the screen. The more tables you use, the slower your page displays.

CSS Positioning (CSS-P) is more accurate than either graphics or tables, and the results are displayed much faster. CSS gives us control over composition in terms of creating margins and borders (see Chapter 6). Beyond that, CSS-P allows us to position elements on the screen either exactly where we want them or in relation to other elements on the screen.

This chapter introduces you to the methods used to position HTML elements using Cascading Style Sheets. Although the code presented here is part of the recently completed Cascading Style Sheets Level 2, it has already been at least partially implemented in the two primary browsers: Internet Explorer 4.0 and Navigator 4.0.

Setting the position type

When you set the attributes of an HTML tag through a selector in a Cascading Style Sheet, you in effect single out any content within that tag's container as being a unique element on the screen. (See **Understanding the element's box?** on page 84.) This unique element can then be manipulated through CSS positioning.

An element can have one of three different position values (see **Table 7.1**). The position type tells the browser how to treat the element when placing it on the screen.

Once elements have been positioned on the screen, you can then use JavaScript or other scripting languages to move, hide, or display them.

✔ Tips

■ Although you can use CSS-P attributes with any HTML that you can use regular CSS with, it is often useful instead to associate the positioning information with an independent class or ID (see pages 22-24). The class or ID can then be applied as needed rather than being assigned automatically with the tag.

■ If you are already familiar with Netscape's Layers (see Chapter 13) then CSS-P should look pretty familiar. For crossbrowser DHTML, though, CSS-P will be used instead of layers.

Table 7.1

A Matter of Position		
NAME	**HOW IT WORKS**	**FOR MORE INFORMATION**
static	Flows the content inline, but position of element can't be touched.	*"Using static positioning"*
relative	Flows the element inline, but allows you to move the element around within the element's natural position on the screen.	*"Using relative positioning"*
absolute	Element is placed independently of other elements on the screen in a specific position in the window.	*"Using absolute positioning"*

Caution: Positioning and older browsers

Use of most of the CSS properties discussed in Chapters 2–6 will not prevent a document from displaying properly in a non-CSS browser. However, if you are relying on position properties for the layout of your document, the document will probably not display well in older browsers and may even be completely unusable. Always test your code in a non-CSS browser to see if the results are acceptable.

Code 7.1 Although the image exists in the HTML...

```
<HTML>
  <HEAD>
    STYLE TYPE="text/css">
    .hide {visibility: hidden; font-weight:
→bold;}
    </STYLE>
  </HEAD>
  <BODY BGCOLOR="#FFFFFF">
  <SPAN CLASS="hide">
    <IMG SRC="../images/alice06a.gif" WIDTH="163"
HEIGHT="200" ALIGN="right">
  </SPAN>
'I wish I hadn't mentioned Dinah!' she said to
herself in a melancholy tone. 'Nobody seems to
like her, down here, and I'm sure she's the best
cat in the world! Oh, my dear Dinah! I wonder if I
shall ever see you any more!'
  </BODY>
</HTML>.
```

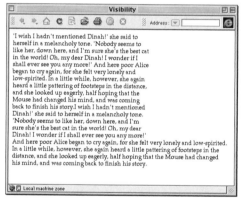

Figure 7.1 ...it does not appear on the screen. Instead there is an empty space where the graphic should be.

Visibility (or not)

The visibility property designates whether an element is visible or not when it is initially put into the window. If visibility is set to hidden, the element will still be in the document, taking up space, but will be invisible and appear as a big empty rectangle where the image should be as **Figure 7.1** shows.

To set an element's visibility:

1. .hide1 {

   Start your CSS rule off with a selector and bracket. I recommend using an ID if you want to define the visibility of a single element on the screen (which you might later use JavaScript to reveal).

2.   visibility:

   Type in the visibility property name with a colon.

3.   hidden

   Now type one of the following keywords for how you want this elements visibility treated:

   - hidden, which causes the element to be invisible when initially rendered on the screen.

   - visible, to cause the element to be visible.

   - inherit, which causes the element to inherit the visibility of its parent element.

4. ; font-weight: bold;}

   Close the definition with a semicolon and a } bracket.

✔ Tip

■ The visibility of an element can be turned on or off using a scripting language (see page 150).

■ Though seemingly similar, visibility differs from the display property (see page 105). When display is set to none, the element is wiped out of the document altogether.

Using absolute positioning

Absolute positioning creates an independent element—a free agent—separate from the rest of the document, into which you can put any type of HTML content you want. Elements that are defined in this way are placed at an exact point in the window using x and y coordinates. The top-left corner of the window or its enclosing element is the origin (that is, coordinates 0,0). Moving it to a position farther to the right is a positive x value, while moving down is a positive y value (see page 118).

Figure 7.2 on the next page shows an absolutely positioned element in the window. Using the top and left properties it has been moved 25 pixels from the left edge of the screen (x) and 50 pixels down from the top of the screen (y).

To define an element that positions itself absolutely:

1. #absElement {

   Give this rule a selector name. Generally for positioned elements you will want to use an ID selector that can then be used to specify the placement of a specific element on the page. This is demonstrated in **Code 7.2**

2.   position:

   Type in the position property name followed by a colon.

3.   absolute

   If you want to have exact control over where this element will appear in the browser window, set the value for the position attribute to absolute.

4. ;top: 25px; left: 50px; width: 200px; color:
   →red; font-weight:bold;}

   Close the definition with a semicolon, and then add any other positioning properties

Code 7.2 Whatever is assigned to the ID absLayer will be absolutely positioned within the window or within its parent element.

```
                        code
<HTML>
  <HEAD>
    <STYLE TYPE="text/css">
      #absElement {position: absolute; top:
→25px; left: 50px; width: 200px; color: red;
→font-weight:bold;}
    </STYLE>
  </HEAD>
  <BODY BGCOLOR="#FFFFFF">
    <P>Alice looked at the jury-box, and saw that,
in her haste, she had put the Lizard in head
downwards…</P>
    <SPAN ID="absElement">
    As soon as the jury had a little recovered
from the shock of being upset, and their slates and
pencils had been found and handed back to them…
    </SPAN>
  </BODY>
</HTML>
```

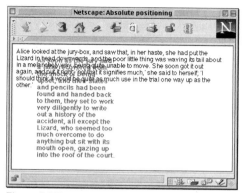

Figure 7.2 The absolutely positioned paragraph is placed 25 pixels down and 50 pixels over, even though the previous paragraph occupies that space.

or CSS properties that you want, before closing the rule with a } bracket. Here we set a top (y) and left (x) value for this element, as well as the width and color.

✔ Tips

■ The contents of elements with a higher z-index (see **Defining the stacking order** on page 122) may obscure an element that has been absolutely positioned.

■ You can position any positioned element in the window using the top and left properties (see **Setting the left and top margins** on page 118).

■ If nested within another positioned element, an absolutely positioned element will treat its parent's top-left corner as its origin. (See **Using relative positioning**, next).

■ If a width value is not specified, the element will stretch to the right side of the window or the right side of its parent element.

■ If a height value is not specified, the element will be made large enough to display all of its content.

Using absolute positioning

Using relative positioning

An element that is defined as being *relatively positioned* will "flow" into place within the window or within its parent element, just as any other HTML element would default to. That is, it appears after everything that's before it in the HTML, and before everything that's after it in the HTML.

A relatively positioned element can be moved from its natural position on the screen using the top and left properties. This is useful for controlling the way elements will appear in relation to other elements on the screen.

In **Figure 7.3** the word "Queen," which has been enlarged in relation to the surrounding text, has been moved up 15 pixels from where it would appear if left alone by using a negative value with the top property.

To define an element that positions itself relative to the flow

1. EM {

   Open the rule by typing a selector. Here we will be telling the emphasis tag how it should position itself in relation to the rest of the text around it.

2.   position:

   Type in the position property name and a colon.

3.   relative

   Add the relative value to the position property to position this element in relationship to its natural position in the flow of the document. Now when the top or left properties are included for this element, it will be positioned with its own top-left corner as its origin.

Code 7.3 The emphasis tag is co-opted, so that the queen can stand out but still be part of the paragraph.

```
code
<HTML>
  <HEAD>
    <STYLE TYPE="text/css">
    EM {position: relative; top: -15px; color:red;
--▶font: normal bold 36pt times, serif; z-order: -
--▶1;}
    </STYLE>
  </HEAD>
  <BODY BGCOLOR="#FFFFFF">
    <P>'I'd rather finish my tea,' said the
Hatter, with an anxious look at the
<EM>Queen</EM>, who was reading the list of
singers.</P>
  </BODY>
</HTML>
```

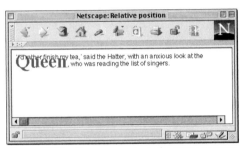

Figure 7.3 The Queen goes where the queen wants to go (within context anyway).

4. ; top: -15px; color:red; font: normal bold 36pt times, serif;}

Close the definition with a semicolon, followed by any other needed positioning properties and CSS properties, and finally the } close bracket. (In this example, we've bumped the font size up, added a bit of color, and offset the text by 15 pixels.)

✔ Tips

■ You can use relative positioning to create superscripted and subscripted text, at least until the align-vertical property becomes standard on all browsers (see **Aligning text vertically** on page 59). If you want to superscript or subscript your text, I recommend creating a class that sets the text to a smaller font size and then uses the top property to raise or lower the text relative to the surrounding elements.

■ Use the top and left properties to move the element around within its natural "in-flow" placement. Negative values move it up and to the left from its natural position, and positive values move it down and to the right.

Using relative positioning

Adding absolute elements to a relative element

We have seen how an element can be positioned on the screen in an exact (absolute) spot. An absolutely positioned element can also be nested within another element that has relative positioning. When you do this, the absolute element will flow from an origin at the top-left corner of the *relative* element rather than the screen.

In **Figure 7.4** the word "ALICE" has been absolutely positioned, but is nested in a relatively positioned element. So rather than appearing at the very top of the page, it gets pushed down 15 pixels along with its parent.

To set up an absolutely positioned element within a relatively positioned element:

1. .relElement{position: relative; margin-top:
   →15px; }

   Create a relatively positioned class in your style sheet, as demonstrated in **Code 7.4**. The one shown here will have a 15 pixel top margin.

2. .title { position: absolute; font-size: 36pt;
   →color: #999999;}

   Set up your absolutely positioned elements as desired. This one will let the element appear in the top left corner of its parent and make its text large and gray.

3. <DIV CLASS="relElement">
       <SPAN CLASS="title">ALICE</SPAN>
       </DIV>

   Now, in the body of the document, surround the absolute elements with a tag using the relElement class. The title is absolutely positioned, but in relation to its parent element and not the screen.

Code 7.4 This sets up a class called relElement that can be positioned relative to other content in the screen, even though its own content is absolutely positioned.

```
<HTML>
  <HEAD>
  <STYLE TYPE="text/css">
    .relElement {
      position: relative;
      margin-top: 15px; }
    .title {
      position: absolute;
      font-size: 36pt;
      color: #999999; }
    </STYLE>
  </HEAD>
  <BODY BGCOLOR="#ffffff">
    <DIV CLASS="relElement">
      <SPAN CLASS="title">ALICE</SPAN>
      <P>There were doors all round the hall, but
they were all locked; and when Alice had been all
the way down one side and up the other, trying
every door, she walked sadly down the middle,
wondering how she was ever to get out again.</P>
      </DIV>
    </BODY>
</HTML>
```

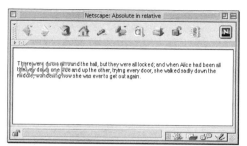

Figure 7.4 The content marked by relElement has a 15-pixel top margin. Then the absolutely positioned content within the relative layer goes on top of it.

✔ Tips

- The above technique for combining relative and absolutely positioned elements can be especially useful if you need to position one or more elements absolutely in relation to *one another*, but not in relation to the screen or other elements on the screen—for example, with a drop shadow. (See page 131).

- Notice that the absolutely positioned text ("ALICE") appears stacked above the other text. Later in this chapter we will learn how to change the "stacking order" of elements to shuffle them around like a deck of cards (see page 122).

Using static positioning

Elements are by default positioned as static on the screen *unless* you define them as being positioned absolutely or relatively. Static elements, like the relatively positioned elements explained in the previous section, flow into a document one after the next. However, static positioning differs in that a static element cannot be explicitly positioned or repositioned. **Figure 7.5** shows a document using all three types of positioning at the same time to create a text collage.

To define a static element:

1. .stat {

Start your rule with a selector and a { bracket. Here we will define a class called stat, as shown in **Code 7.5**.

2. position:

Type in the position property name.

3. static

To create an element that cannot be repositioned, add the static value for the position property.

4. ; font: bold 45pt helvetica;}

Close the definition with a semicolon, type any other applicable definitions, and close the rule with a bracket.

✔ Tips

■ A child element that is positioned as either relative or absolute will not treat any static element as a parent.

■ You don't have to explicitly define an element as static; if left undefined, an element's position will automatically be set to static. But all of you compulsives out there will be happy to know that you can, if you *really* want to.

Code 7.5 This sets up three classes, each with a different positioning type.

```
<HTML>
  <HEAD>
    <STYLE TYPE="text/css">
    .stat {position: static; font: bold 45pt
→helvetica;}
    .rel {position: relative; top: 0px; left:
→45px; font: bold 15pt times; color: red;}
    .abs {position: absolute;top: 25px; left:
→175px; width: 150px; font: bold 35pt helvetica;
→color: pink;}

    </STYLE>
  </HEAD>
  <BODY BGCOLOR="#FFFFFF">
    <P CLASS="stat"> 'Oh my ears and whiskers, how
late it's getting!'</P>
    <P CLASS="abs"> 'Oh my ears and whiskers, how
late it's getting!'</P>
    <P CLASS="rel"> 'Oh my ears and whiskers, how
late it's getting!'</P>
  </BODY>
</HTML>
```

Figure 7.5 The results of Code 7.4 are the static text at the top of the page with the relative text below it, and the absolute text over top of both of these.

Code 7.6 The first paragraph is set to relative positioning and wrapping left, while the second paragraph is absolute positioned.

```
                    code
<HTML>
  <BODY BGCOLOR="#FFFFFF">
    <P STYLE="position: relative; float: left;
——>width: 200px;">At this the whole pack rose up
into the air, and came flying down upon her: she
gave a little scream...</P>
    <P STYLE="position: absolute;"> 'Oh, I've had
such a curious dream!' said Alice, and she told her
sister...</P>
  </BODY>
</HTML>
```

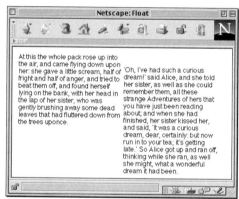

Figure 7.6 The absolute paragraph still wraps around the relative paragraph because the margins have not been set in **Code 7.6**.

Making floating elements with positions

We learned how to create a floating element in Chapter 6. This allows us to cause text in one element to wrap around another element. Defining an element's position as absolute (see previous), though, will determine whether text will be allowed to flow around it.

Floating behavior around positioned elements

Here are some things to remember about the interaction of floating elements and positioned elements:

- If position: absolute; has been set, and the margins (top, left) or the width have been set, the text in the floating element will not wrap around other elements.

- If position: absolute; has been set but the margins and width are not set, other elements will wrap around this element as shown in **Code 7.6**.

- Other elements will never wrap around an absolutely positioned element. (This is unfortunate because it would be a really useful design tool, allowing you to place a pull quote between columns of text.)

Setting the left and top margins

In addition to the margins, which can be specified as part of the box properties (see page 86), a positioned element can also have a top value and a left value.

Figure 7.7 shows an element which has been moved over 9em from the left edge of the screen and 75 pixels down.

To define the left and top margins:

1. #ht42 {

Set up the selector that you want to use to define the element that you will be positioning on the screen. In **Code 7.7** we are setting up an ID selector.

2.   position: absolute;

In order to position an element using the left and/or top properties, we have to include the position property in the same rule.

3.   left:

Type the left property name.

4.   9em

Now type in a value for how far to the left the element should appear. You can enter any of the following:

- A length value, like the 9em in this example, to define the element's distance from the left edge of the window or parent.

- A percentage value such as 55%. The left displacement will be relative to the parent element's width.

- auto which allows the browser to calculate the value if the position is set to absolute; otherwise, left will be 0.

5. ;

Close this definition with a semicolon.

Code 7.7 This code sets up an ID selector that, when applied, will offset the element 9em units from the left and 75 pixels down.

```
code
<HTML>
   <HEAD>
     <STYLE TYPE="text/css">
     #ht42{position: absolute; left: 9em; top:
→ 75px;}
     </STYLE>
   </HEAD>
   <BODY BGCOLOR="#FFFFFF">
<SPAN ID="ht42" STYLE="width: 250px; border: red
5px solid; padding: 5px;">
 'I wonder if I shall fall right through the earth!
</SPAN>
   </BODY>
</HTML>
```

In relation to what?

These values set the position of the top-left corner of the element (including its margin) in relation to the top-left corner of the element's parent. If the element is not nested in any other elements, this position will be the top-left corner of the screen for absolutely positioned elements. For relatively positioned elements this will always be the top left corner of where it would normally appear in the page.

Figure 7.7 The element is moved down and over. The border has been turned on to give you a better feel of exactly what is being moved and where.

6. top:

   Type in the top property name.

7. 75px

   Now type in a value for how far from the top the element should appear. You can enter any of the following:

   • A length value, such as the 25px in this example, to define the element's distance from the top edge of the window or parent.

   • A percentage value such as 55%. The top displacement will be relative to the window or parent element's width.

   • The value auto, which allows the browser to calculate the value if the position is set to absolute; otherwise, top will be 0.

7. ;}

   Close the definition with a semicolon, and the rule with a } bracket.

✔ Tips

■ You can use negative values to move the content up and to the right instead of down and to the left.

■ With an element whose position is defined as relative, the margins remain unaffected by the top and left properties. This means that setting the top and left margins may cause the content to move outside of its naturally defined box and overlap other content

■ Although top and left are not inherited by an elements children, nested elements will be offset along with their parent.

Using width and the height with positioning

Chapter 6 shows how to set an element's width and height. However, when an element's position is set to absolute, width and height behave slightly differently.

1. If width is defined as auto, the element will stretch across the screen to the right edge of its parent element.

2. If a percentage value is used for either width or height, they are relative to the parent element's width or height.

Setting the left and top margins

Clipping the element

Unlike setting the width and the height of an element, which controls its dimensions, clipping an element designates how much of that element is actually visible on the screen. The rest of the element's content will still be there, but it will be invisible to the visitor and treated as empty space by the browser. In **Figure 7.8** The first picture of Alice shows the whole story while the second one has been expurgated.

To define the clip area of an element:

1. **.halfNhalf {**

   Open your rule with a selector and bracket. In this example a class called halfNhalf is set up which can then be applied to any HTML tag.

2. **position: relative;**

   Set the position property to either relative or absolute.

3. **clip:**

   Type in the clip property name followed by a colon.

4. **rect(100 143)**

   Now type:

   rect to define the shape of the clip as a rectangle.

   Now type an opening parenthesis and two values separated by a space, and then a closing parenthesis. (The first value in parentheses represents the width of the display area; the second is the height of the display area.)

   Both values can be either a length value or auto, which will allow the browser to determine the clip size (usually 100%).

5. **;}**

   Finish by typing a semicolon and a } bracket.

Code 7.8 The paragraph tag will be clipped in Navigator to 100 by 143 pixels. Navigator has difficulty applying styles directly to the image tag, so here it is nested in the paragraph tag instead.

```
<HTML>
  <HEAD>
    <STYLE TYPE="text/css">
      .halfNhalf {position: relative; clip:
→rect(100 143);}
    </STYLE>
  </HEAD>
  <BODY BGCOLOR="#FFFFFF">
  <IMG SRC="../images/alice40a.gif" WIDTH="200"
HEIGHT="246" ALIGN="left">
  <P CLASS="halfNhalf">
  <IMG SRC="../images/alice40a.gif" WIDTH="200"
HEIGHT="246" ALIGN="left"></P>
  </BODY>
</HTML>.
```

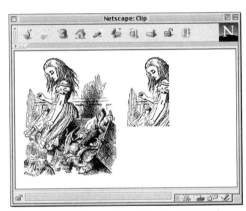

Figure 7.8 The first version of the illustration isn't clipped at all; the second gets clipped in half horizontally and vertically.

✔ Tips

■ Clipping is not supported by Internet Explorer.

■ Officially, clipping works a little differently from how it's specified here. Instead of two values, you include up to four to define the clipped area of the element. Including all four values, however, prevents a clipped element from appearing in Navigator 4.0.

■ Currently, clips can only be rectangular, but future versions of CSS promise to have other shapes.

Where does the overflow go?

If you clip an area, obviously there will be content that does not get displayed. The overflow property allows you to specify how this extra content is treated. Currently neither of the DHTML-capable browsers support this property so the extra content just disappears. Maybe in the next generation. For now let's just see how to set it up.

To define the overflow control:

1. #ht678 {

Begin your definition.

2. clip: rect(150 200);

For there to be overflow in an element, you have to clip it first. (If you need help with this step, see the preceding section.)

3. overflow:

Type the overflow property.

4. scroll

Now type in one of the following *keywords* to tell the browser how to treat overflow from the clip:

• scroll, which sets scroll bars around the visible area to allow the visitor to scroll through the element's content.

• hidden, which hides the overflow.

• visible, to cause even the clipped part of the element show up.

• auto, which allows the browser to decide how to treat extra material after clipping.

5. ;}

Close the definition with a ; and close the rule with a bracket.

Clipping the element

Defining the stacking order

The various elements in a browser window can be placed on the screen by giving them left and top values. These correspond to x and y coordinates on the screen, using the top-left corner as the origin. Despite the fact that the screen is a two-dimensional area, elements that are positioned can be given a third-dimension: a stacking order in relationship to one another.

In **Figure 7.9**, you can see how each positioned element is automatically assigned a stacking number, starting with 0, in the order that the element appears in the HTML and relative to its parents and siblings. This is called the z-index. An elements z-index number is a value that shows its relation to other elements in the window.

If the content of elements overlap each other, the element with a higher number in the stacking order will appear over top of the element with a lower number.

You can override the "natural" order of the elements on the page by setting the z-index property directly. **Figure 7.10** shows several elements that have been reordered from their natural order (**Figure 7.11**) in **Code 7.9**.

To define an element's z-index:

1. #element0 {

Set up your selector.

2. position: absolute;

In order to layer an element on the screen, it has to have the position property defined (as shown in **Code 7.9**).

3. z-index:

Type in the z-index property name.

Code 7.9 This sets up four IDs, layer0 through layer3, used to position our images on the screen. The z-indexes have been set so that the elements positioned farther down and to the right will appear on top.

```
<HTML>
  <HEAD>
    <STYLE TYPE="text/css"><!
      #element1 { position: absolute; z-index:
→3; top: 175px; left: 255px }
      #element2 { position: absolute; z-index:
→2; top: 100px; left: 170px }
      #element3 { position: absolute; z-index:
→1; top: 65px; left: 85px }
      #element4 { position: absolute; z-index:
→0; top: 5px; left: 5px }-->
    </STYLE>
  </HEAD>
  <BODY BGCOLOR="#ffffff">
    <SPAN ID="element1">
    <IMG SRC="../images/alice22a.gif" WIDTH="100"
HEIGHT="147"><BR CLEAR="all">
    Element 1
    </SPAN>
    <SPAN ID="element2">
    <IMG SRC="../images/alice32a.gif" WIDTH="139"
HEIGHT="200"><BR CLEAR="all">
    Element 2
    </SPAN>
    <SPAN ID="element3">
    <IMG SRC="../images/alice15a.gif" WIDTH="151"
HEIGHT="200"><BR CLEAR="all">
    Element 3
    </SPAN>
    <SPAN ID="element4">
    <IMG SRC="../images/alice29a.gif" WIDTH="200"
HEIGHT="236"><BR CLEAR="all">
    Element 4
    </SPAN>
  </BODY>
</HTML>
```

element	z-index
<E1>	← 0
<E2></E2>	← 1
</E1>	
<E3>	← 1
</E3>	
<E4>	← 2
<E5>	← 1
<E6></E6>	← 1
<E7></E7>	← 2
<E8></E8>	← 3
</E5>	
<E9></E9>	← 2
</E4>	
<E10></E10>	← 3

Figure 7.9 Natural stacking order. The first element <E1> has a z-index of 0. The second element <E2>, which is nested in <E1>, gets a z-index of 1. The third element <E3> also gets a z-index of 1; however, <E2> will be beneath it because <E2>'s parent, <E1>, has a z-index of 0. Skipping down, <E6> also gets a z-index of 1. But <E6> will appear over all of the other elements because they are z-index=1's whereas <E6>'s top parent, <E4>, is a z-index=2.

Figure 7.10 The results of **Code 7.9**. Notice that despite the fact that the Element 1 should be on the bottom of the stack, its z-index has been set to 3; so it now appears on top.

Figure 7.11 The same document, if we had not set the z-index but had allowed it to be defined by the natural stacking order. Notice that Element 1 is now underneath everything else because its natural z-index is 0.

4.   0

Now type in a number, either positive or negative, or 0. This sets the element's z-index in relation to its siblings where 0 is on the same level.

Or type auto to allow the browser to determine the element z-order.

5. ; top: 5px; left: 5px; 0;}

Close the definition with a semicolon and a } bracket.

✔ Tips

- Using a negative number for the z-index will cause an element to be stacked that many levels beneath its parents instead of above.

- If two elements that have the same z-index number appear in the same space, the element whose top level parent came last goes on top.

Defining the stacking order

REAL-WORLD CSS

There are as many different ways to use Cascading Style Sheets as there are ways to lay out Web pages. Yet CSS is still a relatively new design tool, and designers are still discovering its abilities and limitations. In addition, many designers are initially captivated by the "gee-whiz" aspects of using CSS to create Dynamic HTML. They overlook some of the nuts-and-bolts issues that are solved by CSS itself, to facilitate solid, compelling page layout on the Web.

In this chapter you will explore some of the valuable solutions offered by CSS to real-world, everyday design issues that you have probably already encountered. For these tasks, CSS has many uses and can achieve a variety of effects on your Web pages.

Creating headlines with graphic backgrounds

One hassle in Web design is headlines created using a graphic, which usually means creating a new graphic for every headline. Using the CSS background property, however, you can create as many different title "graphics" as you want—without having to actually create new graphics and without incurring the additional download time.

To create a headline with a graphic background

1. Create and save your background in a graphics program. **Figure 8.1** shows a sample background. Call the graphic something like background_headline.gif or whatever works for you.

2. H1 {background: white url(../images/back
   → ground_headline.gif) no-repeat; font: bold
   → 18pt helvetica,sans-serif; color: white;
   → height: 150px; width: 400px;
   → padding:10px;}

   Make a CSS rule with the Level 1 header tag, as shown in **Code 8.1**. In the example here, background_headline.gif is the location of our background graphic.

3. <H1>CHAPTER VII
   A Mad Tea-Party </H1>

   Whenever you use Level 1 headings in your document, as in **Code 8.1**, they will have your background graphic behind them as shown in **Figure 8.2**.

✔ Tips

- The other head levels can be set in the same way as described in this chapter. You can use different graphics, or use the same graphic by grouping the selectors together.

Code 8.1 Setting up the rule for your headline.

```
code
<HTML>
  <HEAD>
   <STYLE TYPE="text/css">
     H1 {background: white
→url(../images/background_headline.gif) no-
→repeat; font: bold 18pt helvetica,sans-serif;
→color: white; height: 150px; width: 400px;
→padding:10px;}
     P {font: normal 10pt/14pt times,sans-serif;
→left-margin: 25px; width: 400;}
   </STYLE>
  </HEAD>
  <BODY BGCOLOR="#FFFFFF">
    <H1>CHAPTER VII<BR>
    A Mad Tea-Party</H1>
    <P>There was a table set out under a tree in
front of the house...
  </BODY>
</HTML>
```

Figure 8.1 The background image for a headline.

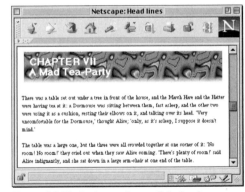

Figure 8.2 The background sets off the header.

Code 8.2 Setting up the side bar with a rule and a table.

```
code
<HTML>
  <HEAD>
    <STYLE TYPE="text/css">
      BODY {background: #cccccc
→url(../images/background_side.gif) repeat-y;}.
    </STYLE>
  </HEAD>
  <BODY>
    <P>
    <TABLE BORDER="0" CELLPADDING="0"
CELLSPACING="5">

    <TR>
<!-- Side bar -->
    <TD WIDTH="151" VALIGN="TOP">
    <CENTER>
    <IMG SRC="../images/b_book.gif" WIDTH="69"
→HEIGHT="81"><BR>
      <IMG SRC="../images/b_portrait.gif"
→WIDTH="69" HEIGHT="81"><BR>
      <IMG SRC="../images/b_portfolio.gif"
→WIDTH="72" HEIGHT="79"><BR>
    </CENTER>
    </TD>
<!-- End Side bar -->
    <TD>
<!-- Main Content -->
    <H2>My Conversation with Alice</H2>
    <P>'I've been to a day-school, too,' said
Alice; 'you needn't be so proud as all that.'</P>
  </BODY>
</HTML>
```

Figure 8.3 The background graphic for the side bar.

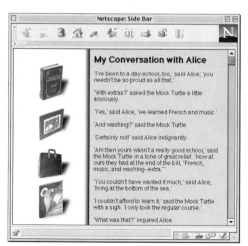

Figure 8.4 A Web page with a side bar.

Creating a side bar

Side bars are possibly the most common method used to set off navigation tools. The traditional method for this arrangement is to create a long, horizontal background graphic that includes the side bar and the background color for the content area. Using CSS, though, we can create a graphic that is just the width of the side bar and then use the **repeat-y** property to tile the image down the left side. This saves download time by reducing the size of the background graphic.

To create a side bar:

1. Make a thin strip the width that you want your side bar to be. **Figure 8.3** shows one used to create a side bar 160 pixels wide.

2. BODY {
   background: #cccccc url(../images/back
   →ground_side.gif) repeat-y;}.

   Set up the body selector in your document to use the graphic you created in step 1, but only repeat it in the y direction as shown in **Code 8.2**. You'll also want to set the background color for the rest of the page.

3. You can now use tables or CSS positioning to set up a left-hand column for the side bar's content and a right-hand column for everything else.

   The result should look something like **Figure 8.4**.

✔ Tip

■ This technique with **repeat-y** will not work in non-CSS browsers since they expect the background graphic to be set in the body tag. These browsers do not have the ability to specify in which direction to repeat the graphic.

Creating drop caps

Drop cap-style letters are a time-honored way of starting a new section or chapter of lengthy text. Medieval monks used drop caps with illuminated manuscripts—and now you can use them on the Web.

The drop cap is created by making the first letter of a paragraph larger than subsequent letters, and moving the first several lines of text over to accommodate the larger letter. This effect is illustrated in **Figure 8.5**.

To set a drop cap using the <SPAN> tag:

1. P { font: normal 10pt/12pt
   →helvetica,arial,sans-serif; }

   Define the paragraph tag to display text in the style you want. Here we used Helvetica 10pt, with a 12pt line spacing. This rule is shown in in **Code 8.3**. (For help with font sizing, see page 44).

2. .dropcap {font: bold 300% times,serif; color:
   →red; float: left;}

   Set up a class that defines its text as bold and three times larger than the text around it. Other text will flow around this emphasized text element—to the right because this drop-cap text will "float" to the left (see page 117).

3. <P> <SPAN class="dropcap">Y</SPAN>our
   →text here.</P>

   To use the dropcap class to create drop cap text, you'll employ the <SPAN> container in your HTML, as shown in **Code 8.3**. In this setup, the letter will appear in a 30pt (3x10pt) size and "dropped down" so that its top aligns with the tops of the rest of the text.

✔ Tip

■ Internet Explorer renders floating letters

Code 8.3 The **dropcap** class sets this text bold, three times larger than neighboring text, in the Times font, and with a nice olive color.

```
                        code
<HTML>
  <HEAD>
    <TITLE>Drop Cap</TITLE>
    <STYLE TYPE="text/css">
        P {font: 10pt/12pt helvetica,arial,sans-
→serif;}
        .dropcap {font: bold 300% times,serif;
→color: red; float: left;}
    </STYLE>
  </HEAD>
  <BODY BGCOLOR="#FFFFFF">
    <H3>CHAPTER VI<BR>
    Pig and Pepper</H3>
    <P><SPAN CLASS="dropcap">F</SPAN>or a minute
or two she stood looking at the house, and
wondering what to do next, when suddenly a footman
in livery came running out of the wood- (she
considered him to be a footman because he was in
livery: otherwise, judging by his face only, she
would have called him a fish...</P>
  </BODY>
</HTML>
```

Creating drop caps

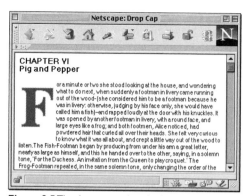

Figure 8.5 The drop cap makes the beginning of the paragraph stand out.

with their baselines even with the rest of the text (that is, the bottoms of letters on the same line); therefore, the letter styled with dropcap will not actually drop down.

Not really an element

There is actually an easier way of creating drop caps: by using the first-letter pseudo-element. A *pseudo-element* is a specific and unique part of an element—such as the first letter or first line of a paragraph—whose appearance can be controlled independently of the rest of the element. For example, we can use the first-letter pseudo-element to set the style of the first letter in a paragraph like this:

```
P:first-letter { font: bold 300% times,serif;
→float: left; }
```

Another pseudo-element is first-line, which allows you to set the appearance of the first line of text.

Unfortunately, neither of these pseudo-elements is supported in either of the DHTML-capable browsers. So for the time being, we are stuck with creating a drop-cap class instead.

Creating drop caps

<table>
<tr><td>

Creating a title bar

Putting content at the top of the page on a unique background different from the rest of the document has always been problematic with HTML. That's because eventually the background graphic repeats somewhere farther down the page, ruining the effect. The repeat-x property prevents this unwanted repetition.

To create a title bar:

1. Create the background graphic you want to use behind the title. The height of the graphic should be the amount of vertical space you want to occupy at the top of the page.

2. BODY { background: white url(title_bar_back →ground.gif) repeat-x; }

   Set the body selector in your document to use the graphic created in step 1, but repeat it only in the x direction, as we've done in **Code 8.4**. You'll also probably want to set the background color for the rest of the page.

3. You can now use tables or CSS Positioning to create the menu at the top of the page that will fit into the title bar header.

   The result should look something like **Figure 8.6**.

</td><td>

Code 8.4 The body tag is set to have its background repeat *only* across the top of the page.

```
code
<HTML>
  <HEAD>
    STYLE TYPE="text/css">
      BODY {background: white
→url(../images/background_title.gif) repeat-x;}
    </STYLE>
  </HEAD>
  <BODY>
<!-- Page Header -->
    <CENTER>
      <P><IMG SRC="../images/b_book.gif"
WIDTH="69" HEIGHT="81"><IMG
SRC="../images/b_hammer.gif" WIDTH="72"
HEIGHT="81"><IMG SRC="../images/b_letter.gif"
WIDTH="72" HEIGHT="79"><IMG
SRC="../images/b_painting.gif" WIDTH="69"
HEIGHT="81"><IMG SRC="../images/b_portfolio.gif"
WIDTH="72" HEIGHT="79"><IMG
SRC="../images/b_portrait.gif" WIDTH="69"
HEIGHT="81"><BR CLEAR="all">
      </P>
    </CENTER>
    <H2> </H2>
    <H2>Choose an item from above.</H2>
<!-- Header area End -->

  <FONT SIZE="2">There was nothing so very
remarkable in that; nor did Alice think it so very
much out of the way to hear the Rabbit say to
itself, 'Oh dear! Oh dear! I shall be late!...
  </BODY>
</HTML>
```

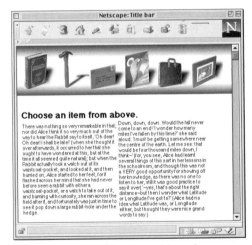

Figure 8.6 The top of the page stands out better because of the unique background.

</td></tr>
</table>

Code 8.5 The external CSS file 8_05.css has three IDs that can be used for creating a drop shadow.

```
code
#text {position: absolute; top: 5px; left: 5px;
→color: #000000; z-index:2;}
#shadow1 {position: absolute; top: 2px; left:
→2px; color: #CCCCCC;  z-index:0;}
#shadow2 {position: absolute; top: 8px; left:
→8px; color: #666666; z-index:1;}
```

Code 8.6 The rules from code 8.5 are imported into this code using the link tag. ...

```
code
<HTML>
  <HEAD>
    <LINK REL=stylesheet HREF="8_05.css">
    <STYLE>
      H1 {font-size: 75pt;}
    </STYLE>
  </HEAD>
  <BODY BGCOLOR="#FFFFFF">
    <SPAN  ID="shadow1"><H1>ALICE</H1></SPAN>
    <SPAN  ID="shadow2"><H1>ALICE</H1></SPAN>
    <SPAN  ID="text"><H1>ALICE</H1></SPAN>
  </BODY>
</HTML>
```

Figure 8.7 The drop shadow is created by using the three classes that offset the word in shades of gray.

Creating a drop shadow

Another popular special effect on the Web is the drop shadow. Drop shadows make your text, especially large headlines and titles, stand out from the rest of the page, adding emphasis and impact. Before CSS, however, the only way to create drop shadows was to create a graphic of the text and its shadow. Now a little CSS trickery lets us do the same thing without having to load graphics.

To create a CSS drop shadow:

1. In your CSS rules list, create three ID selectors called text, shadow1, and shadow2, as shown in **Code 8.5**.

2. Set up three identical versions of the text that you want to appear in drop shadow. Then use the <SPAN> tag to code the first version as shadow1, the second version as shadow2, and the third version as text, as shown in **Code 8.6**.

   Save this file and load it into a browser. Its display should look something like **Figure 8.7**.

✔ Tip

■ One caution: A non-CSS browser reading a page using this drop shadow technique will display the text one line after the next, which might not look very appealing.

Creating distinctive titles

Titles are used to guide the viewer's eye around the screen and highlight important areas and ideas, but without becoming obnoxious or overwhelming. With CSS positioning, you can create titles in which text of various sizes and colors overlap. Of course the possibilities for this application are limitless, but here's one idea to get you started.

To create an overlapping title:

1. Create an external CSS file that contains the code shown in **Code 8.7**. This sets up header Levels 2 and 3 to be relatively positioned elements.

2. In your HTML, type in your own desired titles, using the <H2> tag. Type the text you want to float on top of that using the <H3> tag. **Code 8.8** shows you what it should look like.

   The results will look something like **Figure 8.8**.

Code 8.7 This code sets header Levels 1 and 2 to create our distinctive title, which is then imported into **Code 8.8**.

```
H2
  {
  position: relative;
  top: 5px;
  left: 5px;
  font: bold italic 72pt times, serif;
  color: #CCCCCC;
  }
H3
  {
  position: relative;
  top: -45px;
  font: bold 18pt helvetica, sans-serif;
  color: #000000;
  margin-left: 0px;
  }
```

Code 8.8 The rules from **Code 8.7** are imported in to this code and then applied to its tags.

```
<HTML>
  <HEAD>
    <LINK REL=stylesheet HREF="titles.css">
  </HEAD>
  <BODY BGCOLOR="#FFFFFF">
    <H2>a l i c e</H2>
    <H3>in Wonderland</H3>
    <P>Alice was beginning to get very tired of
sitting by her sister on the bank, and of having
nothing to do: once or twice she had peeped into
the book her sister was reading, but it had no
pictures or conversations in it, 'and what is the
use of a book,' thought Alice 'without pictures or
conversation?'</P>
  </BODY>
```

Figure 8.8 The word "alice" appears below the phrase "in Wonderland" to make a distinct title.

Code 8.9 Setting the links' three different states.

```
code
<HTML>
  <HEAD>
    <TITLE>CSS links</TITLE>
    <STYLE TYPE="text/css">
      A:link {color: purple; font-weight: bold;}
      A:active {color: darkgoldenrod; font-size:
→larger;}
      A:visited {color: mediumpurple; font-size:
→80%; font weight: normal;}
      P {font-size: 12;}
    </STYLE>
  </HEAD>
  <BODY BGCOLOR="#FFFFFF">
    <P>You can go to this <A HREF="link.html">Link
</A> .</P>
    <P>You are going to this <A HREF="a_link.html
">Active Link.</A></P>
    <P>But you have already been to this <A HREF=
"inline.html">Visited Link .</A></P>
  </BODY>
</HTML>
```

Figure 8.9 This is the display of **Code 8.9** after the second link has been accessed and the third one is in the process of being clicked.

Not *really* a class

Certain special classes are automatically recognized by CSS-supporting browsers. *Pseudo-classes* represent tags that have special unique attributes that can be defined separately from each other. For example the anchor tag includes link, active, and visited attributes. These pseudo-classes can be defined individually just as if they were HTML selectors.

Setting the appearance of an anchor link

Most browsers allow you to specify link colors (for a link, a visited link, and an active link) in the body tag of the document. With CSS you can not only define these colors but also any other properties that you want the links to have.

Although an anchor is a tag—**<A>**—its individual attributes are not, so to set these properties we have to use the pseudo-classes associated with each one. The various link types are illustrated in **Figure 8.9**.

To set contrasting link appearances:

1. A:link {color: purple; font-style: bold;}

   This will set all unvisited links to be bold and purple, to stand out from surrounding text.

2. A:active {color: darkgoldenrod; font-size:
   →larger;}

   This will cause links that are being selected to darken slightly and grow larger.

3. A:visited {color: mediumpurple; font-size:
   →80%; font weight: normal;}

   This will set all visited links back to purple, but in italic rather than bold text, and in a slightly smaller size.

✔ Tips

- The active and visited pseudo-classes are not currently supported in Navigator 4.0.

- The Web is a hypertextual medium, so it is important that users be able to distinguish between text, links, and visited links. Since you can't always count on users having their "underline links" option turned on, it's a good idea to set the link appearance for every document.

Creating columns

Multiple columns have a variety of roles in
Web pages: They can save space on the screen,
for instance; and they are easier to read than a
single, massively wide column. Before CSS,
the only way to create columns was with
tables. The problem with tables, however, is
that they were never intended to be used for
layout and present several design difficulties
as a result. Also, they can take a while to
download and set up in the browser window.

To set up columns:

1. Set up an external CSS file modeled after
the code shown in **Code 8.10**. This sets up
three IDs, each defining a column on the
screen. These elements will be absolutely
positioned, so each one has to be positioned to the left of the preceding one.

2. Create the three columns of content in
your HTML document, as demonstrated
in **Code 8.11**. Notice that the image in
column 2 has been left-aligned. The image
has to have an established alignment, or
else the text will slip underneath it.

   The results should look something like
Figure 8.10. The relElement style from
Chapter 7 makes an appearance here, as
well. This arrangement has the columns
flowing in under the title; otherwise, they
would just appear on top of it.

✔ Tips

- Although using CSS positioning to set up
columns is easier and faster than tables,
browser support for tables is more universal.

- Watch out: Using HTML positioning can
cause havoc if the visitor's browser does
not support CSS. For example, if the code
used for **Figure 8.10** is displayed in a
non-CSS browser, the text will appear as

Code 8.10 This sets up IDs that can be used to create
three different columns when imported into an HTML
document.

```
#column1 {position: absolute; top: .5in; left:
→.1in; width: 2.5in; font:  12pt/14pt time,
→serif;}
#column2 {position: absolute; top: .5in; left:
→2.8in; width: 2.5in;font:  12pt/14pt time,
→serif;}
#column3 {position: absolute; top: .5in; left:
→5.5in; width: 1.5in; font: bold 9pt/24pt
→helvetica, sans-serif; color: red;}
.relElement {position: relative; margin: 10px;}
```

Code 8.11 The code above is linked into this document
and then used to set up the content into three columns.

```
<HTML>
  <HEAD>
    <LINK REL=stylesheet HREF="8_09.css">
  </HEAD>
<BODY BGCOLOR="#FFFFFF">
    <H3>Alice in Wonderland</H3>
    <DIV CLASS="relElement">
    <SPAN ID="column1">Down, down, down. There was
nothing else to do, so Alice soon began talking
again. 'Dinah'll miss me very much to-night, I
should think!'</SPAN>
    <SPAN ID="column2">
    <IMG SRC="../images/alice02a.gif" WIDTH="144"
HEIGHT="216" ALIGN="left">
<BR CLEAR="all">
Alice was not a bit hurt, and she jumped up on to
her feet in a moment: she looked up, but it was all
dark overhead;..
    </SPAN>
    <SPAN ID="column3">There were doors all round
the hall, but they were all locked.</SPAN>
    </DIV>
  </BODY>
</HTML>
```

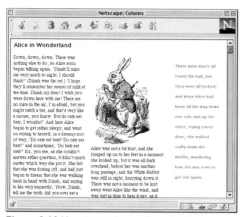

Figure 8.10 Here is our three column layout.

one solid lump, without breaks. If you are worried about backwards-compatibility, consider using the column IDs with a <P> tag instead of <SPAN>, since this arrangement will at least separate the paragraphs.

Creating columns

THE DOCUMENT OBJECT MODEL

As powerful as Cascading Style Sheets are, they aren't really dynamic per se. They give us control over how the document looks when it is first put onto the screen, but what about after that?

Web pages created with Cascading Style Sheets can have their properties changed while on the screen (that is, dynamically)—through the use of a scripting language.

The ability to change a Web page dynamically is made possible by the Document Object Model (DOM) which can connect any element on the screen to a JavaScript function. The DOM is quickly becoming the definitive concept for dealing with Web pages, second only to HTML.

The bad news (you knew it couldn't be that easy!) is that Navigator and Internet Explorer have implemented their DOMs differently. In this chapter we will focus on the differences between the two DOMs and how to create DHTML that works on both platforms.

Since JavaScript (JScript in Internet Explorer) is available almost universally, that is the scripting language we will use in this book. However, CSS can be affected by any scripting language that your particular browser can handle—VBScript in Internet Explorer, for instance.

What is a Document Object Model?

The Document Object Model, known as DOM, is the road map through which you can locate any element in your HTML document and use a script, such as JavaScript, to change the element's properties. A DOM can address any element on the screen that is either a replaced element, such as an image with a name, or any element that is identified by an ID. The key is that the element must have a unique identity on the screen.

Each element on the screen can be identified using a NAME or an ID attribute to give it its own unique "address" as if it were on a city map. If we were writing a letter, we would address the envelope for a particular house on that map. We would describe the city, the street, and number:

atlanta.mainSt.2210

The DOM is like a map of your web page: you describe a *path* starting with the HTML document itself, down to the various elements on the Web page. For instance, the DOM for an image called button1 would be

document.images.button1

which tells the browser that the document contains an image called button1. You can use this path to allow a JavaScript function to send that element a message (such as what image it should be displaying).

At least that's the grand idea.

Unfortunately, the DHTML browsers don't agree on the same map to get to elements defined using CSS. Fortunately we can use JavaScript to make sure that both browsers are "reading off the same page." (see **Creating a cross-browser DOM**, page 146).

Table 9.1

What the DOM Allows	
ABILITY	BROWSER
Change the CSS properties of an element while it is on the screen	Internet Explorer
Change the z-index of elements	Both
Hide or show elements on the screen	Both
Control the position of elements relative to the visitor's setup	Both
Move elements on screen	Both
Allow visitors to move objects around on the screen	Both
Reclip the visible area of an element	Navigator

The future of the DOM

Currently the World Wide Web consortium is working on a standard DOM, which will more than likely be the basis of future browsers. But the bad news is that even if the standard is born soon, there will still be legacy browsers that won't work with the specification.

Code 9.1 The image called button1 one is changed from button_off.gif to button_on.gif when a visitor click on it.

```
                    code
 <A HREF="next.html" onMouseOver="
→document.images.button1.src="button_on.gif"
→">
 <IMG SRC="button_off.gif" NAME="button1">
 </A>
```

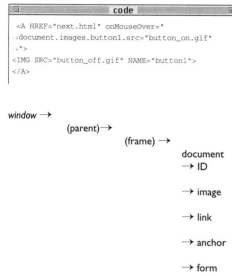

Figure 9.1 The DOM works by tracing a path from the script down to the individual element to be acted upon within the HTML document. Each object is a subset of the object before it.

How a DOM works

If you have used any type of scripting language with an HTML page, then you have more than likely seen a Document Object Model in action. The DOM works by describing the path from a JavaScript function to an element on the screen, usually in response to something that happens on the screen. (See **Figure 9.1**.)

Setting up a DOM:

document.images.button1.src = "button_on.gif"

describes a path starting with the current document, down to its images, and through to the source location of an image called button 1. If associated with an event handler as shown in **Code 9.1**—onMouseOver, for instance—that is within a link surrounding the graphic named button1, this action would change the source of the graphic from whatever it was, to button_on.gif. (See **New event handlers**, coming up.)

New event handlers

In the world of JavaScript, *events* occur when something happens in the browser window, usually initiated by the visitor. One example is when the visitor clicks on a link; this generates an onClick *event*. Events can also occur when the browser does something, such as loading a new document. An *event handler* connects an event to a JavaScript, which in turn performs some function in the browser window.

Many events that are prevalent in HTML documents can be employed with elements defined using CSS. Some of the more common ones are listed in **Table 9.2**

And with Dynamic HTML come several new event handlers to allow even greater control. **Table 9.3** defines the new events, which can be used with any CSS-defined element.

Figure 9.2 shows what happens when you click on an image with an onClick event handler that changes the images source.

To use an event handler:

1. <A HREF="next.html"

Set up an HTML element that can have an event associated with it. In **Code 9.2** we are using a link.

2. onMouseDown="document.image.button1.
→src='button_on.gif">

Add your event handler, along with the action you want taken when the conditions are met (that is, when the event occurs). Here we use the onMouseDown event handler, which causes the images source file for the image called button1 to change.

Code 9.2 When the image is first loaded, the button is turned off. When the visitor clicks on the button, the image source is replaced by the "On" version of the graphic. The browser knows which graphic to replace by following the DOM.

```
<A HREF="next.html" onMouseDown="
→document.images.button1.src='b_on.gif'">
  <IMG SRC='b_off.gif' NAME="button1" BORDER="0">
</A>
```

Figure 9.2 The first graphic is the button in Off mode. When the visitor clicks on the graphic, it appears to turn as the graphic switches between On and Off states.

Table 9.2

Common Event Handlers

EVENT HANDLER	WHEN IT HAPPENS	ELEMENTS AFFECTED
onLoad	After an object is loaded	Documents and images
onUnload	After the object is no longer loaded	Documents and images
onFocus	When an element is selected	Documents and forms
onBlur	When an element is deselected	Documents and forms
onMouseOver	When the mouse pointer passes over an area	Links and image map areas
onMouseOut	When the mouse pointer passes out of an area	Links and image map areas
onClick	When the mouse button is clicked over an area	Links, image map areas, forms

Table 9.3

New DHTML Event Handlers

EVENT HANDLER	WHEN IT HAPPENS	ELEMENTS AFFECTED
onMouseDown	While the mouse button is depressed	Links, image map areas, forms
onMouseUp	When the mouse button is released	Links, image map areas, forms
onMouseMove	As the mouse is moved	Document
onKeyDown	While a keyboard key is depressed	Forms
onKeyUp	When a keyboard key is released	Forms
onKeyPress	When a keyboard key is depressed and immediately released	Forms
onMove*	When the window is moved	Document
onResize*	When the window or frame is resized	Document

*Not supported by Internet Explorer

3.   `<IMG SRC="button_off.gif" name="` ⇢`button1"></A>`

Here is the linked image called button1 and the closing link tag.

✔ Tip

■ At first glance onClick and onMouseUp may seem to do the same thing. However, the Click event only occurs after the mouse has been pressed down and then released. MouseDown and MouseUp break this into two separate events each of which can have a different action.

New event handlers

The Netscape Navigator DOM

The Navigator DOM allows you to write scripts to control elements created using the <LAYER> tag (see Chapter 13, **Netscape Layers**) and elements created using CSS positioning. This lets you control the position, visibility, and clipping of the element. Changes made to these properties, using either layers or CSS positioning, will occur immediately on the page.

However, unlike Internet Explorer, Navigator does not provide access to CSS properties other than the positioning properties.

Under the Navigator DOM, an element's CSS properties are accessed using an index number, name, or ID of the element name as shown in **Figure 9.3**.

 Code 9.3 shows a JavaScript function using the Navigator DOM. It describes a path to a particular element's position and then reassigns that position. **Figure 9.4** shows the element moving from its original position across the screen in response to the function.

Code 9.3 The Navigator DOM in action, creating a function that can change the position of an element.

```
function NAVmoveElement(elementName){
  document.elementName.left = 120;
  document.elementName.top = 120;
}
```

Keyword that lets the browser know where you want to make changes (i.e., this document) | The name given to the HTML element | The CSS property you want to change

document . elementName . styleProperty

Figure 9.3 The Navigator DOM for accessing CSS

Figure 9.4 The function NAVmoveElement() is used to move this element across the screen—but only in Netscape Navigator.

Code 9.4 The Internet Explorer DOM in action, to change the position of an element.

```
                      code
function IEmoveElement(elementName){
  document.all.elementName.style.left = 120;
  document.all.elementName.style.top = 120;
}
```

Figure 9.5 The function IEmoveElement() is used to move this element across the screen—but only in Internet Explorer.

The Internet Explorer DOM

The Internet Explorer DOM allows you to write scripts that can access any element on the screen—at least, any element that Internet Explorer understands. That includes CSS properties and CSS positioning. This lets you control the position and visibility of elements on the screen, as well as their appearance. Any changes made to these properties will occur immediately on the page and Internet Explorer will re-render the page to comply.

An element's properties can be accessed by Internet Explorer 4 using document.all with an index number, name, or ID as the elementName and then the word style as shown in **Figure 9.6**.

Code 9.4 shows a JavaScript function using the Internet Explorer DOM while **Figure 9.5** shows how this function can move an element in Internet Explorer 4.

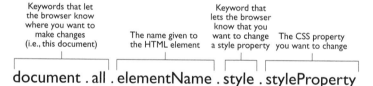

Keywords that let the browser know where you want to make changes (i.e., this document) — The name given to the HTML element — Keyword that lets the browser know that you want to change a style property — The CSS property you want to change

`document . all . elementName . style . styleProperty`

Figure 9.6 The Internet Explorer DOM for accessing CSS

Sensing the browser type and version

Since each browser has its own way of implementing the DOM, we could code two different versions of our page to accommodate these differences. That's hard. Instead, we'll create our own DOM to use in our JavaScript functions. To do that, though, we first have to tell the computer how to tell the difference between Internet Explorer and Netscape Navigator. We want to be sure and include the version number so that we can check and make sure that the code is in fact running in a DHTML-capable browser.

For their version 5.0 browsers, both Netscape and Microsoft have pledged to follow the common standards being set down by the W3C. Therefore, we also have to include in this code a test for whether the browser version is 5 or higher. But we don't have to determine which browser type it is, because (hopefully) it will not matter.

To determine browser type and version:

1. Add **Code 9.5** and **Code 9.6** to the head of your document.

   All of this code will run as soon as the page is loaded into the browser window. The first script (**9.5**) initializes several variables to 0 (False), which will be used later to record whether the browser is Netscape 4, Internet Explorer 4, or a newer browser. The second code (**9.6**) tests to determine the browser and assign the appropriate variable to 1 (True). Since the language has been set to JavaScript 1.2, the script will only run in one of the 4.x browsers or higher (that is, a DHTML browser).

Code 9.5 In the first JavaScript example, we initialize the variables to 0 (False). Later on we'll use these to determine whether this is a DHTML browser or not.

```
<HTML>
<HEAD>
<SCRIPT LANGUAGE="JavaScript">
/* Browser sensing */
/* Set up Boolean variables to record the browser
type */
var isNew = 0;
var isNS4 = 0;
var isIE4 = 0;
</SCRIPT>
```

Code 9.6 This code checks the browser name and version and then changes the appropriate variable to 1 (True). Since we have set the language for this code as JavaScript1.2, the script will only run on the 4.0 or later browsers.

```
<SCRIPT LANGUAGE="JavaScript1.2">
/* Determines the browser name and browser version
*/
var brow = ((navigator.appName) +
→(parseInt(navigator.appVersion)));
/* reassign variable depending on the browser */
if (parseInt(navigator.appVersion >= 5)) {
isNew = 1}
else if (brow == "Netscape4")
  {isNS4 = 1;}
  else if (brow == "Microsoft Internet
→Explorer4")
  {isIE4 = 1;}
</SCRIPT>
```

Code 9.7 Using browser sensing in JavaScript. If any of the values (isNS4, isIE4, or isNew) is 1, then the first piece of code will be used; otherwise the second piece of code is run.

```
</HEAD>
<BODY>
<SCRIPT LANGUAGE="JavaScript">
if (isNS4 || isIE4 || isNew) {
  document.writeln('I am a Dynamic HTML capable
→browser!');
}
  else {
    document.writeln('I can not run Dynamic HTML.
→Sorry.')
  }
</SCRIPT>
</BODY>
```

Figure 9.7 The first browser shows this code running in Navigator 3.0, and the second running in Internet

2. if (isNS4 || isIE4 || isNew) {DHTML code}

   You can now employ browser sensing in JavaScript, as shown in **Code 9.7**. If any of the variables isNS4, isIE4, or isNew has been set to 1, then the first script is run.

3.   else{non-DHTML code}

   Otherwise, the second script is run.

✔ Tip

■ Of course new browsers will be coming along, and you will probably need to change this browser-sensing code as time goes by to stay up-to-date. By including the isNew variable, however, future compatibility problems can be avoided.

Creating a cross-browser DOM

One way around the issue of having two different DOMs is to detect which browser is in use, and then employ variables to create a generic DOM that will work on either browser. The two DOMs differ in the properties used to access the document and the styles, so we initialize two variables to reflect these differences depending on which browser the visitor is using.

We can then use these variables in functions to control CSS positioned elements without having to code twice for each browser.

To use the cross-browser DOM with a JavaScript function:

1. ```
   <SCRIPT LANGUAGE="JavaScript1.2"
   →SRC="browser_sensing.js"></SCRIPT>
   ```

   Add the browser-sensing code shown in the preceding section to your JavaScript. In **Code 9.8** we have set up an external text file that contains the JavaScript we need, and then used the SRC attribute with the <SCRIPT> tag to import the file into our document.

2. ```
   docObj = (isNS4) ? 'document' :
   →'document.all';
           styleObj = (isNS4) ? " : '.style';
   ```

   Add **Code 9.9** to your JavaScript. This code will run as soon as the page is loaded into the browser window, and will initialize the variables for our generic DOM to work on that browser. If this is Navigator 4 the variable docObj will get the value "document" and styleObj will remain blank. Otherwise the variables get IE 4's "document.all." and ".style".

Code 9.8 This will initialize the variables to be used in our generic DOM. When we need to access a particular browser's DOM using JavaScript, we can use the generic DOM.

```
                              code
<HTML>
  <HEAD>
    <SCRIPT LANGUAGE="JavaScript1.2"
→SRC="browser_sensing.js"></SCRIPT>
//Loads the browser-sensing JavaScript.
    <SCRIPT LANGUAGE="JavaScript">
<!-- Hide from old browsers
```

Code 9.9 This code assigns the variable docObj a value of document if the browser is Navigator 4, or document.all if it's another browser.

```
if (isNS4||isIE4||isNew) {
  docObj = (isNS4) ? 'document' : 'document.all';
  styleObj = (isNS4) ? '' : '.style';
  }
/*Assigns the variable styleObj a blank value if
the browser is Navigator 4, or .style if it is
not.*/

function checkDOM(elementName){
  if (isNS4||isIE4||isNew){
    dom = eval(docObj + '.' + elementName +
→styleObj);
```

Figure 9.8 The Alert windows tell you which DOM is being used.

Code 9.10 If Netscape 4: dom = document.elementName (object layer). If Internet Explorer 4: dom = document. all.elementName.style (object style).

```
    alert('This browser uses the ' + dom + '
→Document Object Model.');
    dom.left = 120;
    dom.top = 120;
  }
}
// Stop hiding from old browsers -->
    </SCRIPT>
    <STYLE>
.banner {position: absolute; font: bold 18pt/25pt
→helvetica; background-color: #333333;
→color:#CCCCCC;}
    </STYLE>
  </HEAD>
  <BODY ONLOAD="checkDOM('b1')">
    <SPAN ID="b1" CLASS="banner" STYLE="left:
20px; top: 20px;">A very pretty HTML element!
</SPAN>
  </BODY>
</HTML>
```

✔ Tips

- In the future, it is anticipated that both Navigator and Internet Explorer will be using the same DOM—which will more than likely resemble the DOM being used today by Internet Explorer. In that case, all you'll have to do to update the generic DOM for browsers 5.x or later is to add isNew to your condition statement, thus:

    if (isNS4||isIE4||isNew)

- Currently Navigator can only use the DOM to change CSS positioning properties; but Internet Explorer can use the DOM to make changes to other CSS properties as well.

3. function checkDOM(elementName)
     if (isNS4||isIE4)

Set up your JavaScript function so that the name of the element to be affected in the script is passed to the function. You'll also want to make sure that this is a DHTML browser.

4.   dom = eval(docObj + '.' +
     →elementName + styleObj);

Using the variables assigned in step 2, you can now assign the variable dom to represent the Document Object Model for this element in this particular browser. If the browser in question is Navigator 4.x, dom will get the value object layer; otherwise, the dom will get the value object style.

5.   alert('This browser uses the '
     →+ dom + ' Document Object Model.');
               dom.left = 120;
               dom.top = 120;}}

Now add the meat of your function shown in **Code 9.10**, using the dom variable along with a CSS positioning property. Just to show you how it works, here we have an Alert window pop up to tell the visitor which DOM they are using. We also change the left and top positioning properties for the element in question.

6. <SPAN ID="b1" CLASS="banner" STYLE="left:
     →20px; top: 20px;">A very pretty HTML ele
     →ment! </SPAN>

Set up the element using the ID attribute. Here we have set up an ID called b1. Notice that we have not set up a CSS rule for this ID type (but we could if we wanted to).

7. <BODY ONLOAD="checkDOM('b1')">

Connect the element to the script using an event handler. In this case we will have the script run after the document has been loaded.

Feature Sensing

There's another way of determining whether the browser that is running your script has what it takes to do the job: Ask it. Finding out if the browser has the feature(s) you need to use is a lot simpler than it sounds, and only requires one added line per function.

In many cases, feature sensing is a better alternative than browser sensing. If the current version of a browser cannot run your script, who is to say that another, more powerful version of the browser won't be released? Feature sensing will let any able browser to run the code.

The drawback to feature sensing is that if you're using several JavaScript features that require checking, you have to check each one separately.

To sense if a particular JavaScript feature is available:

1. if (document.images)

Within a JavaScript container, set up a conditional statement as shown in **Code 9.11.** Within the parentheses of the if statement, place the DOM for the JavaScript feature you need to use. In this example, we are checking to see if the browser can handle the image object.

2. { document.writeln('Yes, I can change
→images.')}

Within {} brackets, type in the JavaScript code you want executed if this feature is in fact available on this browser.

3. else { document.writeln(' Sorry. I can't
→change images.')}

You can also include an else statement specifying the code to be run in the event that the JavaScript feature you are testing for is not available.

Code 9.11 The code in the if statement will run if the browser is capable of dealing with images; otherwise, the else code will run.

```
if (document.images) {
  document.writeln('Yes, I can change images.')
/*JavaScript to be run on Navigator 4, Internet
Explorer 4, or if the browser is more recent than
those.*/
}
  else {
    document.writeln('Sorry. I can't change
→images.')
//JavaScript Code to be run on other browsers
  }
```

Figure 9.9 This window shows **Code 9.11** running in Internet Explorer 3.0.

Figure 9.10 The second window is the same code in Navigator 4.0.

DYNAMIC TECHNIQUES

In the past Web pages have been more or less static entities—once the page is loaded into the browser window, it's impossible to make changes. But today's Web pages have much more life and JavaScript has been responsible for some of this evolution. Even so, until recently there has been no way to add or subtract elements from the screen without loading a whole new HTML document.

Using Cascading Style Sheets, along with JavaScript and the cross-browser Document Object Model you met in Chapter 9, I will show you the basic techniques you need to know to create dynamic documents. This includes hiding and showing elements, moving elements, changing an elements stacking level, finding your location on the screen, dynamic content between frames, placing external content into the document and how to select any element on the screen.

Showing and hiding elements

As you learned in Chapter 7, the visibility property lets you designate whether an element on the screen will be visible or invisible on the web page. Using JavaScript to control this property, you can dynamically toggle the element's visibility on and off.

In **Figure 10.1** we see how the screen appears before the toggle button is pressed and **Figure 10.2** shows what happens after the button is pressed.

To toggle the visibility of an element:

1. Add browser sensing and DOM initialization to the JavaScript in the head of your document (see **Creating a cross-browser DOM**, page 146) so that the functions below will know whether they are running in a DHTML browser.

2. function toggleVis(currElem)

    Add the function **toggleVis()** (as shown in **Code 10.1**) to the JavaScript in the head of your document, which checks on the current state of the visibility of the element in question and then switches it.

    ```
    dom = eval(docObj + '.' + currElem +
    →styleObj);
    state = dom.visibility;
    ```

    This function sets our generic DOM for the element being controlled and then assigns that elements current visibility to the variable **state**.

    ```
    if (state == "visible" || state == "show")
    →{dom.visibility = "hidden";}
    ```

    The function then checks to see if the element is visible and if it is, the function hides the element.

Code 10.1 The toggleVis() function turns visibility to hidden if the element is visible, or to visible if it's hidden.

```
                        code
<HTML>
<HEAD>
<SCRIPT SRC="browser-sensing.js">
</SCRIPT>
<SCRIPT>
/* Toggles an elements visibility between hidden
and visible */
function toggleVis(currElem){
  dom = eval(docObj + '.' + currElem +
→styleObj);
  state = dom.visibility;
  if (state == "visible" || state == "show")
    {dom.visibility = "hidden";}
  else {dom.visibility = "visible";*}
}
</SCRIPT>
</HEAD>
```

Code 10.2 The input button in the form calls toggleVis() to make the element meep hidden or visible. Notice that we didn't have to set up an ID rule for meep in order for this to work. All we have to do is include an ID attribute with the tag in order to identify it.

```
<BODY>
  <FORM ACTION="" METHOD="get">
    <DIV ID="meep" STYLE="position: relative;
→visibility: hidden; font: bold 18pt/18pt
→helvetica;">
      <IMG SRC="../images/coco.jpg">
      MEEP!
    </DIV>
    <BR>
    <INPUT TYPE="BUTTON" Value="Toggle"
→ONCLICK="toggleVis('meep')">
  </FORM>
</BODY>
</HTML>
```

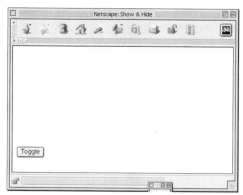

Figure 10.1 The toggle button allows us to see the content of the element (or not).

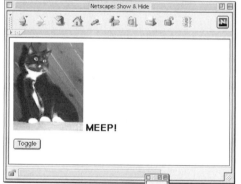

Figure 10.2 Here the toggle button has been pressed, and the element's content is visible: CoCo the cat.

else {dom.visibility = "visible";}

If the element is not visible, this function will be set to visible.

3. <DIV ID="meep" STYLE="position:
→relative; visibility: hidden; font: bold
→18pt/18pt helvetica;">Here I am!</DIV>

Set up a CSS positioned element using an ID selector in your HTML. Set the visibility property to either visible or hidden, as shown in **Code 10.2**.

4. <INPUT TYPE="BUTTON" Value="Toggle"
→ONCLICK="toggleVis('meep')">

Add an event handler that calls the toggleVis() function, using the ID name of your positioned element. You can see how this works in **Code 10.2**. In this example we have set up a form button so that, when clicked, will run the toggleVis() function on the "meep" element.

✔ Tips

■ You'll notice in the toggleVis() function that we check two states for visibility: visible or show. Although the CSS-P standards for visibility are the values visible and hidden, Navigator 4 uses the values show and hide. Navigator 4 does allow you to assign visible or hidden to the visibility property, but the browser then automatically translates those values to show or hide.

■ You could split the toggleVis() function up into two parts, if you wish: one that turns the visibility on, and one that turns visibility off. Why? Sometimes when programming a Web page, you may just want to make sure that the visibility is on or off, without necessarily knowing its current state.

■ Why meep for the ID? It's the sound my cat CoCo makes instead of meow.

Showing and hiding elements

Toggling graphics

One popular dynamic effect that uses JavaScript is to replace a graphic when a screen event happens. For instance, when visitors pass their mouse over a button, it's nice to have that button respond by showing that it is ready to be pressed. In **Figure 10.3** we make the button "glow" when the mouse is over it by switching the image to its "active" version.

To toggle between graphics:

1. Add **Code 10.3** to the JavaScript in the head of your document. This code will initialize an array and record the location of the graphics we are using (b_on.gif and b_off.gif).

2. imag[1] = "images/b_on.gif";

   Add this code for each graphic that you want enabled for toggling in your document. Each graphic gets a different number (imag[0]... imag[1]... imag[2]) and a different location (="url").

3. Add the function toggleImg(), as shown in **Code 10.4**, to the JavaScript in your document. This function will change the source of the image imgName and replace it with the graphic in the array from step 2, noted by the variable num.

4. <A HREF="top.html"
   ONMOUSEOUT="toggle(b1,0)"
   ONMOUSEOVER="toggle(b1,1)"
   ONCLICK="toggle(b3,2)"

   Now you can set up your event handlers to cover several possible events. The events call the function toggleImg() with the name of the graphic you want to change, and the array number of the graphic you want to replace it with. This effect is demonstrated in **Figure 10.3**.

Code 10.3 This sets up a simple array to record the URLs of our different graphics.

```
code
<HTML>
<HEAD>
<SCRIPT>
if (document.image)
  {
  imag = new Array();
  imag[0] = "images/b_off.gif";
  imag[1] = "images/b_on.gif";
  imag[2] = "images/b_active.gif";
  im = new Array();
  for (var i = 0; i <= imag.length; i++)
    {
    im[i] = new Image();
    im[i].src = imag[i];
    }
  }

function toggleImg(imgName,num)
  {
  if (document.image){
    document.imgName.src = im[num].src
    }
  }
</SCRIPT>
</HEAD>
```

Code 10.4 If the mouse is moved onto the graphic, the graphic b_on.gif is used. When the mouse moves away from the graphic, it reverts back to b_off.gif. When the button is clicked, it gets the b_active.gif graphic.

```
<BODY BGCOLOR="#FFFFFF">
  <A HREF="top.html"
ONMOUSEOUT="toggle(b1,0)"
ONMOUSEOVER="toggle(b1,1)"
ONCLICK="toggle(b1,2)">
    <IMG SRC="../images/b_off.gif" BORDER="0"
→WIDTH="25" HEIGHT="25" NAME="b1" ALIGN="left">
    Home Page
  </A>
  <BR CLEAR="all">
  <A HREF="news/index.html"
→ONMOUSEOUT="toggle(b3,0)"
→ONMOUSEOVER="toggle(b3,1)"
→ONCLICK="toggle(b3,2)">
    <IMG SRC="../images/b_off.gif" BORDER="0"
→WIDTH="25" HEIGHT="25" NAME="b3" ALIGN="left">
    News of the World
  </A>
</BODY>
</HTML>
```

Figure 10.3 When the mouse pointer is on the graphic, it glows.

✔ Tips

■ For image toggling, I recommend using feature sensing rather than browser sensing because only one particular feature is in question (whether the browser can accommodate the image object or not).

■ User feedback is one of the important features of a site using DHTML. Letting visitors know—graphically—the state of a link they are using not only makes the site more interesting but adds layers of information, as well.

Changing the stacking order

Using CSS positioning, we can "stack" various elements, overlapping one on top of the other in the browser window. With a little clever JavaScripting, we can arrange for a click on any element to bring that element to the front of the stack. **Figure 10.4** shows what the document looks like when first loaded and **Figure 10.5** is what happens when Element 2 is clicked on.

To change the stacking order:

1. **<SCRIPT LANGUAGE="JavaScript" SRC="browser_sensing.js"></SCRIPT>**

   Add browser sensing and DOM initialization to the JavaScript in the head of your document (see **Creating a cross-browser DOM**, page 146), so that we can initialize a DOM for the browser the code runs in. In **Code 10.5**, the code necessary for these operations is linked from an external file.

2. **var currTop='elem1';**

   Initialize the variable currTop to elem1. This tells the browser which element is starting out on top. You could actually make currTop any of the selector IDs that you are using.

3. **function bringForward(newTop)**

   Add the function bringForward() (shown in **Code 10.6**) to your JavaScript. This function sets the element that is currently on top to z-index 0, and then sets the clicked-on element to z-index 100, which should place it above all other elements.

   domTop = eval(docObj + '.' + currTop + →styleObj);

   domNew = eval(docObj + '.' + newTop + →styleObj);

   We first set up two DOMs, one for the element that is currently on top and one for

Code 10.5 This script moves the element that is currently on top back down to the 0 level in the z-index, and the one that gets selected moves to the top.

```
<HTML>
<HEAD>
<SCRIPT LANGUAGE="JavaScript"
SRC="browser_sensing.js"></SCRIPT>
<SCRIPT LANGUAGE="JavaScript">
var currTop ='elem1';
function bringForward(newTop) {
  if (isNS4||isIE4||isNew){
  domTop = eval(docObj +  '.' + currTop +
→styleObj);
  domNew = eval(docObj +  '.' + newTop +
→styleObj);
  domTop.zIndex = "0";
  domNew.zIndex = "10";
  currTop = newTop;
  }
}
</SCRIPT>
```

Code 10.6 The styles are set up as ID "layers" (elem1 through elem4) which can then be switched around.

```
<STYLE TYPE="text/css">
#elem1 {
position: absolute; top: 5px; left: 5px; z-index: 0;}
#elem2 {
position: absolute; top: 51px; left: 75px; z-
→index: 0;}
#elem3 {
position: absolute; top: 60px; left: 150px; z-
→index: 0;}
#elem4 {
position: absolute; top: 123px; left: 225px; z-
→index: 0;}
</STYLE>
```

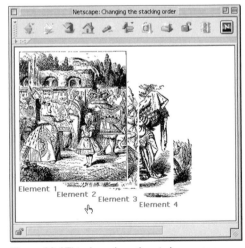

Figure 10.4 This shows how the window appears when loaded.

Code 10.7 The HTML used to set up our layers. The function call to bringForward() is actually in the <HREF> link, so that when the visitor clicks on an element, that element comes to the front.

```
<BODY BGCOLOR="#FFFFFF">
  <SPAN ID="elem4">
<A HREF="JAVASCRIPT:bringForward('elem4')">
<IMG SRC="../images/alice22a.gif" WIDTH="100"
→HEIGHT="147" BORDER="0"> <BR CLEAR="all">
  <B>Element 4</B> </A></SPAN>
  <SPAN ID="elem3">
<A HREF="JAVASCRIPT:bringForward('elem3')">
<IMG SRC="../images/alice32a.gif" WIDTH="139"
→HEIGHT="200" BORDER="0"> <BR CLEAR="all">
  <B>Element 3</B> </A></SPAN>
  <SPAN ID="elem2">
<A HREF="JAVASCRIPT:bringForward('elem2')">
→<IMG SRC="../images/alice15a.gif" WIDTH="151"
→HEIGHT="200" BORDER="0"> <BR CLEAR="all">
  <B>Element 2</B> </A></SPAN>
  <SPAN ID="elem1">
<A HREF="JAVASCRIPT:bringForward('elem1')">
<IMG SRC="../images/alice29a.gif" WIDTH="200"
→HEIGHT="236" BORDER="0"> <BR CLEAR="all">
  <B>Element 1</B></A> </SPAN>
  </BODY>
</HTML>
```

Figure 10.5 This shows what happens when you click on one of the pictures.

the element that is being moved to the top.

```
domTop.zIndex = "0";
domNew.zIndex = "100";
```

Now we set the z-index value for the current top element to 0, moving it back down, and the z-index for the new top element to 100 moving it above other elements on the screen.

```
currTop = newTop;
```

Finally we set the new top element as the top element.

4. #elem1 {position: absolute; top: 5px; left: 5px; z-index: 0;}

Create a separate ID selector for each element and set their positions as desired. Set all of their z-indexes to 0.

5. <SPAN ID="elem1"><A HREF="JAVASCRIPT:
   →bringForward('elem1')"><IMG SRC="../
   →images/alice29a.gif" WIDTH="200"
   →HEIGHT="236" BORDER="0"> <BR
   →CLEAR="all">
   <B>Element 1</B></A> </SPAN>

Use the <SPAN> tag and CSS-P to create the elements that will be "shuffled." Include a <LINK> tag with a call to the function bringForward(). The result? When a visitor clicks one of these elements on the page, the function will be executed and that element will come to the front.

✔ Tips

■ Element stacking is a powerful feature that has multiple uses. For instance, you could set up several stacked menus, each one having a tab showing. Visitors can click any menu's tab to move it to the top.

■ With non-DHTML browsers, the elements that were overlapping using CSS-P should simply appear one under the next on the page without overlapping. Not as nice looking, but it will still work.

Moving elements from point to point

You can move elements from place to place on the screen by changing the top and left properties for an element. The first window in **Figure 10.6** shows how the document originally loads. After entering 250,10 into the fields and pressing the move button, the element moves to those coordinates, as shown in the **Figure 10.7**.

To move an element:

1. Add browser sensing and DOM initialization to the JavaScript in the head of your document (see **Creating a cross-browser DOM**, page 146).

2. function moveElement(curElem,mTop,mLeft)

   Add the function moveElement() to the JavaScript in the head of your document. This function (**Code 10.8**) is used to move the element from its current position to a new position in the window.

       dom = eval(docObj + '.' + curElem +
       →styleObj);

   First, the function sets the DOM for this element.

       dom.top = mTop;
       dom.left = mLeft;

   These lines set the top and left properties for this element to the top and left values which have been passed.

3. Next set up a CSS positioned element that has been positioned using the top and left properties, as demonstrated in **Code 10.9**.

4. Add a form field that allows the visitor to enter the coordinates of the position they want to move the element to, and then create a form button that calls the function moveElement(). Use the ID for the element you want moved, and the values entered in the form fields. (**Code 10.8**

Code 10.8 This function relocates an object on the screen, depending on how the object was initially positioned (relative or absolute).

```
code
<HTML>
<HEAD>
<SCRIPT SRC="browser-sensing.js>
</SCRIPT>
function moveElement(curElem,mTop,mLeft){
   dom = eval(docObj + '.' + curElem + styleObj);
   dom.top = mTop;
   dom.left = mLeft;
}
```

Code 10.9 Input lines are placed in the body to let the visitor give the coordinates that will move the element.

```
<BODY>
   <DIV ID="meep2" STYLE="position: absolute;
→left: 60px; top: 60px; font: bold 24pt/24pt
→times;">
      Here I am!
   </DIV>
   <FORM ACTION="(Empty Reference!)" NAME="bob"
→METHOD="get">
      x:<INPUT TYPE="TEXT" NAME="leftVal"
→SIZE="3"><BR>
      y:<INPUT TYPE="TEXT" NAME="topVal"
→SIZE="3"><BR>
      <INPUT TYPE="button" VALUE="Move"
→onClick="moveElement('meep2',document.bob.topV
→al.value,document.bob.leftVal.value)">
   </FORM>
</BODY>
</HTML>
```

Figure 10.6 Enter coordinates to move the element meep2.

Figure 10.7 The element meep2 has moved from its original position at 60,60 to a new position at 250,10.

shows you what this looks like.) Pushing this button will cause the element to move to the coordinates specified.

✔ Tip

■ There are other ways to determine the coordinates to which you want an object moved—you don't have to get them from the user. See **Finding your location**, coming up in the next section.

Moving elements from point to point

Finding your location

All events in the browser window generate certain information about what occurred, where it occurred, and how. The most important piece of information for our purposes here is the screen location of the event.

In **Figure 10.8** we have set up the image so that when you click in it, the coordinates of the click appear in the two form fields. In this case clicking on the branch behind the caterpillar yields 50,96.

To find your location:

1. <SCRIPT LANGUAGE="JavaScript1.2"
→SRC="browser_sensing.js"></SCRIPT>

Add browser sensing to the JavaScript in your document so that the functions can check whether they are running in DHTML browsers or not.

2. function locate(evt)

Add the function locate() to the JavaScript in your heading tag. The event will be passed to the function through the **evt** variable.

3. leftVal = eval(event.x)

The left position value.

topVal = eval(event.y)

The top position value.

Internet Explorer 4 can access the event object directly without having to use the evt variable. This code takes advantage of this ability, feeding the x,y coordinates of the event directly into our variables.

4. leftVal = eval(evt.pageX)

The left position value.

leftVal = eval(evt.pageY)

The top position value

For the more-quirky Navigator, notice that we have to use the **evt** variable, which has been passed the event object from the event handler (see step 2).

Code 10.10 The function locate() will display the x,y coordinates of the mouse.

```
<HTML>
  <HEAD>
    <SCRIPT LANGUAGE="JavaScript1.2"
→SRC="browser_sensing.js"></SCRIPT>
    <SCRIPT LANGUAGE="JavaScript">
<!-- Hide from old browsers
function locate(evt){
  if (isNS4||isIE4){
    if (isNS4) {
      topVal = eval(evt.pageY);
      leftVal = eval(evt.pageX);}
    else {
      topVal = eval(event.y);
      leftVal = eval(event.x);}
    document.coords.xcoord.value = leftVal;
    document.coords.ycoord.value = topVal;
  }
}
function nodda() {null;}
// Stop hiding from old browsers -->
</SCRIPT>
  </HEAD>
  <BODY BGCOLOR="#FFFFFF">
    <P><FORM ACTION="test" METHOD="get"
NAME="coords">
    x:<INPUT TYPE="TEXT" NAME="xcoord" SIZE="3">
y:<INPUT TYPE="TEXT" NAME="ycoord" SIZE="3"></P>
    </FORM>
    <A HREF="JAVASCRIPT:nodda()"
→ONCLICK="locate(event)">
<IMG SRC="../images/alice15a.gif" WIDTH="300"
→HEIGHT="200"></A>
  </BODY>
</HTML>
```

Figure 10.8 When the graphic is clicked, the x,y coordinates for the mouse pointer are displayed in the form fields.

5. The variables leftVal and topVal now contain the x,y position of the mouse click, with the top-left corner of the window display area being the origin (0,0).

✔ Tip

■ You can use this technique to position elements on the screen in relation to where the visitor clicks (see **Creating pop-up elements**, page 170).

Finding your location

Sensing events anywhere on the screen

For the most part, events are confined to stuff that happens to an element as a result of mouse movements and clicks. In this section you'll examine a method that allows you to detect an event that happens anywhere in the browser window—regardless of whether it happens to be associated with a particular element or not.

Figure 10.9 shows the initial appearance of the screen. When a visitor clicks anywhere on the screen, a message pops up telling them not to do that, as shown **Figure 10.10**.

To set up global sensing:

1. <SCRIPT LANGUAGE="JavaScript1.2"
→SRC="browser_sensing.js"></SCRIPT>

Add browser sensing and DOM initialization to the JavaScript in the head of your document.

2. function defaultEvents()

Add the function defaultEvents() to the JavaScript in the head of your document, as demonstrated in **Code 10.11**.

3. if (isNS4) {document.captureEvents
→(Event.MOUSEDOWN | Event.MOUSEUP) }

This function first initializes universal or "global" detection if the visitor's browser is Navigator 4. Internet Explorer does not need to do this as it can automatically detect events anywhere on the screen.

4. document.onmousedown = errorOn;
document.onmouseup = errorOff;

This function now assigns the functions to be executed if one of several specified events occurs anywhere in the window. The first function is for the mouseDown event, which triggers the errorOn() function. The second is for the mouseUp event, which triggers the errorOff() function.

Code 10.11 This code sets up default functions to be run when particular events happen anywhere in the window, regardless of whether an element is associated with it or not.

```
code

<HTML>
<HEAD>
<SCRIPT LANGUAGE="JavaScript1.2"
→SRC="browser_sensing.js"></SCRIPT>
<SCRIPT LANGUAGE="JavaScript">
<!-- Hide from old browsers
function defaultEvents() {
  if (isNS4) {
// Gives Navigator 4 global event capturing
     document.captureEvents(Event.MOUSEDOWN |
→Event.MOUSEUP)
  }
  if (isNS4||isIE4){
/* Sets up event capturing in both
Navigator 4 and Internet Explorer 4 */
  document.onmousedown = errorOn;
  document.onmouseup = errorOff;
  dom = eval(docObj + '.errMess' + styleObj);
  }
}

function errorOn() {
  dom.visibility = "visible";
  return false;
}

function errorOff() {
  dom.visibility = "hidden";
  return false;
}
// Stop hiding from old browsers -->
</SCRIPT>
    <STYLE>
#errMess {
position: absolute; top: 30%; left: 40%;
→visibility: hidden; border: red 5pt solid;
→background-color: white;  layer-background-
→color: white; z-index: 10;}
</STYLE>
    </HEAD>
    <BODY BGCOLOR="#FFFFFF" ONLOAD="defaultEvents()">
        <CENTER>
            <SPAN ID="errMess">Please Do Not Click
There!</SPAN>
            <IMG SRC="../images/alice42a.gif"
WIDTH="180" HEIGHT="240">
        </CENTER>
    </BODY>
</HTML>
```

Figure 10.9 When you click anywhere on the screen...

Figure 10.10 ... the error message is displayed.

5.   dom = eval(docObj + '.errMess' + styleObj);

Finally the function initializes the DOM for the element we will be using when an event occurs on the screen.

6. Add the functions errorOn() and errorOff(), which are executed from the function defaultEvents(). These functions will cause the element called errMess to appear and disappear.

7. <BODY BGCOLOR="#FFFFFF"
    →ONLOAD="defaultEvents()">

In the <BODY> tag, add an onLoad event handler to run the defaultEvents() function as soon as the document is loaded in the browser window.

✔ Tip

- Global events can be overridden by event handlers that are associated with a particular element in the window.

Placing external content

In traditional Web pages, all content is included within a single HTML document. By using the new <LAYER> tag (introduced in Chapter 13), the <OBJECT> tag, and a bit of clever JavaScripting, we can import content into our document from anywhere we want, as shown in **Figure 10.11**.

To place external content:

1. <B><FONT SIZE="5" COLOR="#CC0033">Hello World!</FONT></B>

In a separate file, type in the content that you will be importing and save the file. For this example, we are calling the file 10_12.html. You only need to include the HTML that would normally appear within the <BODY> tag, as shown in **Code 10.12**.

2. <SCRIPT LANGUAGE="JavaScript1.2"
→SRC="browser_sensing.js"></SCRIPT>

Add browser sensing to your document, as demonstrated in **Code 10.13**.

3. if (isNS4) {
document.writeln('<LAYER SRC="10_12.
→html"></LAYER>')}

Within the body, add JavaScript that will write a <LAYER> tag into your document. The SRC attribute should point to your external content.

4. else {
document.writeln('<OBJECT SRC="external.
→html"></OBJECT>')}

If the browser being used is not Navigator 4 then the code writes in the <OBJECT> tag. The SRC attribute can point to the same external document, or to a different one depending on your need.

Code 10.12 The HTML to be imported into the document shown in Code 10.13. (The file is 10–12.html)

```
                      code
<B>
<FONT SIZE="5" COLOR="#CC0033">
Hello World!
</FONT>
</B>
```

Code 10.13 The code in Code 10.12 is imported into the document.

```
                      code
<HEAD>
  <SCRIPT LANGUAGE="JavaScript1.2"
SRC="browser_sensing.js"></SCRIPT>
</HEAD>
<BODY BGCOLOR="#FFFFFF">
  <SCRIPT LANGUAGE="JavaScript">
<!-- Hide from old browsers
if (isNS4) {
→document.writeln('<LAYER SRC="10-12.html">
→</LAYER>')}
  else {
→document.writeln('<OBJECT SRC="external.html">
→</OBJECT>')}
// Stop hiding from old browsers -->
  </SCRIPT>
</BODY>
```

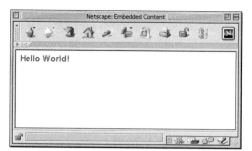

Figure 10.11 The imported code displays just as if it were a part of the document, regardless of browser.

✔ Tip

■ Theoretically, for this example we could have simply included both tags without the JavaScript. Navigator 4 ignores the <OBJECT> tag, and Internet Explorer ignores the <LAYER> tag. But by including both tags we create a potential compatibility issue: We cannot know if future versions of the browsers will *not* include both tags, in which case the content would be imported twice. By using JavaScript, we can avoid this repetition.

Placing external content

Selecting an element

Whenever an event occurs on the screen, (such as a mouse-over or a click) if you want to use the element that sparked that mouse event (like an image) you have to pass the name of that element as a variable to your function. Using DHTML though, we can actually have the browser determine which element on the screen the event occurred at. With Internet Explorer, in fact, this is a very easy task because the name of the element is a part of the event object. Navigator will take a little more work and we will have to rely on its layers abilities (see Chapter 13) to make this work.

In **Figure 10.12** a function has been set up so that when the mouse passes over an image on the screen, an alert comes up to tell you what image it is.

To determine which element the event occurred at:

1. <SCRIPT LANGUAGE="JavaScript"
→SRC="browser_sensing.js"></SCRIPT>

Add browser sensing functionality to the JavaScript in the head of your document so that the following code can tell whether it is running in a DHTML browser and which one. In this example we are importing the code from an external file.

2. function whichElement(evt)

Add the function whichElement() to the JavaScript in the head of your document as shown in **Code 10.14**. This script is used to determine which CSS Element on the screen the event occurred at and then displays an alert telling you which one it is.

if (isNS4)

If the code is running in Navigator, the function will determine the position of the mouse and then check each layer in its array of layers to determine which one this position corresponds to.

Code 10.14 The WhichElement() function is used to determine which element on the screen an event came from without have to pass that as a variable to the function.

```
<HTML>
  <HEAD>
    <SCRIPT LANGUAGE="JavaScript1.2"
→SRC="browser_sensing.js"></SCRIPT>
    <SCRIPT LANGUAGE="JavaScript1.2">
<!--
var name = null;
function whichElement(evt) {
  if (isNS4) {
    var testElem;
    var xPos = evt.pageX;
    var yPos = evt.pageY;
    // In Netscape, cycles through the layers
    // if the mouse pointer is in one of them
    for (var i = document.layers.length - 1; i >=
→0; i--) {
      testElem = document.layers[i];
      if ((xPos > testElem.left) &&
      (xPos < testElem.left +
→testElem.clip.width) &&
      (yPos > testElem.top) &&
      (yPos < testElem.top +
→testElem.clip.height)) {
        name = testElem.name;
        alert('You are on ' + name + '.');
        return
      }
    }
  }
  else {
    // accesses the element that generated
    // the event and gets its ID name
    name = event.srcElement.name;
    alert('You are on ' + name + '.');
    return;
  }
  return;
}
// -->
    </SCRIPT>
    <STYLE><!--
      #alice1 { top: 5px; left: 5px }
      #alice2 { top: 150px; left: 200px }
      #alice3 { top: 5px; left: 300px }
      .alice { position: absolute }-->
    </STYLE>
  </HEAD>
  <BODY BGCOLOR="#ffffff">
    <SPAN ID="alice1" CLASS="alice">
<A HREF="which_element.html"
→ONMOUSEOVER="whichElement(event)"><IMG
SRC="../images/alice20a.gif" BORDER="0"
WIDTH="134" HEIGHT="161" NAME="alice1"></A>
</SPAN>
<SPAN ID="alice2" CLASS="alice">
<A HREF="which_element.html"
→ONMOUSEOVER="whichElement(event)"><IMG
SRC="../images/alice12a.gif" BORDER="0"
WIDTH="134" HEIGHT="192" NAME="alice2">
</A></SPAN>
<SPAN ID="alice3" CLASS="alice">
<A HREF="which_element.html"
→ONMOUSEOVER="whichElement(event)"><IMG
SRC="../images/alice11a.gif" BORDER="0"
WIDTH="187" HEIGHT="131" NAME="alice3"></A></SPAN>
  </BODY>
</HTML>
```

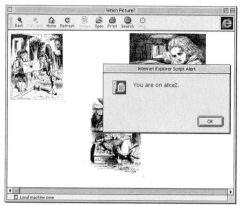

Figure 10.12 The alert window pops up to let you know which image your mouse is passing over.

3. else

> Otherwise (if it is running in Internet Explorer 4) the code simply uses the event objects name—which will be the name of the element that the event comes from.

4. Set up your CSS elements using whatever style properties you want. In this example we set up three images (alice1, alice2, and alice 3) each with their own unique ID.

✔ Tips

- Notice that we also specified a name in each image tag as well as an ID in the Span tag. Netscape uses the name of the ID while Internet Explorer uses the name of the actual image. Include both to remain cross browser.

- This function will come in especially handy in Chapter 11 when we learn to drag elements around on the screen.

Selecting an element

Dynamic content between frames

Elements in one frame can be controlled using JavaScript in another frame without much trouble. The only big change will come in the way we construct our cross-browser DOM which will now need to find a path to an element in another frame.

Figure 10.13 shows a window with two frames. The link in the bottom frame will cause the rabbit in the top frame to move from the right side of the screen to the left side of the screen.

To control elements in other frames:

1. Set up your frames document making sure to name the frames that will have dynamic content in them. In **Code 10.15** we have set up a frame document with two frames named topFrame and bottomFrame which have as their sources top_frame.html and bottom_frame.html respectively.

2. Now set up an HTML document with your CSS elements to be controlled from the other frame. In **Code 10.16** the picture of the rabbit has been given the appropriate ID rabbit. This is the code for top_frame.html.

3. Set up the HTML document that will control the element in the other frame. In **Code 10.17**, (which is saved as bottom_frame.html), we are using a variation on the moveElement which we used earlier in this chapter. The main difference is in the syntax we use to set the DOM:

    var dom = eval('parent.' + frameName + + →docObj + '.' + currElem + styleObj);

    We not only include the docObj, currElem, and stylObj variables as in past examples, but also 'parent.' and the new frameName

Code 10.15 The frame document used in this example.

```
code
<HTML>
  <FRAMESET ROWS="*,35">
    <FRAME SRC="top_frame.html" NAME="topFrame">
    <FRAME SRC="bottom_frame.html"
→NAME="bottomFrame">
  </FRAMESET>
</HTML>
```

Code 10.16 The image in this frame has been given an ID called rabbit. (This file is top_frame.html)

```
code
<HTML>
  <HEAD>
    <STYLE TYPE="text/css
      #rabbit { position: absolute; top: 25px;
→left: 350px }
    </STYLE>
  </HEAD>
  <BODY BGCOLOR="#ffffff">
    <SPAN ID="rabbit">
    <IMG SRC="../../images/alice02a.gif"
WIDTH="134" HEIGHT="201">
    </SPAN>
  </BODY>
</HTML>
```

Code 10.17 The function moveElement in this document has been given a little extra information about how to track down the rabbit in the frame document.

```
code
<HTML>
  <HEAD>
    <SCRIPT LANGUAGE="JavaScript1.2"
→SRC="../browser_sensing.js"></SCRIPT>
    <SCRIPT LANGUAGE="JavaScript">
function moveElement(currElem,frameName,top,left){
  var dom = eval('parent.' + frameName + docObj +
→currElem + styleObj);
  dom.top = top;
  dom.left = left;

}
    </SCRIPT>
  </HEAD>
  <BODY>
    <A HREF="rabbit.html"
→ONMOUSEOVER="moveElement('.rabbit','topFrame.'
→,10,10)"
→ONMOUSEOUT="moveElement('.rabbit','topFrame.',
→25,350)">Run Rabbit, Run!</A>
  </BODY>
</HTML>
```

variable which will locate the element we want to effect within the frame document.

4. <A HREF="rabbit.html"
→ONMOUSEOVER="moveElement('rabbit',
→'topFrame.',10,10)"
→ONMOUSEOUT="moveElement('rabbit',
→'topFrame.',25,350)">Run Rabbit, Run!</A>

In **Code 10.17** we have also set up a link that calls the new moveElement function. This passes to the function the name of the element to be moved and the name of the frame where that element is located. When the mouse passes over this link, the rabbit moves from the right to the left and back again when the mouse moves away.

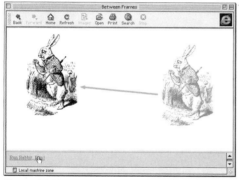

Figure 10.13 The rabbit may be in a different frame but the DOM hunts him down and makes him run.

DYNAMIC SOLUTIONS

The last two chapters have presented the various abilities associated with cross-browser DHTML. The only limitation to the application of these techniques is how many different needs you can find to put them to!

Now, let's look at ways to combine some DHTML techniques in order to solve particular problems—such as pop-up menus, animation, and other tricks. To get you started, this chapter introduces you to some relatively simple uses of DHTML in these situations.

Creating pop-up elements

The ability to have content appear and disappear as needed is probably the most important feature available to you as a designer using DHTML. We have already seen how to toggle the visibility of an element, and how to move it to a particular spot in the window.

This next example shows you how to have an element pop up on the screen, right under the mouse pointer. Although this is a fairly simple and straightforward concept, make no mistake—this is a powerful feature for any Web page. **Figure 11.1** shows the mouse moving onto a link causing a paragraph of Hypertext to popup explaining what the linked text means in greater detail. (**Figure 11.2**)

To create a pop-up element:

1. <SCRIPT LANGUAGE="JavaScript"
   →SRC="browser_sensing.js">

   Add browser sensing and DOM initialization to your JavaScript (see **Creating a cross-browser DOM**, page 146). In **Code 11.1**, the necessary code is linked from an external file called browser_sensing.js which you have to set up and save separately.

2. function popUp(evt,currElem)

   Add the function popUp() to your JavaScript as shown in **Code 11.1**. This function resembles the toggleVis() function presented in **Showing and hiding elements** in Chapter 10. However, popUp() adds a new variable—evt— which "captures" information about the event generated by the event handler in the HTML. This is for use by Navigator.

3. .hyperText {

   Create a general class that describes how the pop-up (hypertextual) element should look on the screen. In this example shown

Code 11.1 The function popUp() moves the element into position under the mouse pointer and then makes it visible. When the mouse moves away from the link, the element is hidden again.

```
<HTML>
  <HEAD>
    <SCRIPT LANGUAGE="JavaScript"
→SRC="browser_sensing.js"></SCRIPT>
<SCRIPT LANGUAGE="JavaScript">
    <!-- Hide from old browsers
function popUp(evt,currElem){
/* Checks to see if this is a DHTML browser and
that currElem is not set to 0, in which case this
was triggered by the HREF and cannot be treated as
an event. */
  if ((isNS4 && currElem != 0) || (isIE4 &&
→currElem != 0)){
     dom = eval(docObj +  '.' + currElem +
→styleObj);
     state = dom.visibility;
     if (state == "visible" || state == "show")
       {dom.visibility = "hidden";}
     else
// finds the position of the mouse
// and then offsets the coordinates slightly
     {
     if (isNS4) {
        topVal = eval(evt.pageY + 2);
        leftVal = eval(evt.pageX - 125);}
     if (isIE4) {
        topVal = eval(event.y + 2);
        leftVal = eval(event.x - 125);}
// keeps the element from going off screen to the
// left
        if(leftVal < 2) {leftVal = 2;}
     dom.top = topVal;
     dom.left = leftVal;
     dom.visibility = "visible";
     }
  }
}
// Stop hiding from old browsers -->
</SCRIPT>
```

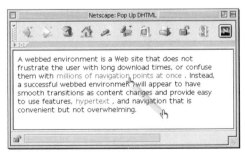

Figure 11.1 The first window is how the document looks when loaded.

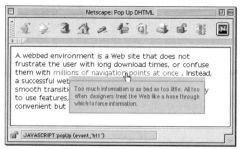

Figure 11.2 The popup appears when you move onto the link

Code 11.2 Set up the styles for the pop-up hypertext. Each one is absolutely positioned, hidden, and with an arbitrary top and left position.

```
<STYLE>
#ht1 {
  position: absolute;
  visibility: hidden;
  z-index: 10;
  top: 0px;
  left: 10px;
  }
#ht2 {
  position: absolute;
  visibility: hidden;
  z-index: 10;
  top: 0px;
  left: 10px;
  }
.hyperText
  {
  background-color: #CCCCCC;
  layer-background-color: #CCCCCC;
  padding: 5px;
  border: 2px solid #999999;
  width: 250px;
  font: normal 10pt/13pt helvetica, sans-serif;
  text-align: justify;
  color: #333333;
  }
</STYLE>
```

in **Code 11.2**, text is on a light-gray background with a dark-gray border.

4. #ht1 {

Create an ID selector that defines your hypertext area. Set its position to be absolute and its visibility to be hidden. Set the z-index high enough so that it will appear on top of any other screen content, I recommend 100. The initial top and left values are unimportant because they will be reset when the visitor places the mouse over the link.

Create a separate ID for each pop-up element.

5. <SPAN ID="ht1" CLASS="hyperText">Too much information is as bad as too little...</SPAN>

Using a <SPAN> tag, set up the content that you want to "pop up" when the link (coming up in step 6) is activated. The full code for this is shown in **Code 11.3**.

6. <A HREF="JAVASCRIPT:popUp (event,'ht1')" →ONMOUSEOUT=" popUp (event,'ht1')" →ONMOUSEOVER="popUp(event,'ht1')"> millions of navigation points at once</A>

Using an anchored link in the HTML, set your event handlers to call the popUp() function. This will place the element below the link.

✔ Tips

- Why use the event (evt) variable to place our hypertext rather than just telling it where to appear on the screen? Because you can never guarantee exactly how a visitor's browser will position text on the screen. By determining where the mouse pointer is when the event occurs, we can guarantee that the pop-up element will always appear close to the link.

- Notice the layer-background-color property in the hypertext class. This is a Netscape

CSS extension and so does not appear in our general discussion of background properties—but that doesn't mean it's not important. If layer-background-color is not included, Netscape browsers will display the padding (the area between the content and the border) as invisible! Not very attractive.

■ In this example we just used text, but we can put anything we want between the <SPAN> tags, including links, graphics, even forms. It's only limited by your imagination.

Code 11.3 In the HTML we set up our two pop-up text areas and then the text of our document with event handlers to make the text "pop-up".

```
<BODY>
<SPAN ID="ht1" CLASS="hyperText">Too much
information is as bad as too little. All too often
designers treat the Web like a hose through which
to force information.</SPAN>
<SPAN ID="ht2" CLASS="hyperText">Hypertext allows
you to include "meta-textual" information for
readers who want to know more.</SPAN>
<P>A webbed environment is a Web site that does not
frustrate the user with long download times, or
confuse them with
<A HREF="JAVASCRIPT:popUp (event,'ht1')"
→ONMOUSEOUT=" popUp (event,'ht1')"
→ONMOUSEOVER="popUp(event,'ht1')">
millions of navigation points at once
</A>
. Instead, a successful webbed environment will
appear to have smooth transitions as content
changes and provide easy to use features,
<A HREF="JAVASCRIPT:popUp (null,0)"
→ONMOUSEOUT=" popUp (event,'ht2')"
→ONMOUSEOVER="popUp(event,'ht2')">
hypertext
</A>
, and navigation that is convenient but not
overwhelming.</P>
</BODY>
```

Creating pop-up elements

Code 11.4 The toggleMenu() function will move the menu up and down. If you change dom.top to dom.left, this same function can cause the menu to pop out from the left side of the screen.

```
                    code
<HTML>
  <HEAD>
  <SCRIPT LANGUAGE="JavaScript1.2"
→SRC="browser_sensing.js"></SCRIPT>
  <SCRIPT LANGUAGE="JavaScript">
function toggleMenu(currElem,repo){
  if (isNS4||isIE4||isNew){
    dom = eval(docObj + '.' + currElem +
→styleObj);
/*This tests whether the menu is retracted or
not.*/

    if (dom.top != -5)
       {dom.top = -5;}
    else
       {dom.top = repo;}
  }
}
  </SCRIPT>
```

Code 11.5 Setting up the CSS for our sliding banner.

```
  <STYLE>
  B {background-color: #ffcccc;}
  .menu {position: absolute; font: 12pt/14pt
→helvetica; width: 75px; background-color:
→#333333; layer-background-color: #333333;
→color:#CCCCCC;}
  </STYLE>
  </HEAD>
</HTML>
```

Figure 11.3 The File menu is open, but the Search menu is still retracted.

Creating a pop-up menu

Pop-up (or pop-down, or pop-out) menus have always been a staple of graphical user interfaces (GUIs). These menus are great for allowing visitors to have quick access to a concise list of menu options in a limited amount of space.

Using JavaScript with positioned elements allows us to move all but a small part of a menu off the screen, and then back onto the screen when needed—through a function we will call toggleMenu().

To make a pop-up menu:

1. <SCRIPT LANGUAGE="JavaScript1.2"
    →SRC="browser_sensing.js">

    Add browser sensing and DOM initialization to your JavaScript. In **Code 11.4**, the necessary code is linked from an external file called browser_sensing.js which you have to set up and save separately.

2. function toggleMenu(currElem,repo)

    Add the function toggleMenu() (**Code 11.4**) to your JavaScript. This function checks to see if the menu is retracted. If it is, the function moves the menu so that it is visible. If the menu is already visible, then it is retracted back into the screen.

3. .menu {position: absolute; font: 12pt/14pt
    →helvetica; width: 75px; background-color:
    →#333333; layer-background-color:
    →#333333; color:#CCCCCC;}

    Code 11.5 shows you how to set up a class for the text options used to create our pop-up menus. Of course we could use graphics in the menu, but HTML text takes less time to download.

4. <SPAN ID="fileMenu" CLASS="menu" STYLE="left: 20px; top: -155px;" >

...

</SPAN>

Using the menu class in a **<SPAN>** tag, set up one or more menus like those in **Code 11.6.** You will also need to include an ID with a unique name in each **<SPAN>** tag and set the left and top position in the STYLE attribute, so that the menu will start with only the bottom tab showing.

5. <A HREF="JAVASCRIPT:toggleMenu
→('fileMenu',-155);"><B>FILE</B></A>

Make the last option in the menu list a link that calls the **toggleMenu()** function, using

- The name of that menu, and

- The number of pixels required to cause it to move off the screen, leaving only the bottom link visible. The upshot of this is that the visitor's click on this tab makes the menu either appear or disappear.

✔ Tip

- Don't add any CSS to an individual HTML tag that is between the menu **<SPAN>** tags. There is a bug in Netscape 4.0 that causes nested styles declared within a positioned element to prevent any more positioned elements from being used.

Code 11.6 Set up your menus in the <BODY> of your document, between <SPAN> tags. The options in the menus can, of course, be hypertextually linked to whatever you want.

```
<BODY>
  <SPAN ID="fileMenu" CLASS="menu" STYLE="left:
→20px; top: -155px;">
    <BR>
    Print
    <HR WIDTH="75" ALIGN="left">
    Show Code
    <HR WIDTH="75" ALIGN="left">
    E-mail Page
    <HR WIDTH="75" ALIGN="left">
    Save
    <HR WIDTH="75" ALIGN="left">
    Close
    <HR WIDTH="75" ALIGN="left">
    <A HREF="JAVASCRIPT:toggleMenu('fileMenu',-
→155);"><B>FILE</B></A>
  </SPAN>
  <SPAN ID="searchMenu" CLASS="menu"
→STYLE="left: 120px; top: -127px;">
    <BR>
    Yahoo
    <HR WIDTH="75" ALIGN="left">
    Excite
    <HR WIDTH="75" ALIGN="left">
    HotBot
    <HR WIDTH="75" ALIGN="left">
    Lycos
    <HR WIDTH="75" ALIGN="left">
    <B<A
HREF="JAVASCRIPT:toggleMenu('searchMenu',-
127);">SEARCH</A></B>
  </SPAN>
</BODY>
</HTML>
```

Code 11.7 The functions setSlide() and slider() move our element across the screen.

```
                     code
<HTML>
  <HEAD>
    <SCRIPT LANGUAGE="JavaScript"
→SRC="browser_sensing.js"></SCRIPT>

<SCRIPT LANGUAGE="JavaScript1.2"
→SRC="browser_sensing.js"></SCRIPT>
<SCRIPT LANGUAGE="JavaScript">
var dom;
function setSlide(currObj,x2,y2){
  if (isNS4||isIE4||isNew){
  dom = eval(docObj + '.' + currObj + styleObj);
/* Determines the element's initial starting
point.*/
  var x1 = dom.left;
  var y1 = dom.top;
  slider(x1,x2,y1,y2);
  }
}
function slider(x1,x2,y1,y2){
/* Checks if the current position (x1) has reached
the final position (x2). It will then add or
subtract from x1 to bring the element closer to x2.
*/

  if (x1 != x2) {
    if ( x1 > x2) {x1 -=1;}
    else {
      if (x1 < x2) {x1 += 1;}
    }
  }
//Same as above, but for the vertical position.
  if (y1 != y2) {
    if ( y1 > y2) {y1 -=1;}
    else {
      if (y1 < y2) {y1 += 1;}
    }
  }
//Moves the element to the new position.
  if ((x1 != x2) || (y1 != y2)) {
    dom.left = x1;
    dom.top = y1;
    setTimeout
('slider('+x1+','+x2+','+y1+','+y2+')', 25);
/* The number "25" determines how fast the element
moves. The smaller the number, the faster it
moves. */
  }
}
</SCRIPT>
</HEAD>
</HTML>
```

Animating elements: The Sliding Banner

The sliding banner represents a two-function process that will move an element incrementally from one point to another. This function is in two parts: The first function, setSlide(), is called and defines which element on the screen is to be moved and its initial position. The second function, slider(), actually moves the element across the screen. **Figure 11.4** shows an element ("Have it your way!") that starts in the lower left corner and slides up and to the right.

To animate an element through a path:

1. <SCRIPT LANGUAGE="JavaScript1.2"
   →SRC="browser_sensing.js"></SCRIPT>

   Add browser sensing and DOM initialization to your JavaScript. In **Code 11.7** we are bringing it in from an external file.

2. Add the functions setSlide() and slider() (see **Code 11.7**) to the JavaScript in the head of your document. The setSlide() function initializes the DOM for our moving element and locates the element's current position; then it runs the slider() function, passing it the starting and stopping coordinates. Then slider() moves the element until it reaches the designated point.

3. .banner {position: absolute; font: bold
   →18pt/25pt helvetica; background-color:
   →#333333; color:#CCCCCC;}

   Create a CSS rule for the element you will be moving, and set it to be absolutely positioned. See **Code 11.8**.

4. ONLOAD="setSlide('A1',150,10)"

   Set an event handler that calls the function setSlide() as shown in **Code 11.9**. The first value for the function is the ID selector for the element you want to move. The second and third values are the final left and top values for the element's final position.

5. `<SPAN ID="A1" CLASS="banner" STYLE="left: 12px; top: 104px;">Have it your Way! </SPAN>`

Set up the element you want to slide across the window, as shown in **Code 11.9**. Set its ID attribute so that it can be located by our two functions, and give the element its initial coordinates (left and top).

✔ Tip

■ These functions, setSlide() and slider(), can deal with any element regardless of where it starts and stops. How the element moves (left to right, top to bottom) depends on the coordinates that you feed it.

Code 11.8 Set up the style for your banner element.

```
<STYLE>
.banner {position: absolute; font: bold
→18pt/25pt helvetica; background-color: #333333;
→color:#CCCCCC;}
</STYLE>
```

Code 11.9 The element to be moved gets started on its way as soon as the document is loaded.

```
<BODY ONLOAD="setSlide('A1',150,10)">
   <SPAN ID="A1" CLASS="banner" STYLE="left:
→10px; top: 100px;">Have it your Way! </SPAN>
</BODY>
```

Figure 11.4 The element slides across the screen.

Code 11.10 Drag-and-drop moving of elements looks simple on the screen but requires several different interdependent functions.

```
              code
<HTML>
  <HEAD>
    <TITLE>Magnetic Poetry Kit</TITLE>
    <SCRIPT LANGUAGE="JavaScript" SRC="
→browser_sensing.js">
    </SCRIPT>
    <SCRIPT LANGUAGE="JavaScript">
    <!-- Hide from old browsers
// Initialize the global variables for this
//document.
var dom = null;
var offsetX, offsetY;
function whichElement(evt) {
  if (isNS4) {
    var testElem;
    var xPos = evt.pageX;
    var yPos = evt.pageY;
/* In Netscape, this cycles through the layers to
see if the mouse pointer is in one of them */
    for (var i = document.layers.length - 1; i >=
→0; i-) {
      testElem = document.layers[i]
      if ((xPos > testElem.left) &&
      (xPos < testElem.left +
→testElem.clip.width) &&
      (yPos > testElem.top) &&
      (yPos < testElem.top +
→testElem.clip.height)) {
        dom = testElem;
        return
      }
    }
  }
  else {
/* Accesses the element that generated  the event,
and gets the element's ID name */
    elementName = event.srcElement.id;
    // checks if this is one of our chips
    if (elementName.indexOf('chip') != -1){
      dom = eval(docObj + '.' + elementName +
→styleObj);
      return;
    }
  }
/* If the event cannot be associated with an
element, then dom is set to 0 (false) */
  dom = 0;
  return;
}
function pickIt(evt) {
  whichElement(evt)
  if (dom) {
// Raise this element above the rest.
    dom.zIndex = 100;
    if (isNS4){
```

Dragging elements: The Magnetic Poetry Kit

Another staple of GUIs is drag-and-drop: the ability to mouse-drag windows, files, and what-not across the screen and drop them into a new element or location. Using most of the techniques we learned in Chapter 10, and some special Navigator and MSIE capabilities that we will explore in more detail in the next section of this book, we can allow our site's visitors to move elements around in the window to suit their needs.

As an example of this technique, we will be creating a refrigerator-magnetic poetry kit for our Web page. You may have one of these games on your own refrigerator right now: Each word is on a magnetic chip, which can be moved around and combined with other chips to make sentences (see **Figure 11.5**).

We will be creating three new JavaScript functions: pickIt(), moveIt(), and dropIt(). We will also use the global event-handling function, defaultEvents(), (discussed in **Sensing events anywhere on the screen** page 160); along with the element-selection function, whichElement().

To set up element dragging:

1. <SCRIPT LANGUAGE="JavaScript1.2"
   →SRC="browser_sensing.js">

   As with most DHTML, we start by adding browser sensing and DOM initialization to your JavaScript. In **Code 11.10** we are bringing it in from an external file.

2. var dom = null; var offsetX, offsetY;

   There are three global variables to initialize: **dom** to record the Document Object Model; and **offsetX** and **offsetY** to record the mouse position within the element for Navigator.

3. function whichElement(evt)

Add the function whichElement() to your JavaScript, as shown in **Code 11.10**. A alternate version of this function is discussed in greater depth in Chapter 10.

4. function pickIt(evt)

Place the pickIt() function into your JavaScript. This function will be triggered whenever the visitor clicks anywhere on the screen. It first runs the whichElement() function to determine which element has been selected; then it sets the z-index of that element to 100, which should place it above all other elements on the page.

In addition, for Navigator 4, this function records the mouse's position relative to the top-left corner of the selected element. This is so that later, when the element is being moved about on the screen, the pointer will stay in the same position relative to the element.

5. function dragIt(evt)

Place the dragIt() function into your JavaScript. Since this function will be triggered by the onMouseMove event, it will move the selected element around on the screen by changing its top and left properties according to wherever the mouse moves. For Navigator, these coordinates are offset so that the pointer will stay in the same place relative to the element. MSIE will drag from the top left corner only.

6. function dropIt()

Place the dropIt() function into your JavaScript. When the mouse button is released, this function is triggered. It resets the dom to null and replaces the element to the 0-level z-index.

7. function defaultEvents()

Place the defaultEvents() function into your JavaScript, as shown in **Code 11.10**.

Code 11.10 (cont.)

```
/* For Netscape, this records the mouse pointer's
position relative to the element's top-left corner
*/
    offsetX = (evt.pageX - dom.left);
    offsetY = (evt.pageY - dom.top);
  }
 }
// Prevents the pop-up menu on the Mac.
 return false;
 }

function dragIt(evt) {
 if (dom) {
// Sets the element's starting position in
//Navigator.
    if (isNS4) {
       dom.left = (evt.pageX - offsetX);
       dom.top = (evt.pageY - offsetY);
    }
/* Sets the element's starting position in other
DHTML browsers. */
    else {
       dom.left = window.event.x;
       dom.top = window.event.y;
    }
  }
 }

function dropIt() {
// Places the element back down to 0.
    dom.zIndex = 0;
    dom = null;
 }

function defaultEvents() {
 if (isNS4) {
// Gives Navigator 4 global event capturing.
       document.captureEvents(Event.MOUSEDOWN |
Event.MOUSEMOVE | Event.MOUSEUP)
   }
  if (isNS4||isIE4){
/* Sets up the default functions to run in both
Navigator 4 and Internet Explorer 4 . */
  document.onmousedown = pickIt;
  document.onmousemove = dragIt;
  document.onmouseup = dropIt;
  }
 }
// Stop hiding from old browsers
-->
</SCRIPT>
```

Figure 11.5 Rearrange the words.

Code 11.11 Set up a class style for designating the appearance of your magnetic poetry chips on the screen.

```
<STYLE TYPE="text/css">
   .chip {position: absolute;  z-index: 0;
→color: black; font: bold 16pt helvetica,sans-
→serif; background-color: #999999;layer-
→background-color: #999999;}
     #chip1 {top: 123px; left: 225px;}
     #chip2 {top: 5px; left: 25px;}
     #chip3 {top: 200px; left: 45px;}
     #chip4 {top: 55px; left: 55px;}
     #chip5 {top: 150px; left: 60px;}
     #chip6 {top: 75px; left: 125px;}
</STYLE>
</HEAD>
```

Code 11.12 Set up all of your chips in the <BODY> of your document.

```
<BODY BGCOLOR="#FFFFFF"
ONLOAD="defaultEvents()">
 <SPAN ID="chip1" CLASS="chip">HELLO</SPAN>
 <SPAN ID="chip2" CLASS="chip">TO</SPAN>
 <SPAN ID="chip3" CLASS="chip">THE</SPAN>
 <SPAN ID="chip4" CLASS="chip">GOOD</SPAN>
 <SPAN ID="chip5" CLASS="chip">PEOPLE</SPAN>
 <SPAN ID="chip6" CLASS="chip">SAY</SPAN></P>
 </BODY>
</HTML>
```

This function will be triggered by an onLoad event handler in the <BODY> tag of your document and set up which functions to run when particular events (onMouseDown, onMouseMove and onMouseUp) occur anywhere within the window. This function is described in greater detail in Chapter 10.

8. .chip {position: absolute; z-index: 0; color:
   →black; font: bold 16pt helvetica,sans-serif;
   →background-color: #999999;
   →layer-background-color: #999999;}

   Set up a class style for designating the appearance of your magnetic poetry chips on the screen. See **Code 11.11**.

9. #chip1 {top: 123px; left: 225px;}

   Set up a different ID selector for each word on the screen (see **Defining an ID selector**, page XXX). Give each ID a starting position.

10. <BODY BGCOLOR="#FFFFFF"
    →onLoad="defaultEvents()">

    Set the function **defaultEvents()** to be run as soon as the document loads. See **Code 11.12**.

11. <SPAN ID="chip1"
    →CLASS="chip">HELLO</SPAN>

    Set up as many word chips as you want, each with its own unique ID.

12. When this code is run in the window, the visitor can click on any of the chips. As the mouse is moved around, the chip will follow, until the visitor releases the mouse button.

✔ Tip

- Watch out: Internet Explorer 4 has a few problems when redrawing elements as they move across the screen.

JavaScript in Netscape's DHTML

Figure 12.1 The splash screen for Netscape's Communicator package featuring Navigator 4.

Netscape has introduced several additions to JavaScript (version 1.2) related to controlling positioned elements. These new features of the scripting language only work with Netscape's version of Dynamic HTML available in the Navigator 4.x browsers (see **Figure 12.1**). One of the enhancements to JavaScript in Navigator 4 is its own version of style sheets based on JavaScript: JavaScript Style Sheets (JSS). The other additions solve some long standing problems that designers have had in finding and controlling the size of the window and the resolution of the screen.

It is unlikely that JSS will ever become a W3C sanctioned standard, since CSS performs most of the functions found in JSS already. In fact, although JSS will be available in future iterations of Navigator, Netscape has announced that it has no plans to develop this technology and will fully support CSS instead.

On the flip side, the rest of the JavaScript presented in this chapter will more than likely become part of standard cross browser JavaScript.

With that in mind, this chapter gives you a crash course in JSS and looks at some of the controls only available using JavaScript in Navigator 4.

What are JavaScript Style Sheets?

Simply put, JavaScript Style Sheets (JSS) are style sheets that use the JavaScript code syntax and can be changed through Netscape's Document Object Model (see **The Netscape Navigator DOM**, page 142).

JSS style sheets will, generally speaking, produce results identical to those produced by Cascading Style Sheets.

If you want to review style concepts in general, see Chapter 1.

JSS vs. CSS: What's the difference?

First thing: DON'T PANIC! Actually JSS and CSS are almost identical, with just a few differences in how the properties are "phrased" and the exact syntax used to set up the rules. The properties that can be applied to your HTML tags and the values that can be associated with them, however, are identical. Of course, JSS does not include all of the CSS properties specified by the W3C, but all of the CSS properties available in Navigator 4.x have a JSS equivalent.

In addition, all of the rules for cascade order, classes, IDs, contextual selectors, inheritance of styles, comments, and external files are virtually identical to CSS except where noted in this chapter.

Table 12.1

Converting CSS Properties to JSS Properties

CSS	JSS
font-size	fontSize
font-family	fontFamily
font-weight	fontWeight
font-style	fontStyle
line-height	lineHeight
text-decoration	textDecoration
text-transform	textTransform
text-align	textAlign
text-indent	textIndent
margin-left	marginLeft
margin-right	marginRight
margin-top	marginTop
margin-bottom	marginBottom
margin	margins(top,right,bottom,left)
padding-left	paddingLeft
padding-right	paddingRight
padding-top	paddingTop
padding-bottom	paddingBottom
padding	paddings(top,right,bottom,left)
border-left-width	borderLeftWidth
border-right-width	borderRightWidth
border-top-width	borderTopWidth
border-bottom-width	borderBottomWidth
border-width	borderWidths(top,right,bottom,left)
border-style	borderStyle
border-color	borderColor
width	width
float	align*
clear	clear
color	color
background-image	backgroundImage
background-color	backgroundColor
display	display
list-style-type	listStyleType
white-space	whiteSpace

* Okay, you found me out. There is one exception: float in CSS becomes align in JSS.

Understanding JSS properties

Although the words used to create JSS properties are almost always identical to the CSS version, properties in JSS are labeled using the JavaScript naming convention. This convention states that if multiple words are used, the first word is lowercase and all subsequent words have their first letter in uppercase with no spaces between the words. For example, margin-left in CSS becomes marginLeft in JSS. **Table 12.1** gives you a list of CSS property names and their equivalent JSS forms.

Other than their names, the values that can be applied to properties and the behavior of those properties are identical to CSS. You can even have CSS and JSS in the same document, as long as they're not within the same <STYLE> tag.

Using JSS Rules

In Chapter 1, we learned the various methods for creating CSS rules. Rest assured that the concepts involved with creating JSS rules and where you can put them are identical to those of CSS, although the actual syntax will look very different. If you aren't comfortable with your knowledge of CSS rules and the various forms they take, I recommend you review those sections of Chapter 1 before going any farther here in this chapter. Once you have reviewed Chapter 1, the concepts presented here should be all too familiar, although the actual execution will be different.

The following 10 pages will show you how to create JSS.

Why use JSS?

Honestly, there are not many good reasons. Generally CSS works better because it is more universally available. However when you are creating solely for the Navigator 4 browser, JSS can offer a few advantages for creating dynamic styles that cannot be achieved using CSS, at least not in Navigator 4.

Code 12.1 The JSS style tag.

```
<HTML>
  <HEAD>
    <STYLE TYPE="text/javascript">
      tags.P.fontWeight="bold";
    </STYLE>
```

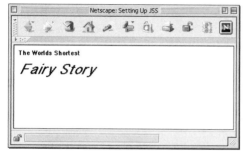

Figure 12.2 The first line, in the paragraph tag, is bold and the second line, in the emphasis tag, is larger.

Setting Up JSS

You set up style sheets using JSS the same way you would CSS style sheets using the <STYLE> tag. The only difference is that in the TYPE attribute you use the value "text/javascript" as shown in **Code 12.1**. **Figure 12.2** shows the results of an HTML document that uses two JavaScript Style Sheets: one set in the HTML document and the other from an external document.

To set up JSS in an HTML document:

1. <STYLE TYPE="text/javascript">

In the head of your HTML document, include the opening style tag with the TYPE attribute set to "text/javascript" (which brands this style sheet as a JSS like the one shown in **Code 12.1**).

2.   tags.P.fontWeight="bold";

Type in your JSS definition. The different definition types are explained on the next several pages. In this example I have set the P selector to have a font weight value of bold.

3. </STYLE>

Close the style container. Now whenever a <P> tag is used in this HTML it text content will be bold faced.

To set up JSS in an external style sheet:

1. tags.EM.fontSize="24pt";

Type JSS definitions—which we will get to in the next sections—into an external text file and save the file as filename.jss. filename can be anything you want it to be. In the example shown in **Code 12.3**, I have set an external file that will set the EM selector to have a font size value of 24 points.

2. <STYLE TYPE="text/javascript"
→SRC="filname.jss">

Include the **<STYLE>** tag within the head container of the document as shown in **Code 12.2**. The type must be "text/javascript". If you are using an external JSS (see step 1), include the source attribute pointing to your external JSS file, as you see in this example.

3. </STYLE>

Type in the closing **</STYLE>** tag without including any style definitions.

✔ Tip

■ You cannot include definitions within a style tag that is calling an external source(the same is true of CSS). However you can include as many different **<STYLE>** tags as you want in the head of the document. You can even mix CSS with JSS by including separate **<STYLE>** tags for each.

Code 12.2 The <STYLE> tag that calls an external JSS called filename.jss.

```
    <STYLE TYPE="text/javascript"
→SRC="filename.jss">
    </STYLE>
  </HEAD>
  <BODY>
    <P>The Worlds Shortest<P>
    <EM>Fairy Story</EM>
  </BODY>
</HTML>
```

Code 12.3 The external JSS called filename.jss.

```
tags.EM.fontSize="24pt";.
```

Code 12.4 JSS for HTML selectors.

```
                    code
<HTML>
  <HEAD>
    <STYLE TYPE="text/javascript">
       tags.H1.color = "red";
       with (tags.H1) {fontWeight = "bold";
→fontFamily = "helvetica, arial, sans-serif";}
    </STYLE>
  </HEAD>
  <BODY BGCOLOR="#FFFFFF">
    <H1>Once a pun a time...</H1>
  </BODY>
</HTML>
```

Figure 12.3 The opening to our story is in red.

Defining an HTML selector with JSS

The main difference between CSS and JSS is the syntax they use to define the selectors used to control the appearance of HTML content. JSS uses a JavaScript syntax that traces the DOM to specify the tag and property to be defined.

To define an HTML selector with JSS:

1. tags.H1.color = "red";

   Type the word **tags**, followed by a dot, then the HTML selector you want to define, another dot, then the property you want to define for that selector, an equal sign, and then the property's value within quotes. In this example I chose to make the color of the content red. Close the definition with a semicolon. This style will now be used with any Level 1 headers in the document.

2. with (tags.H1) {fontWeight = "bold";
   →fontFamily = "helvetica, arial, sans-serif";}

   To define several properties at once for a single HTML selector, type in **with**, followed by an opening parenthesis, then the word **tags**, a dot, and a closing parenthesis. Then, within { } brackets, type in your definitions. A definition is the property name, an equal sign, and then the value in quotes followed by a semicolon. Here I am making the text bold and displayed in the Helvetica or Arial font.

187

Defining a class with JSS

Like CSS, JSS can also use classes to define the appearance of HTML tags without having to directly change the nature of every HTML tag used for that style.

To define JSS classes:

1. classes.mainTitle.all.color = "#339933";

Type in the word classes, a dot, then the name of your class (whatever you wish), another dot, then the word all, another dot, then the name of the property you want to define, an equal sign, and finally the property's value within quotes. Close the definition with a semicolon. In **Code 12.5** a class called mainTitle has been set up that will turn its content a greenish color.

2. with (classes.mainTitle.all) {fontSize =
→"36pt"; fontStyle = "italic";
→borderWidths("2pt","4pt","6pt","8pt");}

To define several properties at once for a single class, type in with, followed by an opening parenthesis, the word classes, a dot, the name of your class (whatever you wish), another dot, the word all, and a closing parenthesis. Then, within { } brackets, type in your definitions. A definition is the property name, an equal sign, and then the value in quotes followed by a semicolon. With this example, shown in **Code 12.5**, the mainTitle class will set up borders around the text, make it larger, and italic.

3. <SPAN CLASS="MAINTITLE">Fairy Tail</SPAN>

To use this class with an HTML element, add the class property to the tag, with the name of the class as its value.

Code 12.5 JSS classes

```
<HTML>
  <HEAD>
    <TITLE>JSS-Classes</TITLE>
    <STYLE TYPE="text/javascript">
      classes.mainTitle.all.color = "#339933";
      with (classes.mainTitle.all) {fontSize =
→"36pt"; fontStyle = "italic";
→borderWidths("2pt","4pt","6pt","8pt");}
    </STYLE>
  </HEAD>
  <BODY BGCOLOR="#FFFFFF">
    <SPAN CLASS="mainTitle">There was a fog
prince.</SPAN>
  </BODY>
</HTML>
```

Figure 12.4 The story is large, slanted, green and in a box.

Code 12.6 JSS IDs

```
code
<HTML>
  <HEAD>
    <TITLE>JSS-IDs</TITLE>
    <STYLE TYPE="text/javascript">
      ids.theEnd. color = "#666666";
      with (ids.theEnd) {fontSize = "24pt";
→textDecoration = "underline";}
    </STYLE>
  </HEAD>
  <BODY BGCOLOR="#FFFFFF">
    <SPAN ID="theEnd">The End</SPAN>
  </BODY>
</HTML>
```

Figure 12.5 The End is large and gray.

Defining IDs with JSS

You define JSS ID selectors in a similar manner to their CSS equivalents too.

To define JSS IDs:

1. ids.theEnd.color = "#666666";

Type in the word ids, a dot, the name of your ID (whatever you wish), another dot, the property you want to define for that selector, an equal sign, and then the property's value within quotes. Close the definition with a semicolon. In **Code 12.6** I have set the drop cap color to be a dark gray.

2. with (ids.theEnd) {fontSize = "24pt";
→textDecoration = "underline";}

To define several properties at once for a single ID, type with, followed by an opening parenthesis, then the word ids, a dot, then the name of your ID (whatever you wish), and a closing parenthesis. Then, within { } brackets, type in your definitions. A definition is the property name, an equal sign, and then the value in quotes followed by a parenthesis. In this example the drop cap ID will be 24 point size and underlined.

3. <SPAN ID="theEnd">The End</SPAN>

To use this ID with an HTML element, add the class property to the tag, with the name of the class as its value.

Defining contextual selectors with JSS

Contextual styles allow you to set up a style that will only be applied to a tag if it is within another tag. In **Figure 12.6** we see the emphasis tag in and out of the level 2 header tag

To define contextual selectors with JSS:

1. contextual(tags.H2,tags.EM)
    → .textDecoration = "underline";

    Type in the word contextual, an opening parenthesis, and then the JSS selectors (HTML, class, or ID) that make up this contextual selector (see **Putting selectors into context**, page 26). Close the parentheses, type a dot, then the property to be used, an equal sign, and then the value within quotes. Close the definition with a semicolon. In the example shown in **Code 12.7** the emphasis tag will be underlined if it is inside of an <H2> tag.

2. <H2>No, there was a <EM>frog</EM></H2>, not <EM>fog</EM>.

    To use the contextual selectors within your HTML, set up the proper nested tags.

Code 12.7 JSS contextual selectors

```
<HTML>
  <HEAD>
    <TITLE>JSS- Contextual Selectors</TITLE>
    <STYLE TYPE="text/javascript">
       contextual(tags.H2,tags.EM).textDecoration
= "underline";
    </STYLE>
  </HEAD>
  <BODY BGCOLOR="#FFFFFF">
    <H2>No,There was a <EM>frog</EM></H2>, not a
<EM>fog</EM>.
  </BODY>
</HTML>
```

Figure 12.6 The emphasized frog is underlined but the emphasized fog is not.

Code 12.8 JSS in HTML

```
                   code
<HTML>
  <HEAD>
    <TITLE>JSS-in an HTML tag</TITLE>
    <STYLE TYPE="text/javascript">
    </STYLE>
  </HEAD>
  <BODY BGCOLOR="#FFFFFF">
    <P STYLE ="color = 'red'; fontWeight =
→'bold'; fontSize = '48pt';">
        The End!
    </P>
  </BODY>
</HTML>
```

Figure 12.7 The End! (Make no mistake about it.)

Defining an individual element with JSS

You can also define JSS rules in individual HTML elements.

To define individual elements with JSS:

1. <STYLE TYPE="text/javascript"></STYLE>

   Remember, in order to use JSS within an HTML tag, a style tag with the TYPE attribute set to "text/javascript" has to be set in the head of the document, as shown in **Code 12.8**, even if no style definitions are declared within it.

2. <P STYLE ="color = 'red'; fontWeight =
   → 'bold'; fontSize='48pt'">The End!</P>

   JSS definitions can be spliced directly into HTML tags using the STYLE property. After the quotes, type in the property name, an equal sign, then your value within quotes, and a semicolon. In **Code 12.8** the text is red, bold and very large. Notice that I used single quotes(') with the values. Double quotes (") are reserved to open and close the STYLE attribute.

Finding the screen's size and number of colors

One of the unknowns of Web design is what type of monitor is being used by a visitor to your site. Primarily there two variables you might need: The size of the monitor (resolution) and the number of colors it can display (color bit depth). JavaScript 1.2 allows you to access these values through the screen object's width, height, and pixelDepth properties.

In **Code 12.9** we have set up a function that determines the screen's resolution, and then opens a window based on the screen size. **Code 12.10** is then loaded into the new window and will check the number of colors available, before it loads a low-color GIF image or a high-color JPEG image.

To open a new window based on screen size:

1. <SCRIPT LANGUAGE="JavaScript1.2">

   Within the <BODY> tag, set up a JavaScript container as shown in **Code 12.9**. This is done so we can check the screen width when the document loads and load an image of the appropriate width.

2. if (screen.width >= 800) {
   →window.open ('12_10.html', 'display',
   → 'width=400,height=200 ');}

   In your JavaScript, set up a conditional statement that checks whether the screen width is 800 pixels or larger. If it is, then open the larger version of the new window.

   - 12_10.html is the name of the HTML document that you want to place into your new window.

   - display is the name you want to give the new window.

   - width and height define the new window's dimensions.

Code 12.9 This will check the width of the screen. If it's 800 pixels or wider, the large version of our window opens. For a smaller screen, the small window gets opened.

```
code
<HTML>
<BODY BGCOLOR="#FFFFFF">
<H2>Checking window resolution...please wait.</H2>
<SCRIPT LANGUAGE="JavaScript1.2">
  if (screen.width >= 800) {
     window.open ('12_10.html', 'display',
→'width=300,height=400');
}
  else {
     window.open ('12_10.html', 'display',
→'width=150,height=200');
}
</SCRIPT>
  </BODY>
</HTML>
```

Code 12.10 This is the document 12_10.html that gets loaded into the new window from Code 12.9. If the monitor has thousands or millions of colors, the JPEG version loads; otherwise, the low-color GIF version gets used.

```
code
<HTML>
<BODY BGCOLOR="#000000">
<SCRIPT LANGUAGE="JavaScript">
  if (screen.pixelDepth >= 16) {
     document.write ('<img SRC="Ophelia.jpg">');
  }
  else {
     document.write ('<img SRC="Ophelia.gif">');
  }
</SCRIPT>
  </BODY>
</HTML>
```

Table 12.2

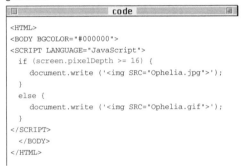

Pixel-Depth Values	
COLOR-BIT DEPTH	# OF COLORS
4	16
8	256
16	65 536
32	16.7 million

Figure 12.8 This shows the JPEG version of the graphic in the larger window.

Figure 12.9 The second window has the GIF version of the graphic displayed in the low-resolution version of the window.

3. else {window.open ('12_10.html',
→ 'display', 'width=200,height=100');}

Set up an else statement to handle a smaller monitor (with a width less than 600 pixels), to open the smaller version of the new window.

To load a graphic based on resolution:

1. <SCRIPT LANGUAGE="JavaScript">

Within the body of your document, place JavaScript tags as shown in **Code 12.8**.

2. if (screen.pixelDepth >= 16) {
→document.write ('<img SRC="Ophelia.jpg"
→>');}

Set up a conditional statement that checks the number of colors (pixelDepth) of the monitor being used. If it has a pixel depth of 16 or greater—which indicates the ability to display thousands or more colors—then display the JPEG version of the graphic.

3. else {document.write (
→ '<img SRC="Ophelia.gif">');}

Otherwise, if the screen can only display 256 colors or less, it uses the low-color GIF version.

✔ Tips

■ Usually any screen with a resolution smaller than 800x600 pixels is considered to be a "small screen."

■ There are four pixel-depth values that correspond to the four basic color-bit depth values. **Table 12.2**, on the previous page, shows the color-bit depth values and the corresponding number of colors possible.

Finding the screen's size and number of colors

Controlling a window's size and position

Navigator's DHTML provides several new ways to dynamically control the size of the window and its location in the screen. In addition, we can specify whether a window always stays on top of other windows or not. **Table 12.3** describes these new properties.

Because the Navigator window control properties are "read/write," they can be dynamically changed using JavaScript functions as shown in **Code 12.11**.

To expand and contract a window:

1. `<SCRIPT LANGUAGE="JavaScript">`

   Set up your JavaScript container in the head of your document.

2. function reduceWin()

   Add the function reduceWin() to your JavaScript. This function reduces the size of the browser window's content area to 100x100 pixels; positions the window in the bottom-right corner of the screen; and sets all other windows to appear on top of this one.

3. function growWin()

   Add the function growWin to your JavaScript. This function enlarges the window to fill the screen and allows it to appear on top of other windows.

Code 12.11 The first function is used to shrink the window and place it down into the bottom-right corner. The second function expands the window out, so that it fills the screen.

```
code
<HTML>
  <HEAD>
    <SCRIPT LANGUAGE="JavaScript">
<!--
//Hide from old browsers
function reduceWin() {
  window.innerWidth = 200;
  window.innerHeight = 200;
  window.screenX = screen.width;
  window.screenY = screen.height;
  alwaysLowered = true;
}

function growWin() {
  window.outerWidth = screen.width;
  window.outerHeight = screen.height;
  window.screenX = 5;
  window.screenY = 5;
  alwaysLowered = false;
}
// Stop hiding from old browsers
-->
    </SCRIPT>

  </HEAD>
  <BODY BGCOLOR="#FFFFFF" ONBLUR="reduceWin()"
ONFOCUS="growWin()">
    <IMG SRC="../images/alice04a.gif" WIDTH="301"
HEIGHT="448">
  </BODY>
</HTML>
```

Table 12.3

Window Size and Position Properties

PROPERTY	WHAT IT CONTROLS	VALUES
innerHeight	Height of the browsers display area	Pixel
innerWidth	Width of the browsers display area	Pixel
outerHeight	Height of entire browser window	Pixel
outerWidth	Width of entire browser window	Pixel
screenX	Vertical location of the left edge of the window in relation to the left edge of the screen	Pixel
screenY	Horizontal location of the top edge of the window in relation to the top edge of the screen	Pixel
alwaysRaised	Will appear above all other windows	True/False
alwaysLowered	Will appear beneath all other windows	True/False

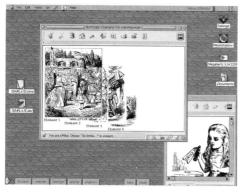

Figure 12.10 When the window is not in use (blurred), it is reduced to the corner of your desktop.

Figure 12.11 When reactivated (focused), it is expanded back out to fill the entire screen.

4. `<BODY BGCOLOR="#FFFFFF"`
`ONBLUR="reduceWin()"`
`ONFOCUS="growWin()">`

In your `<BODY>` tag, set up the blur event to run the reduceWin() function, and the focus event to run the growWin() function. This will cause the window to shrink when it is inactive (blurred) (**Figure 12.10**) and expand when it is active (focused) (**Figure 12.11**).

NETSCAPE LAYERS

Layers are a way to create independent elements in the browser window—elements that can be positioned, repositioned, turned on or off, and stacked on top of each other at will. Sounds like CSS-Positioned elements, doesn't it? That's because layers and CSS-P both do basically the same thing, but slightly differently.

Like the JavaScript Style Sheets you studied in Chapter 12, Netscape will continue to support layers in future iterations of the Navigator browser, but it is highly unlikely that layers will ever become a standard since you can accomplish most of the same effects using CSS-P elements.

Still, layers offer some substantial features for Navigator that are *not* available using CSS-P. We'll examine those features here in this chapter.

What is a layer?

A layer is an independent "chunk" of Web content within an HTML document, set off using one of the two LAYER tag pairs. You can place as many layers into a single page as you want, and each layer can have its own properties controlled dynamically using JavaScript. In this chapter you'll learn to create layers, use layers, and access layers with JavaScript.

Generally speaking, whatever you can do with CSS-Positioning you can do with layers. Like CSS-P elements, layers can be stacked on top of each other and shuffled around as desired. They can be made transparent (with hide) or opaque (with show). In addition, you can specify background images and colors.

The greatest advantage layers offer is their ability to easily include content from an external URL and to dynamically change that content. However, even that can be approximated in CSS, using layers for Navigator and the <OBJECT> tag for MSIE (see **Placing external content**, page 162).

Aside from all that, the greatest advantage of layers is that you can associate them to JavaScript event handlers—something CSS-P cannot do in Netscape, only in Internet Explorer. Rather than relying on the link tag, a layer can include the event handler needed to respond to mouse events on the screen.

Layers vs. CSS-Positioning

The main difference between layers and CSS-P is in Netscape's differing philosophy toward solving the problem of positioning elements on the screen. Netscape, continuing a popular trend started with its first browser, added new tags hoping to extend the capabilities of HTML. Conversely, the World Wide Web Consortium, in an attempt to preserve HTML as a true "mark-up language," added new properties to its style sheet standard. However, both Navigator and Internet Explorer have now pledged to follow the W3C's lead in future versions of their browsers. Thus, CSS-P is the future of dynamic content on the Web.

Code 13.1 Five different layers; five different locations.

```
code

<HTML>
  <HEAD>
    <TITLE>Layers</TITLE>
  </HEAD>
  <BODY BGCOLOR="#FFFFFF">
    <LAYER TOP="150" LEFT="300" BGCOLOR="#666666">
      <H2>Layer 1</H2>
    </LAYER>
    <LAYER TOP="-5" LEFT="-5" BGCOLOR="#CCCCCC">
      <H2>Layer 2</H2>
      <LAYER TOP="100" LEFT="100"
BGCOLOR="#999999"><H2>Layer 3</H2></LAYER>
    </LAYER>
    <LAYER TOP="150" LEFT="85" BGCOLOR="#666666">
      <H2>Layer 4</H2>
      <ILAYER TOP="0" LEFT="100"
BGCOLOR="#CCCCCC"><H2>Layer 5</H2></ILAYER>
    </LAYER>
  </BODY>
</HTML>
```

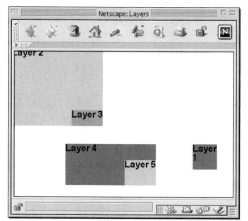

Figure 13.1 The five layers in a Navigator window. Notice that Layer 3 has positioned itself relative to the layer it is in, rather than to the entire window.

Creating layers

Unlike CSS-P, layers require the use of one of two new HTML tags (Netscape extensions to HTML) that will specify whether the layer's content is to be freely positioned on the screen. Absolutely positioned layers use the <LAYER>...</LAYER> tags. Relative layers use the <ILAYER>...</ILAYER> tags.

Figure 13.1 shows 5 layers:

- The first layer is absolutely positioned.

- The third layer is absolutely positioned within the second layer.

- The fifth layer is positioned relative to the fourth layer.

To set up a layer:

1. `<LAYER`

   Within your HTML, open your layer tag as shown in **Code 13.1**.

2. `TOP="150" LEFT="300"`
   `→BGCOLOR="#666666">`

   Type in the attributes you want to use with this layer, as shown in Appendix B. Close the tag with a >. In this example, we have moved the element over 150 pixels and down 300 pixels, and have given it a dark-gray background.

3. `<H2>Layer 1</H2>`

   Within the layer container, include whatever content you desire for this layer. Content in a layer can be anything that might normally appear in an HTML document.

4. `</LAYER>`

   Close the layer with the appropriate closing tag (</LAYER> or </ILAYER>).

✔ Tip

- The inline layer tag, <ILAYER>, is set up identically to the <LAYER> tag described here.

Creating layers

199

Using layers

Like most HTML tags, the <LAYER> tag has a bevy of attributes that control the layer's appearance and behavior. These attributes are listed in Appendix B. For the most part, the layer attributes are identical to those used with CSS or CSS-P, with a few notable exceptions:

- PAGEX and PAGEY. These allow you to position any absolutely positioned layer in the window with the top-left corner of the document as the origin, even when nested in other layers.

- SRC. Allows you to specify an external file to be included within the document.

- ABOVE and BELOW. These are used to specify which layers should be above or below the current layer in the z-index.

In **Figure 13.2**, four layers have been set up. layer1 has pulled in an external file with the Mad Hatter and, despite being defined before layer2, appears on top of it because of the ABOVE attribute set in layer2. layer4 has been nested in layer3, but, because it has been positioned using PAGEX and PAGEY it is still absolutely positioned in relation to the document and not in relation to layer3.

To add attributes to a layer:

1. <LAYER

Open your layer tag.

2. SRC="external.html" ID="layer1"
→BGCOLOR="#CCCCCC">

Type in the attributes you want to use to define this layer. In this example, an external source document is being loaded into the layer. The layer is being identified with a name (layer1) as well as a background color for that layer.

3. </LAYER>

Close your layer container.

Code 13.2 The external content to be used in **Code 13.3**.

```
<H2>Layer 1</H2>
<P><IMG SRC="../images/alice26a.gif" WIDTH="134" HEIGHT="149">
```

Code 13.3 Sets up four layers for us, to play around with the unique attributes of Netscape layers.

```
<HTML>
  <BODY BGCOLOR="#FFFFFF">
    <LAYER ID="layer1" SRC="13_2.html"
→BGCOLOR="#CCCCCC">                          .
    </LAYER>
    <LAYER ID="layer2" ABOVE="layer1" WIDTH="100"
→HEIGHT="100" TOP="125" LEFT="125"
→BGCOLOR="#666666">
      <H2 ALIGN="right">Layer 2</H2>
    </LAYER>
    <LAYER ID="layer3" TOP="10" LEFT="350"
→BGCOLOR="#CCCCCC">
      <H2>Layer 3</H2>
      <LAYER ID="layer4" PAGEY="125" PAGEX="250"
→BGCOLOR="#666666" WIDTH="100" HEIGHT="100">
        <H2>Layer 4</H2>
      </LAYER>
    </LAYER>
  </BODY>
</HTML>
```

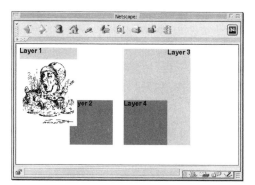

Figure 13.2 Layer 1 shows the Mad Hatter, which comes from the external file. Notice that despite the fact that Layer 3 is positioned at 350,10, it is stretched down and to the left because Layer 4 is nested within Layer 3 and positioned using PAGEY and PAGEX.

✔ Tip

- If you define an external source using the SRC attribute for a layer, you cannot include any other content within the layer container tags.

Accessing layers with JavaScript

In addition to a layer's attributes, the <LAYER> tag can also have the event handlers onMouseOver, onMouseOut, onFocus, onBlur, and onLoad. These event handlers can be associated with the layer to access JavaScript functions, which is something that CSS-P cannot directly do.

To refer to a layer in a JavaScript function, you use the layer object, with which you can specify a layer either by ID (or name), or by the layer's position in the layer index for that page:

- document.layerName

- document.layer[layerName]

- document.layer[index]

Appendix B shows all of the properties associated with the layer object and whether they can be modified by the user.

In **Figure 13.3**, there are three layers set up, labeled layer1, layer2, and layer3. **Code 13.4** establishes these layers and associates an event handler with each one. When triggered, the event handlers will cause the third layer to either appear or disappear.

To access layers through JavaScript:

1. document.layer3.visibility="hide";
document.layers["layer3"].visibility="show";
document.layers[2].visibility="hide";

You can set up the layer object to access a property in one of the three ways shown above. In **Code 13.4**, we have created each type of layer object in a function called revealLayer(), which will show or hide layer 3 depending on which layer the mouse passes over.

Code 13.4 The function hideLayer() will hide or show the third layer depending on which layer the mouse moves over. Despite the fact that all three references have a different syntax, they are all making reference to layer 3.

```
code
<HTML>
  <HEAD>
    <TITLE>Layers with JavaScript</TITLE>
<SCRIPT LANGUAGE="JavaScript">
function hideLayer(lx){
  if (lx == "l1")
→{document.layer3.visibility="hide";}
  else if (lx == "l2")
→{document.layers["layer3"].visibility="show";}
  else if (lx == "l3")
→{document.layers[2].visibility="hide";}
}
</SCRIPT>
  </HEAD>
  <BODY BGCOLOR="#FFFFFF">
    <LAYER ID="layer1" BGCOLOR="#CCCCCC"
→WIDTH="100" HEIGHT="100" TOP="10" LEFT="10"
→onmouseover="hideLayer('l1')">
      <H2 ALIGN="center">Layer 1</H2>
    </LAYER>
    <LAYER ID="layer2" BGCOLOR="#999999"
→WIDTH="100" HEIGHT="100" TOP="10" LEFT="200"
→onmouseover="hideLayer('l2')">
      <H2 ALIGN="center">Layer 2</H2>
    </LAYER>
    <LAYER ID="layer3" BGCOLOR="#666666"
→WIDTH="100" HEIGHT="100" TOP="200" LEFT="100"
→onmouseover="hideLayer('l3')">
      <H2 ALIGN="center">Layer 3</H2>
    </LAYER>
  </BODY>
</HTML>
```

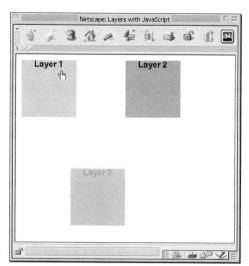

Figure 13.3 When the mouse pointer passes over layer 1, layer 3 does a disappearing act.

2. `<LAYER onmouseover="hideLayer('l1')"`
   `→ID="layer1" BGCOLOR="#CCCCCC"`
   `→WIDTH="100" HEIGHT="100" TOP="10"`
   `→LEFT="10">`

In the layer tag, type in your event handler and the function you want it to execute. In this case, when the mouse passes over the layer, it runs the revealLayer() function and tells it which layer this event is coming from.

✔ Tips

■ Whether you are using layers or CSS-P to position your content, Navigator 4 still accesses these different elements using the layer JavaScript Object. With CSS-P, Navigator treats the various IDs as if they were layers, which can then be accessed through its DOM (see **Selecting an element** on page 164 in Chapter 10).

■ In the layers array, as with most arrays, the first layer is always 0; so the third layer defined in the document is actually number 2 (0,1,2) in the array.

■ Unlike most elements that can have associated event handlers, events that are associated with layers have to call a function. You cannot just place JavaScript into the quotes after the event handler.

Accessing layers with JavaScript

Modifying layers with JavaScript

In addition to the various properties that can be changed through the layer object, there are several layer object methods, which can perform a variety of tasks on a layer. These methods are listed in **Appendix B**. A *method* is a predefined JavaScript function that can save you a lot of time and make simple tasks, such as moving the layer on the screen, that much easier.

Figure 13.4 shows one of these methods, resizeTo, in action. This method expands the size of the layer when visitors move their mouse over it.

To expand the layer:

1. function cheshireLayer(x,y){

    document.layer1.resizeTo(x,y);

}

Set up a function that uses the layer object and the method you want to perform on it. In this example the resizeTo method is being used which will change the size of layer1.

2. <LAYER ID="layer1" clip="200,175"

→ONMOUSEOVER="cheshireLayer(400,271)"

→ONMOUSEOUT="cheshireLayer(200,175)">

Create your layer with event handlers to run the function set up in step 1. Here, the function call sends the cheshireLayer function the coordinates to resize the layer to. When the layer first loads, it is clipped down to 200,175. When the mouse moves over the layer (the visible part), the layer grows to 400,271. When the mouse moves out of the layer, it shrinks back to 200,175.

Code 13.5 The cheshireLayer() function resizes the layer to reveal more of the picture.

```
<HTML>
  <HEAD>
    <TITLE>Layers with JavaScript</TITLE>
    <SCRIPT LANGUAGE="JavaScript">
      function cheshireLayer(x,y){
        document.layer1.resizeTo(x,y);
      }
    </SCRIPT>
  </HEAD>
  <BODY BGCOLOR="#FFFFFF">
    <LAYER ID="layer1" clip="200,175"
→ONMOUSEOVER="cheshireLayer(400,271)"
→ONMOUSEOUT="cheshireLayer(200,175)">
      <IMG SRC="../images/alice24a.gif"
→WIDTH="400" ALIGN="left" HEIGHT="271">
    </LAYER>
  </BODY>
</HTML>
```

Figure 13.4 Moving the mouse over the layer reveals the Cheshire Cat. Move the mouse away and the cat disappears.

Code 13.6 The daily specials are available inserted into the menu as a layer for Navigator 4 or as a link in other browsers.

```
code
<HTML>
  <HEAD>
    <TITLE>Content for Non-layers browsers</TITLE>
  </HEAD>
  <BODY BGCOLOR="#FFFFFF">
  <H1>Chez' Layer</H1>
  <H3>DAILY SPECIAL</H3>
    <ILAYER ID="special" TOP="10" HEIGHT="10"
→SRC="daily_special.html">
    </ILAYER>
    <NOLAYER>
      <A HREF="daily_special.html">
      The Daily Specials are available here!
      </A>
    </NOLAYER>
  </BODY>
</HTML>
```

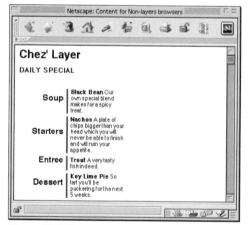

Figure 13.5 The first browser window is Netscape 4 which displays our daily dinner special menu.

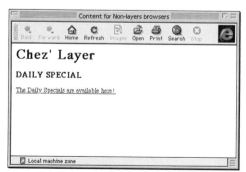

Figure 13.6 The second window shows the same file in Internet Explorer, with a link to the daily specials.

Providing content for non-layer browsers

Similar to the way a frame document can include content to be displayed in browsers that do not understand frames, a special no-layers tag allows you to place content into your document for use by browsers that do not support layers.

The first figure (**Figure 13.5**) shows HTML displayed in Navigator 4.05, with a layer that has a daily special menu for Café Layers being pulled in from an external file. This obviously will not work in a non-layer browser (**Figure 13.6**); instead, the non-layer browser includes a link to the same content.

To add non-layer content:

1. Add whatever layers content you want to your document. In **Code 13.6**, a layer is importing an external HTML file.

2. `<NOLAYER>`

   Open the non-layers area of your document with the `<NOLAYER>` tag.

3. `<A HREF="daily_special.html">`
   `The Daily Specials are available here!`
   `</A>`

   Add the content you want displayed in browsers that cannot handle layers. Here we have added a link to the content that is being inserted into our layer.

4. `</NOLAYER>`

   Close the non-layer content.

VISUAL CONTROLS IN INTERNET EXPLORER

Figure 14.1 Internet Explorer 4.0 start-up screen.

Internet Explorer 4.0 (see **Figure 14.1**) introduced several built-in special effects that can be used to add visual dynamism to your Web pages.

But one word of caution: Although these IE 4.0 special effects are pretty cool, I advise you to use them sparingly. Not only do they not work on the Navigator browser, they do not even work on the Macintosh and UNIX versions of Internet Explorer 4.0. This is because these abilities are based on a proprietary technology controlled solely by Microsoft called ActiveX which currently only works in the Windows operating system. Unlike JavaScript or other Web technologies, ActiveX "controls" are not an open standard and there are no plans to make them so.

Fading between elements
(Windows only)

You can set up two images, or a pair of any screen elements, to fade in and out, or to fade between the two elements. In **Figure 14.2** you can see the two images "mid-fade."

To fade elements:

1. function fadeElement()

Add the function fadeElement() to the JavaScript in the head of your document, as shown in **Code 14.1**. This function applies the blendTrans filter between the current source image for image1 (alice04a.gif in our example) and its replacement alice05a.gif.

2. <IMG ID=" image1"
→SRC="../images/alice04a.gif"

Set up the initial image to be displayed when the screen first loads.

3. STYLE="filter:blendTrans(duration=3)"
→ONCLICK="fadeElement()">

In the STYLE attribute for image1, add a call to IE4's blendTrans filter and set its fade duration to 3 (seconds). This filter will not be acted upon until the image is clicked and the fadeElement() function is executed.

Code 14.1 The function fadeElement(), when activated, will cause image1 to fade from one picture to the next.

```
<HTML>
  <HEAD>
  <SCRIPT LANGUAGE="JavaScript">
    var isFade = 0;
    function fadeElement() {
      if (document.all && isFade == 0) {
      isFade = 1;
      image1.filters.blendTrans.Apply();
      image1.src = "../images/alice05a.gif";
      image1.filters.blendTrans.Play();
      }
    }
  </SCRIPT>
  </HEAD>
  <BODY>
    <IMG ID=" image1"
→SRC="../images/alice04a.gif"
→STYLE="filter:blendTrans(duration=3)"
→ONCLICK="fadeElement()"><BR>
  </BODY>
</HTML>
```

Figure 14.2 One image fades in as the other fades out.

Table 1.5

IE Transition Filters	
TRANSITION	REFERENCE #
Box In	0
Box Out	1
Circle In	2
Circle Out	3
Wipe Up	4
Wipe Down	5
Wipe Right	6
Wipe Left	7
Vertical Blinds	8
Horizontal Blinds	9
Checkerboard Across	10
Checkerboard Down	11
Random Dissolve	12
Split Vertical In	13
Split Vertical Out	14
Split Horizontal In	15
Split Horizontal Out	16
Strips Left Down	17
Strips Left Up	18
Strips Right Down	19
Strips Right Up	20
Random Bars Horizontal	21
Random Bars Vertical	22
Random	23

Transitions between pages (Windows only)

When you're jumping between Web pages, it's always a bit disconcerting when the first page blinks out and is then slowly replaced by the next page piece by piece. Using the RevealTrans() filters, however, you can produce transitions between Web pages that are more "cinematic." **Table 14.1** lists the transition filter effects that are available. **Figure 14.3** shows a Web page in the process of loading with a transition that causes one page to spiral into the next.

To set up a transition between Web pages:

1. <META http-equiv="Page-Enter"

Set up a <META> tag in the head of your document, as shown in **Code 14.2.** Set the http-equiv attribute to Page-Enter.

2. CONTENT = "RevealTrans (Duration=2,
→Transition=2)>

Set the CONTENT attribute for this <META> tag to execute the RevealTrans() filter, and set its duration to 2 (seconds). Then add the name of the transition of your choice from **Table 14.1**. For this example, I chose the Circle In effect, to have the page "spiral" in.

3. <META http-equiv="Page-Exit" CONTENT =
→"RevealTrans (Duration=2, Transition=3)>

To set a filter to run when the visitor leaves this page, type another <META> tag for Page-Exit. For this one, I selected the Circle Out filter.

✔ Tip

■ You can also use the RevealTrans() filters with individual images or CSS elements, as shown in **Fading between elements** in the previous spread. Conversely, you can also use the fade filter to fade between Web pages.

Code 14.2 Here, the <META> tag is used to execute transition filters when the document is opened and when it is closed.

```
code

<HTML>
  <META HTTP-EQUIV="Page-Enter"
→CONTENT="RevealTrans (Duration=2,
→Transition=2)">
  <META http-equiv="Page-Exit"
→CONTENT="RevealTrans (Duration=2,
Transition=3)">
  <BODY BGCOLOR=" #FF9999">
    <CENTER>
    <A HREF="pict2.html">
    <IMG SRC="../images/alice01a.gif"
→HEIGHT="90%"><BR>
    Next Picture —&gt;</A>
    </CENTER>
  </BODY>
</HTML>
```

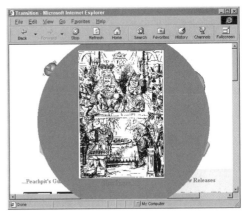

Figure 14.3 The page is shown in mid-transition as the content spins in.

Transitions between pages

Code 14.3 The blurOn() function will cause the image to slowly blur across the screen.

```
                    code
<HTML>
  <HEAD>
  <SCRIPT LANGUAGE="JAVASCRIPT">
  function blurOn(currStrength,currDirection){
    if (document.all && currStrength < 360) {
      currStrength += 1;
      currDirection += 1;
      document.all.blurMe.style.filter =
→"blur(strength= " + currStrength + "," +
→currDirection + ")";
      setTimeout("blurOn(" + currStrength + "," +
→currDirection + ")",100);
    }
  }
  </SCRIPT>
  <BODY BGCOLOR="#ffffff" onLoad="blurOn(15,15)">
    <CENTER>
    <IMG ID="blurMe" SRC="../images/alice01.gif"
→HEIGHT="95%" STYLE="FILTER:blur(strength=0,
→direction=5)"}>
    </CENTER>
  </BODY>
</HTML>
```

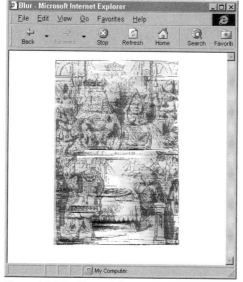

Figure 14.4 The King and Queen going for a trip.

Making an element blur

Blurring can make an element—text or graphic—look as if it is moving by simulating the blurring caused by motion. **Figure 14.4** shows the image of the king and queen smudged across the screen. The blurOn() function in **Code 14.3** will actually cause the image to slowly blur across the screen.

To blur an element:

1. function blurOn(
   →currStrength,currDirection)

   Add the blurOn() function to the JavaScript in the head of your document, as demonstrated in **Code 14.3**. This function will recursively apply the blur filter to the image named blurMe until it reaches a strength of 360. The strength attribute refers to how far the element should be blurred.

2. <IMG ID="blurMe"
   →SRC="../images/alice01a.gif"
   →HEIGHT="95%"
   →STYLE="FILTER:blur(strength=0,
   →direction=0)">

   In the body of your document, add the image you want to blur. In the <IMG> tag, add the STYLE attribute with the blur filter. Set its initial strength to 0; set direction to 0, as well.

3. <BODY BGCOLOR="#ffffff"
   →onLoad="blurOn(15,15)">

   In the <BODY> tag, add an onLoad that runs the blurOn() function from step 1. When the document loads, the function runs, causing the image from step 2 to blur across the page as shown in **Figure 14.4**.

Making an element wave

The wave filter causes an image or other element to distort in a rippling effect, like a flag undulating in the wind. **Figure 14.5** shows what this looks like.

To make an element look wavy:

1. <IMG SRC="../images/alice08a.gif"
   →HEIGHT="95%"

   Set up an image in the body of your document, as demonstrated in **Code 14.4**.

2. STYLE="FILTER:wave(freq=12, strength=45)">

   Add the style property to your image, using the wave filter with the frequency set to 3. (This number controls the number of ridges in the wave.) Set the strength to 6 (which controls the size of the ripples).

Code 14.4 The wave filter is applied to the image alice08.gf.

```
code
<HTML>
  <BODY BGCOLOR="#ffffff">
    <CENTER>
    <IMG SRC="../images/alice08a.gif"
→HEIGHT="95%" STYLE="FILTER:wave(freq=3,
→strength=6)">
    </CENTER>
  </BODY>
</HTML>
```

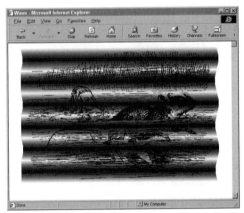

Figure 14.5 The image appears to be rippled as Alice swims away.

Dynamic CSS in Internet Explorer

Internet Explorer's Dynamic Object Model allows for some interesting effects when creating Dynamic HTML with Cascading Style Sheets. In contrast to Navigator 4, which only allows you to make changes to the CSS Position properties, Internet Explorer recognizes changes to any of the CSS properties available to it (see Appendix A). This allows you to dynamically control your CSS in the window: Dynamic CSS.

For instance, you can change not only the color of a link, but the size of the link's text, and whether it is being displayed or not. In addition, Internet Explorer can either disable or apply a style sheet if the document is being printed rather than displayed on a screen.

The other good news is that a lot of the stuff presented in this chapter, though not cross-browser, is at least cross-platform. In addition, these abilities are part of the new CSS Level 2 specification and will more than likely be available in Navigator 5.

Changing a style property

One obvious use for Dynamic CSS is to change the CSS properties of a particular element on the screen. **Figure 15.1** shows the screen when it's first loaded. Then in **Figure 15.2** you can see how the color and size of the hypertext link changes when the visitor's mouse passes over it. This visually indicates to the visitor that this link is ready to be used.

To change a style property:

1. A { color: blue; }

   Set up your style sheet for the document, defining the anchor <A> tag with a color. I chose blue for this example, as shown in **Code 15.1**.

2. <A HREF="next.html"

   Place an anchor link in the body of your document.

3. onmouseover="this.style.color = 'red';
   →this.style.font = 'bold 18pt helvetica'"

   Add an onMouseOver event handler to the link. This event accesses the style for this selector (A, as defined in step 1) and then changes its color property, and the same again for its font properties. Here I chose to make the link red, bold, larger, and in the Helvetica font.

4. onmouseout="this.style.color = 'blue';
   →this.style.font = 'normal 12pt times'">

   Add an onMouseOut event to change the link's appearance back to its original state when the visitor's mouse moves away.

Code 15.1 The code to make your links more dynamic.

```
<HTML>
  <HEAD>
    <TITLE>Changing Styles</TITLE>
    <STYLE TYPE="text/css">
      BODY { font: normal 12pt times; }
      A { color: blue; }
    </STYLE>
  </HEAD>
<BODY BGCOLOR="#FFFFFF">
You can
<A HREF="next.html"
onmouseover="this.style.color = 'red';
→this.style.font = 'bold 18pt helvetica'"
onmouseout="this.style.color = 'blue';
→this.style.font = 'normal 12pt times'">
Go to the next screen</A>
if you want.
</BODY>
</HTML>
```

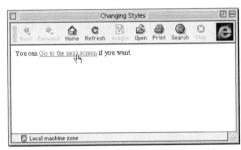

Figure 15.1 When the screen loads, the link is blue and underlined.

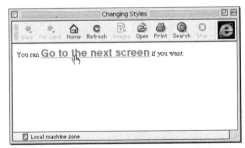

Figure 15.2 When the mouse moves over the link, it changes color, size, and font. Also, notice that the rest of the text has adjusted itself to make room for the link's new size.

Code 15.2 The tiny and huge classes can be swapped back and forth by accessing the element's styleName property.

```
<HTML>
  <HEAD>
    <STYLE TYPE="text/css">
      .tiny {
        color: red;
        font-size: 6pt;}
      .huge {
        color: blue;
        font-size: 100pt;}
    </STYLE>
  </HEAD>
  <BODY BGCOLOR="#FFFFFF">
    <P CLASS="tiny"
    onmouseover="this.className = 'huge'"
    onmouseout="this.className = 'tiny'">
    Can you read me Now?</P>
  </BODY>
</HTML>.
```

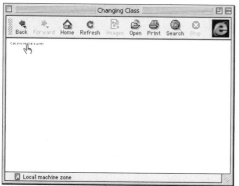

Figure 15.3 When the window first loads, you can't really see what the text says...

Figure 15.4 ...but place your mouse over the link, and you'd have to be blind to miss it

Changing an element's class

Rather than changing each CSS property separately, as shown in the preceding example, it's likely that swapping that element's class will be easier to do. This allows you to change a number of properties without having to continually type them out for each event.

In **Figure 15.3**, the text starts out really tiny, but in **Figure 15.4** it becomes huge.

To change an element's class:

1. .tiny { color: red; font-size: 6pt; }

.huge { color: blue; font-size: 100pt;}

Set up the classes that you want to use in this document. For **Code 15.2**, I set up two classes: tiny and huge.

2. <P CLASS="tiny"

Now set up an element in your HTML and define its starting class—the one in which it will display when the Web page is first loaded. In this example, the text will start out with the tiny class, so the text in the <P> tag will start out really small.

3.   onmouseover="this.className = 'huge'"

Add an onMouseOver event handler to this tag, to detect when the mouse is over top of it and to change the className for this element to huge. Notice that we can add the event handler to an individual tag without using a link, something we cannot do in Navigator.

4.   onmouseout="this.className = 'tiny'">

Add an onMouseOut event handler to change the class back to tiny when the visitor moves the mouse away.

5.   Can you read me Now?</P>

Add any content you want for this element, and then type the end tag.

Creating collapsing and expanding menus

We saw in Chapter 6 how to tell an element on the screen how it should appear, or whether it should be displayed at all. Now we can dynamically control whether the element is displayed at all—with some very eye catching results.

Anyone who has used a graphical user interface (GUI)—whether Macintosh, Windows, or UNIX-based, it doesn't matter—has watched menus in a window collapse and expand. Click on a directory, and its contents are displayed right below, while the other files and directories move down to accommodate the expanded content. In Microsoft Windows, it's done by clicking on the little plus and minus signs. On the Mac, it's done using the little triangles. We can achieve a similar effect here by using the display property.

Figure 15.5 shows our two menu options when they first load. And in **Figure 15.6** you can see the same window after the first menu option has been expanded.

To create a collapsing/ expanding menu:

1. #menu1 { display : none; }

Create an ID rule for each of your collapsible menus, setting the display property to none as shown in **Code 15.3**. This way, the menus will not appear when the document is first loaded.

2. <SPAN ...><B>Menu 1</B></SPAN>

In the body of your document, set up a <SPAN> tag surrounding the element (graphic or text) that will be clicked on to reveal the menu.

Code 15.3 This code sets up the menu styles used to set up our menus, and then includes event handlers to cause our menus to appear and disappear.

```
                        code
<HTML>
  <HEAD>
    <TITLE>Display</TITLE>
    <STYLE TYPE="text/css">
      #menu1 { display : none; }
      #menu2 { display : none; }
    </STYLE>
  </HEAD>
  <BODY BGCOLOR="#FFFFFF">
  <SPAN onclick="if
→(document.all.menu1.style.display =='block') {
→document.all.menu1.style.display='none';} else
→{document.all.menu1.style.display='block';}">
<B>Menu 1</B></SPAN><BR>
  <SPAN ID="menu1">
  Option 1<BR>
  Option 2<BR>
  Option 3<BR>
  Option 4<BR>
  </SPAN>
  <P>
  <SPAN onclick="if
→(document.all.menu2.style.display =='block') {
→document.all.menu2.style.display='none';} else
→{document.all.menu2.style.display='block';}">
<B>Menu 2</B><BR>
</SPAN>
  <SPAN ID="menu2">
  Option 1<BR>
  Option 2<BR>
  Option 3<BR>
  Option 4<BR>
  </SPAN>
  </BODY>
</HTML>
```

Creating collapsing and expanding menus

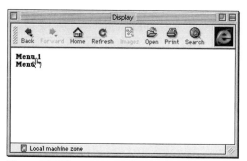

Figure 15.5 The screen as it first loads, with its menus collapsed.

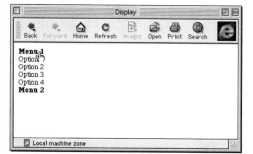

Figure 15.6 After clicking on the Menu I option, the menu expands. Notice that the second menu head has moved down to accommodate the first menu

3. onclick="if (document.all.menu1.style.display
→== 'block') {
document.all.menu1.style.display = 'none';}
else
{document.all.menu1.style.display='block';}">

In the <SPAN> tag, add an onClick event handler that checks to see whether the menu is currently visible ('block'). If it is, then onClick sets that element's display property to none; otherwise, display is set to block.

4. <SPAN ID="menu1">

Option 1

Option 2

Option 3

Option 4

</SPAN>

Now set up the actual menu, giving it an ID name to match the DOM used in step 3.

✔ Tips

- You can, of course, use any type of elements in these menus, including graphics. The exact design is up to you.

- Why don't we simply have the onClick event call a function that runs all of this code? That *does* work in Windows (see **Adding a new rule dynamically** later in this chapter). The Macintosh version of Internet Explorer, however, has problems using CSS in a function.

- This expanding/collapsing menu technique will not work on Navigator 4. Moreover, since the display for the menus gets set to none, the menus will not appear at all. One possible solution is to test for the browser being used, and then set up JavaScript to write the style sheet for Internet Explorer only.

Creating collapsing and expanding menus

Disabling CSS

(Windows only)

Sometimes your visitors might want to see just the text, without all of those fancy styles. Their loss—but everyone has their own tastes. Internet Explorer allows you to disable (turn off) a particular style, and then turn it back on again to suit your needs.

In **Figure 15.7,** the text is displayed in a garish green color. By clicking on the link beneath the text, we can turn the style off and revert to a default H1 style, as shown in **Figure 15.8.**

To disable a style sheet:

1. Set up a style sheet in the head of your document, as shown in **Code 15.4.** Give the <STYLE> tag the ID attribute and a name. In this example, I created a style sheet called strangeStyle that will cause the <H1> tag to display its text in large green letters.

2. <SPAN onclick=
   "document.styleSheets.strangeStyle.
   disabled=true; document.all.styleOff.style.
   display='none';">here</SPAN>

   Set up a <SPAN> tag with an onClick event handler. When the element is clicked, the value for the disabled property of the strangeStyle style sheet is set to true. This turns the style sheet off, and any elements on the screen using this style sheet will revert to the original condition, as if the style sheet did not exist. We also set the display for this element—the one with the onClick event in it—to none, so that it disappears along with the style and will not confuse our visitor since the style is already turned off.

Code 15.4 This code can be used to turn the strangeStyle off, if desired.

```
<HTML>
  <HEAD>
    <TITLE></TITLE>
    <STYLE ID="strangeStyle">
      H1 { color: limegreen; font: italic 36pt
→fantasy; }
    </STYLE>
  </HEAD>
  <BODY BGCOLOR="#FFFFFF">
  <H1 CLASS="bizzaro">Greetings and
Salutations?</H1><BR>
  <SPAN ID="styleOff">If you can not read the
above, click
<SPAN onclick="document.styleSheets.strangeStyle.
→disabled=true;
→document.all.styleOff.style.display='none';">
here</SPAN>
  </SPAN>
  </BODY>
</HTML>
```

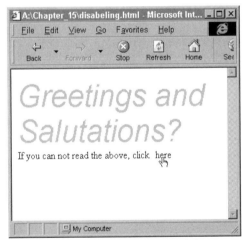

Figure 15.7 The original version is kind of obnoxious.

Figure 15.8 So we get rid of the style. Notice that we have hidden the place for the visitor to click to disable the style, since the style is already disabled.

✔ Tip

■ Rather than setting the disabled property to true, you can set it to false in order to enable a style sheet that was previously inactive.

Adding a new rule dynamically
(Windows only)

By placing Dynamic CSS calls into a JavaScript (or JScript, since this is Internet Explorer), we gain the advantage of creating functions to control our CSS. The one drawback to this ability is that the Macintosh version of Internet Explorer cannot run such scripts.

In this example we will use a JScript function to use the addRule method. This method does just what it says: It adds a new rule to a style sheet, which is immediately used in the document. You can see the window when it first loads in **Figure 15.9**, and then after the screen is clicked and we get a reddish background in **Figure 15.10**.

To dynamically add a rule to a style sheet:

1. function addARule(selector,definition) {
   →document.styleSheets.headerStyles.addRule
   →(selector,definition)
   }
   Add the function addARule to the JScript in the head of your document, as shown in **Code 15.5.** This function has two variables: selector (the name of a particular selector) and definition (the definition to be applied to that selector). The function will then use the addRule method to add a new rule to the style sheet called derStyles.

2. <STYLE ID="derStyles">
   In the head of your document, add a style sheet with the ID attribute, and call it derStyles.

3. <BODY BGCOLOR="#FFFFFF"
   →onClick="addARule('P','color:red')">
   You can now add an event handler in your document that calls the function addARule, feeding it the name of the selector for which you want to add a rule, and the definition you want to assign to that selector.

Code 15.5 The addARule function takes a selector and a definition and adds them as a rule to your style sheet.

```
<HTML>
  <HEAD>
    <TITLE>Scripting</TITLE>
    <SCRIPT LANGUAGE="JScript">
    function addARule(selector,definition) {
    document.styleSheets.MyStyles.addRule
→(selector,definition)
    }
    </SCRIPT>
    <STYLE ID="derStyles">
      BODY  {font-size: 24pt;}
    </STYLE>
  </HEAD>
  <BODY BGCOLOR="#FFFFFF"
→onClick="addARule('P','color:red')">
    <P>Click any where to change me to red!</P>
    <SPAN onclick="addARule('BODY','background-
→color:salmon')">Or here to change the
→background color</SPAN>
  </BODY>
</HTML>
```

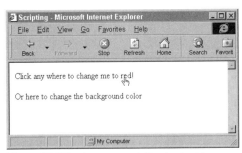

Figure 15.9 The document as it first loads with a white background.

Figure 15.10 When the visitor clicks anywhere on the screen, the background turns a nice salmon-pink color.

Code 15.6 The screen.css style sheet will be used when the document is displayed on a computer monitor.

```
code
body    {
   color: white;
   background-color: black;
   }
```

Code 15.7 print.css will be used if the document is being printed.

```
code
body    {
   color: black;
   background-color: white;
   }
```

Code 15.8 The two different style sheets are linked to this document and used based on the output media.

```
code
<HTML>
   <HEAD>
      <TITLE>Printing</TITLE>
      <LINK rel="stylesheet" type="text/css"
→media="print" href="print.css">
      <LINK rel="stylesheet" type="text/css"
→media="screen" href="screen.css">
   </HEAD>
   <BODY>

   <P>ALICE'S ADVENTURES IN WONDERLAND<BR>
      Lewis Carroll<BR>
      THE MILLENNIUM FULCRUM EDITION 3.0</P>
      <P><BR>
      <BR>
      CHAPTER I<BR>
      Down the Rabbit-Hole</P>
      <P>Alice was beginning to get very tired of
sitting by her sister on the bank, and of having
nothing to do: once or twice she had peeped into
the book her sister was reading, but it had no
pictures or conversations in it, 'and what is the
use of a book,' thought Alice 'without pictures or
conversation?'</P>
   </BODY>
</HTML>
```

Defining CSS for print
(Windows only)

Originally, the Web did not accommodate design features such as background colors and background graphics. A Web document looked pretty much the same displayed on a computer monitor as it did printed on a piece of paper.

Today, a Web page that appears on a dark background or textured graphic may look fine on the screen, but when printed it's likely to be totally illegible. The media property can be used to tell the browser to use a particular style sheet, depending on the document's intended output form. **Figure 15.11** shows the document from **Code 15.8** as it will appear in a browser window. **Figure 15.12** shows the same document, printed out.

1. body {
   color: white; background-color: black; }

   Set up the CSS for the screen version of your document; put it in an external file and call it screen.css. In **Code 15.6,** I have set the background color to black, with white text.

2. body {
   color: black; background-color: white; }

   Set up the CSS for the print version of your document; save this one in an external file called print.css. In **Code 15.7,** I have set the text color to be black and the background color to be white, which will work better on paper than the screen version would.

3. <LINK rel="stylesheet" type="text/css"
   →media="print" href="print.css">

   In the head of your document, link the print style sheet created in step 2, and add the media attribute set to print. This style sheet will be used when the document is printed.

4. `<LINK rel="stylesheet" type="text/css"`
   `→media="screen" href="screen.css">`

After the link to the print CSS, add a link to the screen version of the style sheet, with the **media** attribute set to **screen**. This style sheet will be used when the document is seen on the screen.

✔ Tips

- Make sure that the screen CSS is linked *after* the print CSS. Not all browsers include the **media** attribute with styles, but they do obey the cascade order. Since **print.css** is a valid style sheet, it would still be used by non-media-discerning browsers as if it were declared last in the cascade order.

- Soon there will be other media types available, including sound and Braille. The **media** property, which is a part of the CSS Level 2 specification, will play an important role in the future, opening Web documents up to more than just screen display.

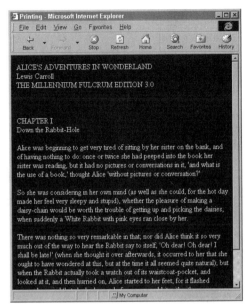

Figure 15.11 The document as seen in a browser window.

ALICE'S ADVENTURES IN WONDERLAND
Lewis Carroll
THE MILLENNIUM FULCRUM EDITION 3.0

CHAPTER I
Down the Rabbit-Hole
Alice was beginning to get very tired of sitting by her sister on the bank, and of having nothing to do: once or twice she had peeped into the book her sister was reading, but it had no pictures or conversations in it, 'and what is the use of a book,' thought Alice 'without pictures or conversation?'

So she was considering in her own mind (as well as she could, for the hot day made her feel very sleepy and stupid), whether the pleasure of making a daisy-chain would be worth the trouble of getting up and picking the daisies, when suddenly a White Rabbit with pink eyes ran close by her.

There was nothing so very remarkable in that; nor did Alice think it so very much out of the way to hear the Rabbit say to itself, 'Oh dear! Oh dear! I shall be late!' (when she thought it over afterwards, it occurred to her that she ought to have wondered at this, but at the time it all seemed quite natural); but when the Rabbit actually took a watch out of its waistcoat-pocket, and looked at it, and then hurried on, Alice started to her feet, for it flashed across her mind that she had never before seen a rabbit with either a waistcoat-pocket, or a watch to take out of it, and burning with curiosity, she ran across the field after

Figure 15.12 The same document printed out on paper.

CSS

QUICK REFERENCE

Chapters 2 through 7 present the properties that can be used with Cascading Style Sheets. Here in this Quick Reference those properties are represented in a slightly more concise format.

- **Table A.1** describes Font Properties

- **Table A.2** describes Text Properties

- **Table A.3** describes List Properties

- **Table A.4** describes Color and Background Properties

- **Table A.5** describes Margin and Border Properties

- **Table A.6** describes Positioning Properties

Quick Reference

You'll find information about the applicability of each property in the various types of HTML tag. Each property is described in terms of what it can be used with, whether or not the property is inherited by its children elements, and whether or not the property is supported in various browsers and operating systems.

Properties marked with a ❷ in the browser columns are only partially implemented or buggy on one or both operating systems. I generally recommend avoiding these properties.

Keep in mind that there are several different versions of each browser, even within a single version number. For instance there is not a Netscape 4, but several, each one with slight differences. The information presented here should be generally correct, but if you want to test the CSS capabilities of your own browser, check out the World Wide Web Consortium's test suite:

http://www.w3.org/Style/CSS/Test/

This utility will help you confirm which properties work on your browser.

Legend

■ = Mac and Windows
○ = Neither
Ⓦ = Windows only
Ⓜ = Mac only
Ⓟ = Problems
Bold face indicates the default value for that property.

Table A.1

Font Properties

PROPERTY NAME	VALUES	APPLIES TO	INHERITED?	NAV4	IE3	IE4
font-family	\<font name\>	All	Yes	■	■	■
	\<generic font\>			■	■	■
font-style	**normal**	All	Yes	■	■	■
	italic			■	■	■
	oblique			○	○	■
font-variant	**normal**	All	Yes	○	○	■
	small-caps			○	○	Ⓟ
font-weight	**normal**	All	Yes	■	○	■
	bold			■	■	■
	bolder			Ⓦ	Ⓦ	■
	lighter			Ⓦ	Ⓦ	■
	100-900*			■	○	■
font-size	\<absolute size\>	All	Yes	■	■	■
	\<relative size\>			■	■	■
	\<length\>			■	■	■
	\<percentage\>			■	■	■
font	\<font-style\>	All	Yes	■	■	■
	\<font-variant\>			○	○	Ⓟ
	\<font-weight\>			■	Ⓟ	■
	\<font-size\>/\<lineheight\>			■	Ⓟ	■
	\<font-family\>			■	■	■

* Requires the visitor's computer to have display-weighted fonts available.

Table A.2

Text Properties

Property Name	Values	Applies To	Inherited?	Nav4	IE3	IE4
word-spacing	**normal**	All	Yes	○	○	○
	<length>			○	○	○
letter-spacing	**normal**	All	Yes	○	○	Ⓦ
	<length>			○	○	Ⓦ
vertical-align	**baseline**	Inline	No	○	○	○
	sub			○	○	Ⓦ
	super			○	○	Ⓦ
	top			○	○	○
	text-top			○	○	○
	middle			○	○	○
	bottom			○	○	○
	text-bottom			○	○	○
	<percentage>			○	○	○
line-height	**normal**	All	Yes	Ⓦ	■	■
	<number>			■	Ⓟ	Ⓟ
	<length>			■	■	■
	<percentage>			■	Ⓟ	Ⓟ
text-decoration	**none**	All	No	■	Ⓜ	Ⓜ
	underline			■	■	■
	overline			○	○	Ⓦ
	line-through			■	■	■
	blink			■	○	○
text-transform	**none**	All	Yes	■	○	Ⓦ
	capitalize			■	○	Ⓦ
	uppercase			■	○	Ⓦ
	lowercase			■	○	Ⓦ
text-alignment	left	Block	Yes	■	■	■
	right			■	■	■
	center			■	■	■
	justify			■	○	Ⓦ
text-indent	<length>	Block	Yes	■	■	■
	<percentage>			■	■	■
white-space	**normal**	Block	Yes	■	○	○
	pre			■	○	○
	nowrap			○	○	○

CSS Quick Reference

Table A.3

List Properties

Property Name	Values	Applies To	Inherited?	Nav4	IE3	IE4
list-style-type	**disc**	All*	Yes	■	○	ⓦ
	circle			■	○	ⓦ
	square			■	○	ⓦ
	decimal			■	○	ⓦ
	lower-roman			■	○	ⓦ
	upper-roman			■	○	ⓦ
	lower-alpha			■	○	ⓦ
	upper-alpha			■	○	ⓦ
	none			○	○	ⓦ
list-style-image	**none**	All*	Yes	○	○	ⓦ
	url(<url>)			○	○	ⓦ
list-style-position	**outside**	All*	Yes	○	○	ⓦ
	inside			○	○	ⓦ
list-style	<list-style-type>	All*	Yes	■	○	ⓦ
	<list-style-position>			○	○	ⓦ
	<list-style-image>			○	○	ⓦ

* In Navigator and Internet Explorer applies only to the list tag. In standard CSS these properties can only be applied to tags that include display: list-item; in the definition.

CSS Quick Reference

Table A.4

Color and Background Properties

Property Name	Values	Applies To	Inherited?	Nav4	IE3	IE4
color	<color>	All	Yes	■	■	■
background-color	**transparent**	All	No	■	■	■
	<color>			■	■	■
background-image	**none**	All	No	■	■	■
	url(<url>)			■	■	■
background-repeat	**repeat**	All	No	■	■	■
	repeat-x			■	■	■
	repeat-y			■	■	■
	no-repeat			■	■	■
background-attachment	**scroll**	All	No	○	■	■
	fixed			○	■	■
background-position	<percentage>	Block	No	○	○	■
	<length>			○	○	■
	top			○	○	■
	center			○	○	■
	bottom			○	○	■
	left			○	○	■
	center			○	○	■
	right			○	○	■
background	<background-color>	All	No	■	■	■
	<background-image>			■	■	■
	<background-repeat>			■	■	■
	<background-attachment>			○	■	■
	<background-position>			○	■	■

CSS Quick Reference

Table A.5

Margin and Border Properties

Property Name	Values	Applies To	Inherited?	Nav4	IE3	IE4
margin-top, -right, -bottom, -left	<length>	All	No	■	P	P
	<percentage>			■	P	■
	auto			P	P	P
margin	<length>	All	No	■	P	P
	<percentage>			■	P	P
	auto			W	P	W
padding-top, -right, -bottom, -left	<length>	All	No	■	○	W
	<percentage>			■	○	W
padding	<length>	All	No	■	○	W
	<percentage>			■	○	W
border-color	<color>	All	No	■	○	W
border-style	**none**	All	No	■	○	○
	dotted			○	○	○
	dashed			○	○	○
	solid			■	○	W
	double			■	○	W
	groove			■	○	W
	ridge			■	○	W
	inset			■	○	W
	outset			■	○	W
border-top, -right, -bottom, left-width	**medium**	All	No	■	○	○
	thin			■	○	○
	thick			■	○	○
border-width	**medium**	All	No	■	○	○
	thin			■	○	○
	thick			■	○	○
border-top, -right, -bottom, -left	<border-width>	All	No	○	○	W
	<border-style>			○	○	W
	<color>			○	○	W
border	<border-width>	All	No	■	○	W
	<border-style>			■	○	W
	<color>			■	○	W
width	**auto**	Block	No	■	○	P
	<length>			■	○	P
	<percentage>			■	○	P
height	**auto**	Block	No	P	○	■
	<length>			P	○	■
float	left	All	No	■	○	■

CSS Quick Reference

Table A.5

Margin and Border Properties (cont.)

PROPERTY NAME	VALUES	APPLIES TO	INHERITED?	NAV4	IE3	IE4
	right			■	○	■
	none			Ⓦ	○	■
clear	**none**	All	No	■	■	■
	left			■	○	Ⓦ
	right			■	○	Ⓦ
	both			■	○	○
display	**block**	All	No	Ⓟ	○	○
	inline			Ⓦ	○	○
	list-item			■	○	○
	none			■	○	■

Table A.6

Positioning Properties

PROPERTY NAME	VALUES	APPLIES TO	INHERITED?	NAV4	IE3	IE4
position	**static**	All	No	■	○	■
	absolute			■	○	■
	relative			■	○	■
left	**auto**	All*	No	■	○	■
	<length>			■	○	■
	<percentage>			■	○	■
top	**auto**	All*	No	■	○	■
	<length>			■	○	■
	<percentage>			■	○	■
clip	**auto**	All*	No	■	○	○
	<shape>			Ⓟ	○	○
overflow	**visible**	All*	No	○	○	○
	hidden			○	○	○
	scroll			○	○	○
	auto			○	○	○
z-index	**auto**	All	No	■	○	■
	number			■	○	■
visibility	**inherit**	All	Yes**	■	○	■
	visibility			■	○	■
	hidden			■	○	■

* The position property must also be set in the same rule, to either absolute or relative.

** If visibility is set to inherit.

LAYERS
QUICK REFERENCE

Although the layer tag (see Chapter 13) might not be around forever, if you are designing solely for the Netscape 4.x platform, some of layers' abilities will come in handy. In addition, many of the JavaScript methods presented below may well become standards in the future for use with Cascading Style Sheets.

In the following tables, values in brackets < > indicate units explained in **Values and units in this book**, on page 11. Other values should be typed in as written.

Table B.1

Layer Tags

TAG NAME	WHAT IT DOES
<LAYER>...</LAYER>	Creates a discrete area of HTML code in Netscape 4 that can be positioned anywhere on the page, and that can be defined using the layer attributes.
<ILAYER>...</ILAYER>	Creates a discrete area of HTML code in Netscape 4 that can be positioned in context to the other elements around it, and that can be defined using the layer attributes.
<NOLAYER>...</NOLAYER>	Hides content intended for non-layers-capable browsers, from layers-capable browsers.

Table B.2

Layer Tag Attributes

ATTRIBUTE NAME	VALUES	WHAT IT DOES
ID	<alpha-numeric>	Identifies the layer for use in JavaScript.
NAME	<alpha-numeric>	Identical to ID. ID is preferred.
LEFT	<length>	Horizontal position relative to parent.
TOP	<length>	Vertical position relative to parent.
PAGEX*	<length>	Horizontal position always relative to window.
PAGEY*	<length>	Vertical position always relative to window.
Z-INDEX	<number>	The stacking order for this layer in relation to others.
ABOVE*	<alpha-numeric>	The name of the layer to appear above this one.
BELOW*	<alpha-numeric>	The name of the layer to appear below this one.
WIDTH	<length> <percentage>	Horizontal length.
HEIGHT	<length> <percentage>	Vertical length.
CLIP	<length, length>	Defines the visible area.
VISIBILITY	show hide inherit	Whether this layer is visible or not.
BGCOLOR	<color>	The color that appears behind the layers contents.
BACKGROUND-COLOR	<color>	Same as BGCOLOR.
BACKGROUND	<url>	An image (GIF or JPEG) that will appear behind the layers contents.
BACKGROUND-IMAGE	<url>	Same as BACKGROUND.
SRC*	<url>	URL of external content to be included.

*No CSS equivalent

Layers Quick Reference

Table B.3

Layer Object Properties

PROPERTY NAME	MODIFIABLE WITH JAVASCRIPT?	WHAT IT DOES
document	No	Every layer can be treated as an independent document used to access its images, applets, embeds, links, anchors, and embedded layers.
name	No	The NAME or ID given to the layer.
left	Yes	The horizontal position of the element. For <LAYER> this will be either absolutely within the page, or relative to surrounding layers. For <ILAYER> this will be relative to its natural position within the document or a surrounding layer.
top	Yes	The vertical position of the element. For <LAYER> this will be either absolutely within the page, or relative to its surrounding layer. For <ILAYER> this will be relative to its natural position within the document or a surrounding layer.
pageX	Yes	The horizontal position of the element relative to the document, regardless of what type of layer it is.
pageY	Yes	The vertical position of the element relative to the document, regardless of what type of layer it is.
zIndex	Yes	The layer's position in the stacking order relative to its siblings.
visibility	Yes	Whether the layer can be seen or not.
clip.width	Yes	The horizontal visible area of the layer.
clip.height	Yes	The vertical visible area of the layer.
bgcolor	Yes	The background color to appear behind the layers content.
background	Yes	The background image to appear behind the layers content.
siblingAbove	No	The NAME or ID of the sibling layer that appears above this layer in the stacking order.
siblingBelow	No	The NAME or ID of the sibling layer that appears below this layer in the stacking order.
above	No	The NAME or ID of the layer in z-order that appears above this layer in the stacking order.
below	No	The NAME or ID of the layer in z-order that appears below this layer in the stacking order.
parentLayer	No	The name of this layers parent. Defaults to the window's name if there is no parent.
src	Yes	The URL of the layer's external source.

Table B.3 shows properties that can be changed using JavaScript. They can receive a value corresponding to its attribute shown in Table B.2.

Layers Quick Reference

Table B.4

Layer Object Methods	

METHOD NAME	WHAT IT DOES
moveBy(x,y)	Moves the layer x pixels to the right and y pixels down from its current position.
moveTo(x,y)	Moves the layer to the specified x,y coordinates within its containing layer or within the document.
moveToAbsolute(x,y)	Moves the layer to the specified x,y coordinates within the document.
resizeBy(x,y)	Resizes the layer x pixels to the right and y pixels down from its current size.
resizeTo(x,y)	Resizes the layer to a width of x pixels and a height of y pixels.
moveAbove(layer)	Moves this layer above the layer specified.
moveBelow(layer)	Moves this layer below the layer specified.
load(URL,width)	Loads the URL specified as the source of the layer with the specified width. You can omit the width to leave that value unchanged.

The methods in Table B.4 can also be applied to CSS-P in Netscape 4.

RESOURCES, RESOURCES, RESOURCES

Looking for more information about
DHTML? There are lots of sources on the Web
if you know where to find them. The following are a few of the sites I used while doing
research for this book. These Web sites are by
no means the only places you can go, but
they're the ones I found most useful.

Dynamic HTML Zone

http://www.dhtmlzone.com/index.html

The Dynamic HTML Zone (**Figure C.1**) is a good place to begin your online exploration of DHTML. This site has a number of well-written articles on the subject, as well as a multitude of live examples and links to other resources on the Web. I especially appreciate the cross-browser approach adopted by the Dynamic HTML Zone site.

One caution here: This site is maintained by Macromedia—makers of the Flash and Shockwave plug-ins, not to mention the Dreamweaver DHTML tool. The site is undeniably biased towards those technologies. In fact, at this site Shockwave is actually mentioned as a component of DHTML! Certainly it is true that both Shockwave and Flash can add dynamism to your Web site, but because they rely on plug-ins to be seen by a browser, they *cannot* be considered an integral part of the Dynamic HTML technology.

Figure C.1 The home page of Macromedia's Dynamic HTML zone. Check this site out for introductory articles about cross-browser dynamic HTML.

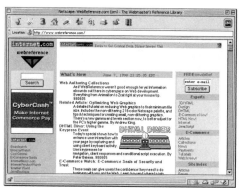

Figure C.2 The Webreference home page. Lots of information, lots of links, some confusion.

Figure C.3 The Webreference DHTML lab gives you step-by-step examples for creating special effects with DHTML.

Web Reference

http://www.webreference.com

Web Reference (**Figure C.2**), produced by internet.com, is intended to be a complete source of information about the various facets of Web development. Here you will find articles on topics ranging from CGI scripting to Web security to JavaScript—and of course, Dynamic HTML. Although there is plenty of useful information at this site, it is often obscured by the overwhelming number of links you have to wade through to get to its diverse topics. It also gets a little "cutesy" at times, bordering on insulting the visitor's intelligence. All in all, though, this Web Reference is worth a look.

http://www.webreference.com/dhtml/

The "DHTML Lab" section of Web Reference (**Figure C.3**) presents various Dynamic HTML scripts that add functionality to your Web page. Generally, these are well laid out and thoroughly explained. However, they require that you have a fair amount of background knowledge in both JavaScript and the various components of DHTML if you want to adapt them to your particular needs.

Web Reference

Web Monkey

http://www.hotwired.com/webmonkey/

HotWired's Web Monkey (**Figure C.4**) presents the bleeding edge of Web development weekly to its readers. If you want to know about something before everybody else does, Web Monkey is a good place to visit. This site includes regularly updated articles on Web technology as well as Web design. Although not everyone likes Wired's visual style, which this site takes to dizzying heights, no one can doubt the effect it has had on the Web.

http://www.hotwired.com/webmonkey/ →collections/dynamic_html.html

If you scratch a bit at the surface of Web Monkey, getting past the glitzy DHTML menus and white text on black background screens, you'll find collections of valuable articles devoted to particular topics. The Dynamic HTML collection of articles (**Figure C.5**) has plenty of good stuff.

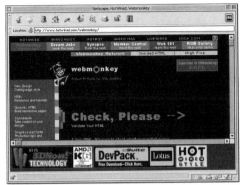

Figure C.4 HotWired's totally cool, totally dynamic front page.

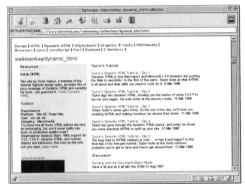

Figure C.5 HotWired's more sedate collection of DHTML articles.

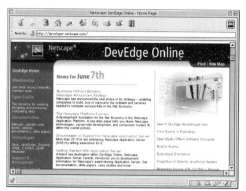

Figure C.6 Netscape's DevEdge Home page for Web developers of every caliber.

Figure C.7 Down a few levels you will find resources for creating cross-browser Dynamic HTML.

Netscape: DevEdge Online

http://developer.netscape.com/

Netscape's DevEdge (**Figure C.6**) is one of the best sources for information about creating Web sites in the Web. There is something here for Web developers ranging in capability from intermediate to advanced. Annotations of the resources at this site could fill a book on their own. Don't worry, though; Netscape has made the DevEdge site easy to use and navigate.

http://developer.netscape.com/tech/
→dynhtml/index.html

The Dynamic HTML section of DevEdge (**Figure C.7**) not only contains information about the specific implementation of DHTML in Navigator 4.x; it also includes numerous articles about creating cross-browser DHTML with Internet Explorer 4.x. This site is definitely one to bookmark and return to.

Netscape: DevEdge Online

Microsoft: SBN Authoring

http://www.microsoft.com/sitebuilder/

The Site Builder Network from Microsoft (**Figure C.8**) contains information and resources for anyone interested in creating Web pages for Microsoft's Internet Explorer line of browsers. Interestingly enough, however, this site seems directed more toward the marketing of Web sites than toward their design and technology.

http://www.microsoft.com/workshop/
→author/dhtml/

The Dynamic HTML side of Microsoft's Site Builder Network (**Figure C.9**) includes thorough descriptions of the Microsoft DHTML implementation. This includes information about IE 4's DOM.

One caution: Several of the pages on this site, because they require Microsoft's proprietary ActiveX technology, will not work unless they are displayed in Internet Explorer 4.x on Windows 95/98/NT.

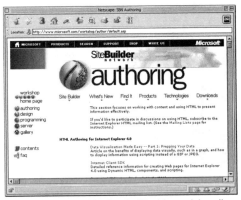

Figure C.8 Microsoft's Site Builder Network has all the information you will need to build Web sites that run on Internet Explorer.

Figure C.9 Learn to use DHTML the Microsoft way.

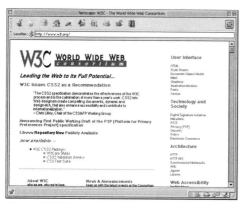

Figure C.10 The source of all standards on the Web: The World Wide Web Consortiums home page.

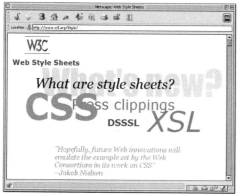

Figure C.11 See how CSS is *supposed* to work at the W3C's Style sheet area.

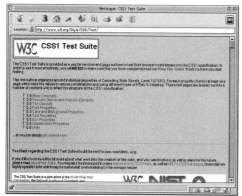

Figure C.12 Check how well your browser conforms to the W3C standard for style sheets using the CSS 1 Test suite.

The World Wide Web Consortium

http://www.w3.org/

The World Wide Web Consortium (**Figure C.10**) is the root source of all information about Cascading Style Sheets and the Dynamic Object Model. What is presented at this site, however, are the standards—and not the actual implementations of those technologies. Still, considering that both Netscape and Microsoft have pledged their future browsers will adhere to these standards, you can't go wrong learning the standards.

http://www.w3.org/Style/

The Style section of the W3C Web site (**Figure C.11**) is a complete resource, including information on CSS (Level 1) and CSS-P, as well as the latest version of the CSS standard (Level 2).

http://www.w3.org/Style/CSS/Test/

One of the most important features of the Style section at the W3C is the CSS 1 Test Suite (**Figure C.12**). These Web pages allow you to test your browser's compliance with CSS Level 1.

The World Wide Web Consortium

The Web Design Group: HTML Help

http://www.htmlhelp.com/

The W3C may be the source of all the standards, but that doesn't mean it's the best place to learn how to understand those standards. The Web Design Group promotes non-browser-specific Web authoring at its HTML Help Web site (**Figure C.13**). Despite its slightly dull design and clip-art graphics, HTML Help is one of the most intelligible sources I have found for getting a grip on the various W3C standards.

http://www.htmlhelp.com/reference/css/

HTML Help also offers the best resource for interpreting the complexities of Cascading Style Sheets (**Figure C.14**). Written in a language that's friendlier than the W3C's own rather dry technical version, this specification includes all of the same information.

Figure C.13 Graphically dull but textually clear: HTML Help home page.

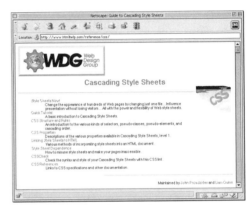

Figure C.14 CSS in a language that non-programmers can understand.

The Visual Quickstart Guide to Dynamic HTML

http://www.webbedenvironments.com/dhtml

At The Visual Quickstart Guide to Dynamic HTML Web site you will be able to find all of the examples and code presented in this book as well as updates and corrections. If you have any problems with the book, check here first and then feel free to write to me at: dhtml@webbedenvironments.com

Also check out the companion site for this book for more information: http://www.peachpit.com/vqs/DHTML

INDEX